Return to Good and Evil

Return to Good and Evil

Flannery O'Connor's Response to Nihilism

Henry T. Edmondson III

LEXINGTON BOOKS
Lanham • Boulder • New York • Toronto • Oxford

LEXINGTON BOOKS

Published in the United States of America
by Lexington Books
An imprint of The Rowman & Littlefield Publishing Group, Inc.
4501 Forbes Boulevard, Suite 200, Lanham, Maryland 20706

PO Box 317
Oxford
OX2 9RU, UK

British Library Cataloguing in Publication Information Available
**The hardback edition of this book was previously cataloged by the Library of
Congress as follows:**

Edmondson, Henry T., 1955–
    Return to good and evil : Flannery O'Connor's response to nihilism / Henry T.
Edmondson, III.
        p. cm.
    Includes bibliographical references and index.
    1. O'Connor, Flannery—Criticism and interpretation. 2. Nihilism (Philosophy)
in literature. 3. O'Connor, Flannery—Philosophy. 4. Good and evil in literature.
5. Nihilism in literature. I. Title.
PS3565.C57 Z664 2002
813'.54—dc21   2002004881

ISBN 0-7391-1105-1 (pbk : alk. paper)
ISBN 0-7391-0421-7 (alk. paper)

Printed in the United States of America

♾™ The paper used in this publication meets the minimum requirements of American
National Standard for Information Sciences—Permanence of Paper for Printed Library
Materials, ANSI/NISO Z39.48–1992.

To
Dennis Patrick McBride
and
Kevin Joseph Murrell
with appreciation and affection

People have been fed enough sweetmeats; it has given them indigestion: they need some bitter medicine, some caustic truths.

—Mikhail Lermontov in *A Hero of Our Time*

Contents

Foreword

Flannery O'Connor, writing her troubled correspondent "A," identifies her audience as "people who think God is dead." She to the contrary, as a believing writer, holds that "the ultimate reality is the Incarnation," eternally present to creation despite its rejection by Modernist man. Given her vision of reality, the challenge to her is formidable, especially given as well that her primary responsibility is to the good of the story itself as a made work and not to the rescue of unbelieving audience. Consequently, her fictional drama rises out of this disparity of her vision to the partial surface view of reality dominant. Her comic grotesque becomes resolution to that dilemma, a frictional drama rising out of this disparity. For the hard of hearing, she remarks, one must "shout" or for the almost blind one must draw "large and startling pictures."

Professor Edmondson's *Return to Good and Evil* explores the intellectual distortion that out of Nietzsche and others promotes the illusion that we are at last "beyond good and evil." His is a careful exploration of the intellectual context which has forgotten or deliberately ignored realities known but set aside which is a part of the "matter" with which O'Connor writes her "incarnational" fiction, recalling us to our reality as intellectual souls incarnate. It is a work most helpful to our understanding the resonances out of faint memories of that human circumstance, resonances both fascinating and disturbing to us on reading her fiction. A commendable tribute to a remarkable maker of fictions.

Marion Montgomery
Author of *Why Flannery O'Connor Stayed Home*,
vol. 1 of the trilogy, *The Prophetic Poet and the Spirit of the Age*

Preface

This book is written as a guide to the works of Flannery O'Connor. Many are attracted to O'Connor's writing but find her work difficult to understand. This has to do, at least in part, with an inadequate understanding of nihilism, the spirit of the modern age with which O'Connor was so concerned. If some ignorance of nihilism might hamper a reading of O'Connor, the problem is also often due to insufficient appreciation of O'Connor's Catholic heritage in general, and her Thomistic philosophy, in particular. The challenges of properly interpreting O'Connor's fiction might be avoided if the reader and critic are only interested in what O'Connor could have said or should have said, in spite of her best intentions to the contrary. But my interest is in what she *did* say, the major contours of which are evident by combining her fiction with her prose and correspondence. Additionally, her work is illuminated by a study of the philosophy, literature, fiction, and experience by which she herself was influenced.

O'Connor understood, as have others, that Friedrich Nietzsche was the most important proponent of nihilism, a philosophy that seeks to dispense with God and traditional values in favor of a brave new world led by those audacious enough to wield their relentless "will to power." Some will complain, however, that O'Connor did not understand the intricate and evolving nature of Nietzsche's thought. They will further object that O'Connor failed to appreciate that Nietzsche's mission was to save nihilism from itself by adding the call for creativity to its destructive impulse in the hope of a better humanity. Nietzsche, himself, argued that his was a positive, "life-affirming" philosophy and not a dark call to destruction. Indeed, Nietzsche believed, as have some of his more sympathetic critics, that even though he accepted some of the premises of nihilism, he was not a nihilist.

O'Connor concluded, however, that despite Nietzsche's brilliance in recognizing the weaknesses of Western civilization, he failed to offer anything of constructive value to replace what he sought to overthrow. Quite the contrary, a distillation of Nietzsche's thought yields little more than a dangerous product of crude sex, raw power, and aimless destruction. O'Connor did agree, however, with Nietzsche's complaint that the modern age is populated by "last men," individuals without faith, vision, purpose, or valor. Her solution, unlike Nietzsche's, was a recovery of the concepts of good and evil, not their rejection. This return to good and evil means that man must recognize anew his need for God and for the operative principle of God's dealings with man, grace. When grace is absent the vacuum will be filled with evil. Thus, far from transcending good and evil, O'Connor believed that nihilism would lead us into a chasm of evil—hence the single-minded urgency of her literary mission.

As a student of Flannery O'Connor's writing, I have immersed myself in her literature, correspondence, prose, and in her personal library. Day after day, I have enjoyed the opportunity of walking out of my office, across the university courtyard, into the Russell Library and up the stairs to the O'Connor Collection on the second floor. In reading the philosophy, literature, and theology that O'Connor owned, I have taken note of what she found especially interesting by following her annotations. These are not hard to discern as she had a distinctive though simple manner of annotation in her personal books. Working in the charming southern town of Milledgeville, Georgia, the place Flannery O'Connor called home from the age of thirteen until her death, I have also enjoyed the rare privilege of meeting some of those who knew her. As a result, I feel I have come to know O'Connor in some small measure, not only as a writer, but also as a person, and for that, I am both grateful and inspired.

Acknowledgments

As always, and most importantly, my loving wife, Dorothy Marie, has been my constant encouragement and support. Her selfless love is even more inspirational than Flannery O'Connor's no-nonsense piety. My children, Nathan, Erin, Jason, and Kerrie always ensure that my focus is on concrete day-to-day experience as opposed to abstract theory, just as O'Connor believed should be the case.

My own department at Georgia College & State University has been consistently supportive and helpful; those individuals who have provided special encouragement and assistance include Mike Digby, Kim Ireland, Maria Gordon, Brandy Rowe, and Tameka Gude.

I acknowledge Professor Gene Miller's stern guidance in my graduate school endeavors and the unrelenting standards he imparts to his students; those standards always seem to lurk nearby, whether their demands are satisfied or not. Professor Tom Lauth, also at the University of Georgia, had the wisdom to give me the creative room to pursue my interests in political philosophy while I was also gaining competence in more "practical" pursuits such as public administration.

I am also grateful to Marion Montgomery for his friendship and encouragement and for his willingness to supply the foreword to the book. William Sessions provided several excellent suggestions very late in this process and gave what guidance he could in the limited space of time I allowed him; if I had made his acquaintance earlier in the endeavor, I'm sure I would have profited from the opportunity. Many other of O'Connor's contemporaries provided insight into her life and work; however, I have come to understand that they treasure their anonymity. Sarah Gordon, of my own university, played a significant though brief role at an important juncture by encouraging both my work in O'Connor and by expressing interest in the thesis I have pursued.

A number of other friends and colleagues have been helpful in reading partial or full drafts of this book; they include Dave Steele, Mike Firmin, Peter Lawler, Bob Schaefer, Daniel Fernald, and Jim Winchester.

My acknowledgment of the help and encouragement of the foregoing individuals should not be construed to mean that they endorse the final product; that, of course, is my responsibility alone.

Specific acknowledgment of earlier publication of some of this material is made to the following:

Henry T. Edmondson III, "Wingless Chickens: Flannery O'Connor's Response to Nihilism in 'Good Country People,'" in *Flannery O'Connor Review*, Vol. 2, 2002. Permission to reprint granted by the editor, *Flannery O'Connor Review*, Georgia College & State University. Reprinted with permission.

Henry T. Edmondson III, "Mystery vs. Modernity in Flannery O'Connor's Short Story 'A View of the Woods,'" in *Interpretation: A Journal of Political Philosophy*, Vol. 29, No. 2, Winter 2001–02. Reprinted with Permission.

Henry T. Edmondson III, "Flannery O'Connor's Teaching on the Nature of Evil in 'The Lame Shall Enter First.'" in *Faith, Reason, and Political Life Today*, edited by Peter Augustine Lawler and Dale McConkey (Lanham, Maryland: Lexington Books, 2001): pp. 243–60. Reprinted with permission.

Abbreviations

Collected Works (New York: Literary Classics of the United States, 1988). Abbreviated as CW.

Letters of Flannery O'Connor: The Habit of Being. Selected and Edited by Sally Fitzgerald (New York: Farrar, Straus and Giroux, 1979). Abbreviated as HB.

Mystery and Manners, Occasional Prose. Selected and Edited by Sally and Robert Fitzgerald (New York: Farrar, Straus & Giroux, 1969) Abbreviated as MM.

"Evil," the counterpart of "good," is an idea that has fallen even more out of fashion apart from the artificial hype of horror movies. Aside from the recent terrorist tragedies, if someone should dare to employ the word as a moral judgment, for example, if a political regime or if human behavior were to be called "evil," the person using the term would risk immediate scorn and isolation. Perhaps, this is because any meaningful use of "evil" entails the exercise of firm moral judgment, if not condemnation, and this in itself violates the prevailing opinion that a "good" person is tolerant and indiscriminate above all else.

We are caught in a perplexing and perilous predicament: neither evil nor good can be defined nor employed in serious discourse. If we want to recover the use of one concept, we must simultaneously regain the usefulness of the other, because neither is meaningful without its opposite. Evil cannot be understood without a sound understanding of good, but good cannot be defined apart from an unambiguous definition of evil.

Thus in a very real sense, we have moved beyond any valid use of the concepts of good and evil. Were he alive today, the German philosopher of nihilism, Friedrich Nietzsche, might be pleased because he advocated the disposal of such concepts, considering them outworn impediments to moral and social human development. Flannery O'Connor, were she among us, would not be surprised, because as early as the middle of the twentieth century she foresaw our present condition with remarkable prescience. She noted with concern that her society had become an age that "is swept this way and that by momentary convictions" and thus likely to find itself in a place without ethical signposts (CW, 820). For that reason, the most important philosophical thrust of her beautifully crafted literature is a refutation of the modern tendency to push beyond the boundaries of good and evil. Her novels and her short stories are a shrewd and artful endeavor to show how we have come to this dangerous point in history and to warn of the disaster to which it will lead. Accordingly, it was O'Connor's hope that her literature might be "a mirror and a guide for society" (CW, 818).

O'Connor sounded the alarm that "[I]f you live today you breathe in nihilism. In or out of the Church, it's the gas you breathe" (HB, 90). The German philosopher Nietzsche is not the only exponent of nihilism, but he is far and away the most important and articulate of its proponents. It was he who popularized the phrase "Beyond Good and Evil" in his book of the same name.[2] Nietzsche predicted that by the destruction of the Western philosophical and moral tradition, the human race would be free to recognize the emergence of a new moral order led by "overmen," those superior individuals among us who would be governed only by the sheer force of their will and who would be unrestrained in facilitating true human progress.

The threat of nihilism, in O'Connor's view, entails and is preceded by a plague of overweening human pride unchecked by self-knowledge and by an attempt to live life according to empty theoretical abstractions at the expense of common sense. Nihilism also, at some point in its progression, involves a cold neglect of the human soul in favor of a preoccupation with materialism, an ignorance of man's need for grace, a depreciation of the redemptive value of human suffering, and an impertinent disrespect for the mystery inherent in human existence. Accordingly, the reader finds all these themes present in her stories.

O'Connor was aware of Nietzsche's writing; she refers to him several times as the next chapter will show. But her references to the more general threat of "nihilism" are more common. Her works are not an attempt to refute directly the Nietzschean philosophical corpus, point-for-point. She was not an expert in his writing and undoubtedly had no desire to be one, nor was she formerly trained as a philosopher. Instead, her work is a general literary response to the pervasive nihilistic influence in philosophy and culture. It may be that Nietzsche's troubled genius lay not so much in his ability to create a new philosophy, but rather, in recognizing and diagnosing an emerging social condition, in foreseeing its influence in a future far beyond his own lifetime, and in providing the philosophical articulation that popularized this modern trend. When he pronounced God's "death" in the middle of the nineteenth century, he was prophetically describing a world in which the Judeo–Christian tradition was no longer dominant or persuasive in matters of morals and policy. Moreover, when Nietzsche attacks "Christian values," he questions "*all* values, since they are the only values he knows, and this seems to question the very purpose and value of human life: existence becomes an insoluble riddle, human life appears to have no meaning."[3] Just as terrorism is identified as an attack not merely on any one country, but on mankind, so also is nihilism not simply a campaign against the Judeo–Christian tradition, but a war against the philosophical and spiritual foundations of civilization itself.

O'Connor's interest, then, lies not in a debate with Nietzsche or any other philosopher, but in identifying and refuting the cultural influence of nihilism more generally understood and offering a remedy to a world rapidly falling under its spell. Both O'Connor and Nietzsche would agree that an experience of "nothingness" is the logical consequence of a world that has for centuries rejected God or at least acted as if He were irrelevant to modern life and affairs. O'Connor argues on many occasions that when God is excluded, then even the exercise of reason becomes overburdened, loses its footing, and is rendered unreliable.

There are others who have, each in their own way, artistically articulated this disturbing phenomenon over which O'Connor brooded. They include the Russian novelists Dostoyevsky and Turgenev and the English playwright George Bernard Shaw. Even contemporary rock musicians such as Jim Morrison and the Doors, the Rolling Stones, and the Moody Blues demonstrate by their lyrics how nihilism has wormed its way into every corner of our culture. Jim Morrison, for example, earnestly demands that we "Break on Through (To the Other Side)" through the aggressive destruction of moral prohibitions against, for example, incest.[4] But it is Nietzsche who most comprehensively explains the main features of nihilism. As one student of O'Connor has keenly noted, "the intensity of [O'Connor's] passion in these choppy seas reminds one again and again of the intense passion of a Nietzsche directed against an indifferent or hostile God."[5]

The reader of O'Connor's works will find her descriptions of the concept of evil far more conspicuous than her discussions of good. This seems to be the case for at least two reasons. The first reason is that good, portrayed by O'Connor as natural and divine grace intervening in human affairs, occurs where it is most needed—in the midst of evil. The second reason is broader: if modern civilization is to recover a sense of good, it must recover as well an appreciation for evil. Just as one color may not be fully defined except by contrast with its opposite, so neither is good fully comprehended except in contrast to its absence. The novelist Walker Percy goes so far as to suggest that evil must be rediscovered *before* good is recovered. His character Lancelot remarks, "'Evil' is surely the clue to this age. . . . For everything and everyone's either wonderful or sick and nothing is evil."[6]

If O'Connor advocates a return to "good and evil," it is fair to ask how she would define the terms. The answer is simple, although it takes the corpus of her fiction, correspondence, and prose to understand it adequately: "good" is the operation of divine and natural grace in human life, and "evil" is the absence of the same. O'Connor follows scripture and Thomistic philosophy in her understanding that the essence of moral and spiritual life is the grace of God, both as it is naturally present in all creation as the residual character of the Maker, and as it operates more supernaturally through purposeful Divine activity. O'Connor illustrates that this grace is often prompted by the pressure of malevolent events and circumstances and consequently leads men and women to that which they need most, redemption. The arrogance of human beings is the greatest hindrance to the operation of grace, yet it is those with such attitudes that are most in need of redemption. For that reason, O'Connor's characters are often violently jolted from their complacency by the stern and disruptive operation of grace in their lives. The process by which grace operates in human lives is neither predictable nor given to easy analysis; rather, its action, like human existence itself, transpires in the swirl of a mystical fog. As the epistle reminds us, we see as "through a glass, darkly."[7]

Why should the reader be especially interested in O'Connor's particular response to the threat of nihilism? After all, she lived a relatively short life and spent most of her time far from the intellectual venues one would expect essential to foster the philosophical insight meaningful to a wider audience. The answer is that somehow O'Connor possessed not only artistic brilliance but also an abundance of philosophical good sense that yielded a universal response to the nihilism she found so troubling. She has managed to offer a diagnosis and prescribe a remedy for what may be man's most serious moral plague to date and the elements of her response to nihilism are the precise elements that should be common to every effort to oppose this most dangerous of philosophies. Such a response is badly needed today, because as she recognized with reference to the Spanish mystic St. John of the Cross, "Right now the whole world seems to be going through a dark night of the soul" (HB, 100). In the same work to which O'Connor makes reference, St. John warns that because of this spiritual and moral benightedness, "At every step we mistake evil for good and good for evil."[8]

PHILOSOPHY AND LITERATURE

O'Connor protested that she was "a novelist and not a philosopher nor a theologian;" but, her literature is profoundly philosophical with vital theological implications (MM, 154). After O'Connor's death, Thomas Merton said he would compare O'Connor, not with modern novelists like Hemingway or Sartre, but with "someone like Sophocles . . . for all the truth and all the craft with which she shows man's fall and his dishonor."[9] As have many other writers of fiction, O'Connor believed that important but complex concepts may be conveyed best through narrative. One might consider, for example, Homer's inimitable portrayals of heroism; equally illustrative is Shakespeare's picture of the nature of tyranny in *Richard III* or the consuming force of ambition in *Macbeth*. Flannery O'Connor understood literature's ability to convey philosophical ideas; but she also recognized the propensity in the modern age to eschew narrative in favor of theory and statistics. In an address at Georgetown University, she admitted

[F]or someone like myself who is not a teacher, and not even a literary person in the accepted sense of the phrase, it's always difficult to throw off the habits of the story-teller and to come up with some abstract statement instead. I'd

much prefer to be reading you one of my stories tonight, but these are times
when stories are considered not quite as satisfying as statements and statements are considered not quite as satisfying as statistics.[10]

Elsewhere O'Connor argued, "A story is a way to say something that
can't be said any other way. . . . You tell a story because a statement would
be inadequate" (MM, 96). In another instance, O'Connor refers to Joseph
Conrad's famous "Preface" in which the Polish-born author reveals that
he tries to teach the reader something of philosophical truth while appealing to his aesthetic sensibilities.

> I suppose when I say that the moral basis of Poetry is the accurate naming of
> the things of God, I mean about the same thing that [Joseph] Conrad meant
> when he said that his aim as an artist was to render the highest possible jus-
> tice to the visible universe. (HB, 128)[11]

By borrowing Conrad's phrase, "the accurate naming of the things of
God," O'Connor means that fiction has the power to identify and articulate the key concepts that underlie human existence. For that reason, and
in respect to other fiction writers, O'Connor complains, "What offends my
taste in fiction is when right is held up as wrong, or wrong as right" (HB,
144). Good fiction, though, does not always produce a lucid, unambiguous view of the world; on the contrary, it may leave "the reader with a
deeper mystery to ponder when the literal mystery has been solved."[12]
The fiction writer, then, does not just tell a story; he must wrap his story
around moral truth. As she explains, "I believe that the fiction writer's
moral sense must coincide with his dramatic sense" (HB, 124). She stops
short, though, of offering a demonstrable theory of exactly how the writer
can accomplish this action as she admits, "The subject of the moral basis
of fiction is one of the most complicated and I don't doubt that I contra-
dict myself on it, for I have no foolproof aesthetic theory" (HB, 123). None
of this is meant to encourage the cold dissection of literature, as some are
prone to do. O'Connor disapproves of the unrestrained search for esoteric
symbolism in literature as well as its violent deconstruction when she
notes, "There was a time when the average reader read a novel simply for
the moral he could get out of it, and however naïve that may have been,
it was a good deal less naïve than some of the more limited objectives he
now has" (CW, 814). The contemporary novelist "is asked to begin with
an examination of statistic rather than with an examination of conscience.
Or if he must examine his conscience, he is asked to do so in the light of
statistics" (MM, 130). O'Connor echoes Aristotle's classic treatise on the
fine arts, the *Poetics*, when she says that the novelist deals with a view of
"absolutes" and this, she continues, "will include a good deal more" than

what is "taken merely in the light provided by a house-to-house survey" (MM, 134).[13]

When O'Connor speaks of her work having a moral thesis, she means that it should change one's life rather than simply supply an abstract notion of right and wrong. The "moral of the story," as she explains, is not a "wild pig that must be hunted down and shot in the underbrush of any novel or short story." On the contrary, the writer's "moral vision" should guide the reader in knowing how to live.

> Centuries ago, St. Cyril of Jerusalem in instructing catechumens, wrote, "The dragon sits by the side of the road, watching those who pass. Beware lest he devour you. We go to the Father of Souls, but it is necessary to pass by the dragon." Moral vision for the artist is the identification of this dragon.[14]

She shared with a friend her excitement that she had made a "lucky find" in St. Thomas Aquinas's sections of the *Summa* and the *De Veritate* on prophecy in which he explained that the "prophetic vision is dependent on the *imagination* of the prophet" (HB, 367).[15] O'Connor's excitement undoubtedly stemmed from the self-recognition that she had something to say of a prophetic nature to the world and that she possessed the imagination to do so aesthetically. Indeed, in her correspondence to her friend Maryat Lee, she often signed her letters with variations of the name of Tarwater, the prophet in her second novel, *The Violent Bear It Away*.[16] Nonetheless, despite her prophetic leanings, she never seemed to take herself too seriously. She commented on her inspiration,

> I wish I had Voices, or anyway distinct voices. I have something that might be a continuing muttering snarl like cats courting under the house, but no clear Voice in years.[17]

Despite no dramatic vision or revelations, she was inspired in her craft insofar as she believed she was invested with the opportunity of serving as a kind of "prophet." In this role, the writer is one who speaks forth truth to his society, not only basing his prophecy on the truth as it is needed and relevant to the reader, but also employing the faculty of the imagination in the service of the prophetic act. The artist has the opportunity, then, to speak as did the Old Testament prophets since the poet, if he is indeed a poet, has the faculty of "sight" that is "essentially prophetic."[18] O'Connor noted, "According to St. Thomas, prophetic vision is not a matter of seeing clearly, but of seeing what is distant, hidden" (HB, 365). She recognized that many other writers saw no transcendent purpose in their art and she explained in a lecture, "Everywhere I go I'm asked if I think the universities stifle writers. My opinion is that they don't stifle enough of them. There's many a best-seller that could have been prevented by a good teacher" (MM, 84-5).[19]

O'CONNOR'S USE OF THE GROTESQUE

In her copy of Jacques Maritain's *Creative Intuition in Art and Poetry*, O'Connor has underlined "art draws beauty from ugly things and monsters."[20] Indeed, Flannery O'Connor's distorted literary characters are a key to her mastery as a moral teacher. By presenting ordinary characters in a distorted, cartoon-like manner, she is able to teach more than she could by simply trying to sketch life in a style restricted to realism. She notes, "Today many readers and critics have set up for the novel a kind of orthodoxy. They demand a realism of fact which may, in the end, limit rather than broaden the novel's scope."[21] O'Connor maintains, "[A] literature which mirrors society would be no fit guide for it. . . . The novelist must be characterized not by his function but by his vision and we must remember that his vision has to be transmitted and that the limitations and blind spots of his audience will very definitely affect the way he is able to show what he sees."[22] "The world of near-perfection," she continues, "seldom makes good fiction."[23]

She explains that if a writer is able to employ distortion effectively, it may indicate that he possesses an undistorted view of normalcy. The grotesque is only grotesque insofar as it is a deviation from what is normal and the ability to create such a deviation presupposes an understanding of the boundaries between the normal and the abnormal. O'Connor explains, "Whenever I'm asked why Southern writers particularly have a penchant for writing about freaks, I say it is because we are still able to recognize one. To be able to recognize a freak you have to have some conception of the whole man" (CW, 817). The existence of the grotesque, furthermore, is a standing contradiction to the dangerous promise of modern philosophy to perfect human nature. It is only

> in these centuries when we are afflicted with the doctrine of the perfectibility of human nature by its efforts that the vision of the freak in fiction is so disturbing [because] he keeps us from forgetting that we share in his state. The only time he should be disturbing to us is when he is held up as a whole man. (MM, 133)

G. K. Chesterton helps O'Connor make her point when he writes, "the real argument about religion turns on the question of whether a man who was born upside down can tell when he comes right way up."[24] The "ordinary condition of man," Chesterton continues, "is not his sane or sensible condition." Rather, "the normal is an abnormality." The French mathematician and Christian apologist Blaise Pascal explains that a sign of "being great" is "to know that one is miserable." He speaks of "the natural poverty of our feeble and mortal condition."[25] "I like Pascal," O'Connor admits, and she echoes him when she insists, "We're all grotesque" (HB, 304; MM, 233). She adds that her stories are grotesque because, "we suffer from Original Sin."[26]

O'Connor employs the technique of grotesqueness to get the attention of an audience moderately literate and morally dull, satisfied with vague discussion and lazy thinking about important matters. She writes, "[To] the hard of hearing, you shout, and for the almost blind you draw large and startling figures" (CW, 806). She also writes, "I can't see any way to write as a Catholic unless you make what you write brutal, since now there aren't any mutually understood words above a certain level."[27] O'Connor's mother once put ruffled curtains in her daughter's room while the writer was away lecturing at Notre Dame University. Upon returning, O'Connor warned her "[T]he curtains have to go, lest they ruin my prose."[28] Walker Percy notes that the traditional religious vocabulary has been rendered meaningless by overuse; hence, as soon as the writer uses the words "salvation or redemption . . . the jig is up."[29] Thus, O'Connor strains for new and alarming ways to get the Christian message across to her audience. For example, in her short story, "The River," and in her second novel *The Violent Bear It Away*, drowning comes to symbolize baptism, because, as Walker Percy has noted, "How else can one possibly write of a baptism as an event of immense significance when baptism is already accepted but accepted by and large as a minor tribal rite somewhat secondary to taking the kids to see Santa at the department store?"[30] In the short story, "Parker's Back," an exploding tractor igniting a tree stands for Moses's burning bush, and to complete the analogy, Parker, like Moses, is rendered shoeless, though involuntarily. After the explosion, "[t]he first thing Parker saw were his shoes. . . . He was not in them" (CW, 665).

In an interview printed in the *Atlanta Journal and Constitution*, O'Connor concedes that not every fiction writer may feel "that he has to shock to get through to the average reader." She continues, "I believe that the 'average' reader, however, is a good deal below average. People say with considerable satisfaction, 'Oh, I'm an average reader,' when the fact is they never learned to read in the first place, and probably never will." Even those who are thought to be "highly educated" often "don't know trashy fiction from any other kind." If one writes contrary to the prevailing values of the time, the writer must "shock" in order to gain attention. If the writer is saying "something that the majority don't believe in or wish to see, then you have to get and hold their attention usually by extreme means."[31] Neither O'Connor's readers nor her critics consistently understood that her use of the grotesque was not an end in itself, but a means to exposing the human condition. She admitted her occasional amusement at seeing some of her stories "described as horror stories . . . because the reviewer always has hold of the wrong horror" (HB, 90).

Finally, O'Connor's preference for the grotesque is explained by one of her most dearly held beliefs, the mystery of human existence. Fiction is able to explore the outer regions of the mysterious, regions to which other disciplines cannot venture. She explains that "if the writer believes that our life is and will remain essentially mysterious . . . then what he sees on the surface will be of interest to him only as he can go through it into an experience of mystery itself."

> His kind of fiction will always be pushing its own limits outward toward the limits of mystery, because for this kind of writer, the meaning of a story does not begin except at a depth where the adequate motivation and the adequate psychology and the various determinations have been exhausted. (CW, 816)

And so, if O'Connor renders her characters and plot grotesque, "that is only done by the violence of a single minded respect for the truth" (MM, 83). "Violence," she asserts, "is a force which can be used for good or evil" (MM, 13). O'Connor endeavors to use it for good. When in her fiction O'Connor distorts action so that violence is exaggerated, then distortion becomes a literary "instrument" (MM, 162). For that reason, "[t]his is not the kind of distortion that destroys; it is the kind that reveals, or should reveal"(MM, 162); it is a "realism which does not hesitate to distort appearance in order to show a hidden truth" (MM, 179). The Christian novelist "will find in modern life distortions which are repugnant to him, and his problem will be to make these appear as distortions to an audience which is used to seeing them as natural." Accordingly, "he may well be forced to take ever more violent means to get his vision across to this hostile audience."

> When you can assume that your audience holds the same beliefs you do, you can relax a little and use more normal ways of talking to it; when you have to assume that it does not, then you have to make your vision apparent by shock. (CW, 805-6)

O'Connor recognized time and again, however, that she ran a risk of misinterpretation when she employed literary distortion. She carried out a short correspondence with Shirley Abbot Tomkieviez, who had written a review of O'Connor's writing. Tomkieviez had erroneously labeled O'Connor an existentialist. O'Connor corrected Tomkieviez in a careful and detailed letter. In a second letter, the author argued that storytelling, even if it employed the grotesque, was her best means of clear self-expression.

> Lately I have been going around (for my sins) talking to ladie's [sic] clubs and several times I have found myself in the same fix—me saying one thing and them thinking I'm saying the exact opposite. You have to spell everything out and leave nothing to the imagination. I have come to think that stories are the only safe things to write.[32]

O'Connor's fascination with things bizarre received early encouragement when at the age of five, she was filmed by a news organization "with her pet bantam chicken who held the distinction of being able to walk backwards as well as forwards." She confessed, "'From that day forward . . . [w]hat had been only a mild interest became a passion, a quest. I had to have more and more chickens. I favored those with one green eye and one orange or with overlong necks and crooked combs. I wanted one with three legs or three wings but nothing in that line turned up.'"[33]

Whereas O'Connor's use of the grotesque elicited misinterpretation from some readers, it invited peculiar attention from a few others. She wrote her editor, "You would be amused at some of the mail I am getting—one from a real west Virginia mountineer to his writer-friend . . . 'I have serious heart and blood vessel condition, don't want a penny or pity but sure do like how your (???) form words—sinsational, WOW, ha ha.' Another letter came from a young man who 'thinks he and I could write one together as good as *Gone With the Wind*.' He then adds that he is 35 years old, weighs 160 pounds, is six feet tall, considered 'handsome, intelligent and great ambition and broke my leg in four place in Miami Florida on April 20 so have plenty time to write.'" One writer, a "Mr. Semple of Cincinnati," having in mind her short story "A Good Man is Hard to Find," "doesn't really see how I can say a good man is hard to find. He is an industrial engineer, likes to play bridge, is the active type, 31 years old, single etc etc." (HB, 86-87). She regaled her friend Maryat Lee with another collection of unsolicited contacts. She described a letter

> from a man in Macon who wants to buy two Chinese geese, letter from a girl in Jonesboro who has an idea for a musical comedy based on the Civil War but is "not versed in literary type writing" and would like me to write it for her, letter from a carpenter in Thomaston ("I seen the pece [sic] in paper about you") who would like to send me his picture, letter from lady in Toccoa enclosing three tracts of Oral Roberts and a magazine called HEALING (crutches in picture).

O'Connor wryly concluded, "All these letters are from people I might have made up" (HB, 359).

THE PERSPECTIVE FROM RURAL GEORGIA

In her correspondence, O'Connor sometimes affected a caricature of Southern dialect and accent, deliberately misspelling words to reflect their idiosyncratic rural pronunciation. She enjoyed humor at her own expense and gently ridiculed the middle Georgia region in which she lived. She once explained that whatever degree of "celebrity" she enjoyed was a "comic distinction shared with Roy Roger's horse and Miss Watermelon of 1955" (HB, 125-6).

To a friend at the *Chicago Review,* she advised, "What you ought to do is get you a Fulbright to Georgia and quit messing around with all those backward places you been at" (HB, 532). In reference to a visit by one of the editorial staff at Harcourt, Brace, & Company, she warned that the editor would have to be "expert in penetrating the Georgia wilderness. The only way to get here is by bus or buzzard" (HB, 77). O'Connor was amused but in no way surprised that her work was often least appreciated in her own region. In correspondence to Ben Griffith, a teacher living in Macon, she said, "I presume you are a foreigner, as nobody in Georgia shows much interest" (HB, 69). She reported, "My uncle Louis [Cline] is always bringing me a message from somebody at [his company] who has read *Wise Blood*. The last was: ask her why she don't write about some nice people." Another Georgia reader conceded that "yeah it was a good book well written and all that but tell her the next time to write about some rich folks, I'm mighty tired of reading about poor folks." (HB, 54) She wrote her publisher, Robert Giroux, "We have a fine new literature commission in this state, composed of a Baptist preacher, a picture-show manager, and some other worthy whom I keep thinking must or should be the warden at the state penitentiary" (HB, 59).

Although her father died when she was fifteen, O'Connor's relationship with her mother, with whom she lived and enjoyed an uncommon but intimate relationship, was a source of never ending wry amusement for the writer. She referred to her mother simply as "my parent," or, more frequently, by her first name, Regina. "Regina is getting very literary. 'Who is this Kafka?' she says. 'People ask me.' A German Jew, I says, I think. He wrote a book about a man that turns into a roach. 'Well, I can't tell people *that*, she says.'" In respect to the English novelist, Evelyn Waugh, Regina asked, "'Who is this Evalin Wow?'" (HB, 33).

Ensconced in the rural South, O'Connor was underappreciated not only for *what* she wrote; she was misunderstood *that* she wrote. After one of her many admissions to the hospital, she wrote a friend from her room,

> When I came in and gave the information about myself at the admitting place, the woman who had carrot-colored hair and eyeglasses to match, asked me by whom was I employed.
> "Self-employed," says I.
> "What's your bidnis?" she says.
> "I'm a writer," I says.
> She looked at me for a while then she says, "How do you spell that?" (HB, 423)

But O'Connor also argued that her geographical and cultural situation was a distinct advantage. She writes, "The Southern writer can outwrite anybody in the country because he has the Bible and a little history" (HB, 444). Living and writing in the South preserved the opportunity for the writer to talk "inside a community" (MM, 53). The South, claims O'Connor, offers some measure of insulation from the worst excesses of overintellectualism. The region helps one to maintain "that balance between principle and fact, between judgment and observation, which is so necessary to maintain if fiction is to be true," whereas the "isolated imagination is easily corrupted by theory" (MM, 53-4). The writer living "inside his community seldom has such a problem," she explains. Therefore, whatever limitations living in the South imposes, its setting "is a gateway to reality" (MM, 54). It is "in these terms" that "being a Georgia writer has some positive significance." But these qualities are not "accessible to the poll-taker," she adds (MM, 57, 58).

O'Connor is a "regional" writer only insofar as she employs her regionalism to transport the reader to another "country," the country of objective truth. She explains, "The one quality which all the best fiction writers have in common is that they are able to use their particular country in such a way that it suggests an ultimate reality." "The serious fiction writer has only one country," she argues, "but his one country suggests so much that when the serious reader travels in it, he may say—'This is a country I never thought could exist but I feel at home here.' Or if the reader does recognize this 'country,' he will appreciate its philosophical profundity in a way he previously had not. He may say, 'This is a place I've always known but there is something mysterious about it now.'" O'Connor explains, "And either of these reactions means that the fiction writer has been successful, that he has given you, at least a hint, of what is your own tremendous country and your true home."[34]

O'Connor reiterates Walker Percy's assertion that losing the Civil War fostered a salubrious climate for Southern writing. She has this in mind when she congratulates Percy in 1962, "I'm glad we lost the War and you won the Nat'l Book Award" (CW, 1159). O'Connor extends Percy's hypothesis by explaining Southerners were under no illusions of a perfectible world. The South's defeat had left the region with "an inburnt knowledge of human limitations."

> What he was saying was that we have had our Fall. We have gone into the modern world . . . with a sense of mystery which could not have developed in our first state of innocence—as it has not sufficiently developed in the rest of our country. (MM, 59)

O'Connor enjoyed the company of a small literary group that met once a week on Wednesday evenings at her dairy farm homestead Andalusia. Their subject material ranged from literature to philosophy. For example, she encouraged a friend to visit the group.

> Wednesday night you must come out and join a bunch that meets out here oncet a week to read things. The past two times it's been Kierkegaard. Next week it is to be Kafka. We hope to proceed to Heidegger, then Camus. Sounds lofty but most of us can't pronounce the names.[35]

Despite her growing international literary reputation, O'Connor did not dominate their gatherings; rather, she only spoke occasionally, but when she did so, others listened carefully.

CONCLUSION AND OVERVIEW

O'Connor's literary style was once described as possessing "a brutal irony, a slam-bang humor and a style of writing as balefully direct as a death sentence."[36] Several of her specific literary habits contribute to the philosophical gravamen of her work. The first is her use of skylines. At a crucial turning point in most of her stories, she invariably will digress to describe the horizon. Thus for her, the artful insertion of a skyline is a signal of a kind of moral climax to the story, and the reader might infer that O'Connor's focus upon the boundary of the earth and sky suggests that the principle at issue is universal in the sense that its implications transcend the philosophical "here-and-now." The juxtaposition of a forest with the skyline is a suggestion of human mystery, most notably in the short story "A View of the Woods." More generally, O'Connor's frequent use of skylines casts a pensive if not somber shadow over the concrete events of the story and suggests that the personal struggle in which the protagonist is engaged is a struggle potentially shared by every reader. For example, in "A Good Man Is Hard to Find," immediately prior to the family's execution and the grandmother's self-revelation, O'Connor writes, "Behind them the line of woods gaped like a dark open mouth" (CW, 146).

A second literary device is O'Connor's description of the human eye. O'Connor often uses the eye to reveal the character if not the soul of her characters. When Tarwater senses his imminent duty to baptize Rayber's child in the lake and thus submit to his transcendent calling, his eyes "were the color of the lake just before dark when the last daylight has faded and the moon has not risen yet" and there appeared to be "something fleeing across the surface of them, a lost light that came from nowhere and vanished into nothing" (CW, 427). This technique reminds one of the Gospel verse, "The eye is the lamp of the body. If your eyes are good, your whole body will be full of light.[37] But if your eyes are bad, your whole body will be full of darkness. If then the light within you is darkness, how great is that darkness!"[38]

Finally, O'Connor's work is rich in its use of symbolism, although she was quick to chasten those who gave her stories bizarre and esoteric interpretations unsupported by the text of the story. She noted to a correspondent that a lot of "foolishness" had been written about her stories.[39] In her letter "To a Professor of English," she responded to a situation in which three faculty members and ninety students in several classes were attempting to interpret "A Good Man is Hard to Find." She began her response, "The interpretation . . . is fantastic and about as far from my intentions as it could get to be. If it were a legitimate interpretation, the story would be little more than a trick and its interest would be simply for abnormal psychology." Although she hoped that the "meaning of a story should go on expanding for the reader the more he thinks about it," she also warned, "If teachers are in the habit of approaching a story as if it were a research problem for which any answer is believable so long as it is not obvious, then I think students will never learn to enjoy fiction" (HB, 437). Attempts to overinterpret her work so disturbed O'Connor that less than two months before her death she eked out a rebuke to another "Professor of English," suggesting, "I think you folks sometimes strain the soup too thin" (HB, 582).

Yet, she admitted that "for the fiction writer himself, symbols are something he uses simply as a matter of course. You might say that these are details that, while having their essential place in the literal level of the story, operate in depth as well as on the surface, increasing the story in every direction" (MM, 71). Just as with her speech, O'Connor's prose is also economical so that in both modes of expression she rarely uses a word or phrase without it being purposefully done. She explains, "The novelist makes his statements by selection, and if he is any good, he selects every word for a reason, every incident for a reason, and arranges them in a certain time sequence for a reason" (MM, 75). O'Connor offers a rationale for the rich symbolism of her work when, following Henry James, she explains that with subjects as complicated as the ones on which she wrote, "the straightforward manner is seldom equal to the complications of the good subject" (MM, 76).

Following this introductory chapter, chapter 2 combines O'Connor's more explicit comments about nihilism with a brief survey of the elements of Nietzsche's thought that seem most pertinent to O'Connor's concerns. The chapter also explains O'Connor's most important philosophical influence, the thought of Thomas Aquinas. Finally, chapter 2 examines two of O'Connor's academic sources from which she learned of nihilism's threat, her college philosophy textbook and an article by Jesuit philosopher Frederick Copleston on Nietzsche and Aquinas.

Chapters 3 and 4 consist of a running commentary on O'Connor's antinihilistic novel, *Wise Blood*. The novel is a modern allegory in which the protagonist Hazel Motes represents man's attempted flight from God through nihilism and his boomerang-like return to God through penance and the proper use of leisure leading to contemplation. These chapters are followed by an explication of O'Connor's most ambitious antinihilistic short story, "Good Country People" in chapter 5, which highlights two features of nihilism as O'Connor understands it, its seductive nature and its philosophical genesis in the hyperrationalistic philosophy of René Descartes.

"The Nature of Evil in 'The Lame Shall Enter First'" is the subject of chapter 6 where the story serves, among other things, to illustrate the Thomistic definition of evil as the absence of good. As the story shows, however, those guilty of inviting evil by denying good may act from the best of intentions; indeed they may be pursuing a misguided conception of goodness, as in well-meaning humanitarian assistance. Chapter 7 on the "Enduring Chill" provides the opportunity to examine O'Connor's social philosophy in which the South provided the closest application. The story suggests that the opposite of prudence, the virtue essential for guiding political and social activity, is not so much rashness as one might expect, but arrogance. Such arrogance demands change but does so in a reckless and often mean-spirited manner. However, for the reader to obtain a fair and balanced view of O'Connor's social philosophy, he must also consider her belief that all men and women are equal at their most fundamental level, their mortality and dependence on God. This belief is most elegantly expressed in her short story, "Revelation," a concise discussion of which is also included in chapter 7. All the elements of her attitude toward social change—moreover, a respect for tradition, a demand for mercy, and an insistence on equality—are antithetical to nihilism.

In her short story, "A View of the Woods," studied in chapter 8, O'Connor is concerned with the theological concept of "mystery," the dimension of human and divine experience that will never be fully comprehensible or controllable. The story begins with the mystery of human nature and the mystery of human suffering; and, by means of a remarkable use of metaphor, shows that these mysteries should lead human beings to the most important mystery of all, the mystery of redemption. In this story, O'Connor is again concerned with the problem of evil. This time Jacques Maritain is especially helpful in explaining the Thomistic dimensions of evil as O'Connor's characters experience it, and Maritain's analysis introduces the possibility that the doctrine of nihilism itself is evil.

Of all of her works, O'Connor's favorite story was "The Artificial Nigger," and this tale, the subject of chapter 9, picks up the theme of redemption introduced in chapter 8. The story is O'Connor's most eloquent call for redemption in which she gives the American black race the honorific role described by the Apostle Paul of "taking up the sufferings of Christ." Finally, chapter 10 elaborates upon the key elements of O'Connor's response to nihilism as they are presented in the preceding chapters, placing special emphasis upon her use of the concept of grace, her belief in the reality of the devil, and the singular role of a prophet in the modern world.

2

O'Connor contra Nihilism

In correspondence, O'Connor once recalled news from the poultry industry involving the experimental breeding of chickens without wings so as to increase the yield of select chicken meat. She then drew a droll but arresting analogy, noting, "[T]he moral sense has been bred out of certain sections of the population, like the wings have been bred off certain chickens to produce more white meat on them. This is a generation of wingless chickens, which I suppose is what Nietzsche meant when he said God was dead" (HB, 90).[1] The opposition of her fiction to the philosophy of nihilism explains, in part, the dark tone of many of her stories. "With such a current to write against, the result almost has to be negative," she said (HB, 97). As O'Connor saw it, nihilism has infected the very act of writing fiction itself, but her aim was to turn fiction against that which nihilism would subvert. She notes, "It is popular to believe that in order to see clearly one must believe nothing," but she argues, "For the fiction writer, to believe nothing is to see nothing; . . . the message I find in the life I see is a moral message."[2]

Of all modern philosophies, nihilism may be the most urgent to understand. Nihilism builds upon the Enlightenment hope in the infinite progress of the human race and teaches that if we are to evolve into an advanced race, traditional values and sentiments must be swept away. In her personal copy of his work, O'Connor has underlined Voegelin's explanation of the progression between the enlightenment promise of "perfectibility" and the later emergence of the nihilistic idea of the "overman." He explains that the modern age begins with the premise that the "nature of man is basically good" and then concludes that the "powers of man can create a society free from want and fear" so that "the ideas of infinite perfectibility, of the superman, and of self-salvation make their appearance."[3] Because religion and tradition are philosophically bankrupt, their decline into "nothingness" must be hastened so as to realize the greatness that is human destiny. Nihilism is, in a sense, worse even than atheism: the atheist is content to disbelieve, whereas, the nihilist must "destroy God" and every vestige of his memory.

O'Connor took a course at Georgia State College for Women entitled "Introduction to Modern Philosophy" during the spring quarter of 1945. The course description as recorded in the 1944–1945 catalog reads, "A first study of philosophic thought from the Renaissance to the post-Romantic period, with selected readings in the key philosophers." The text for the class was the well-regarded, *The Making of the Modern Mind* by John Randall.[4] This was, presumably, O'Connor's first formal introduction to philosophy in general, and nihilism in particular. The text explains that, according to Nietzsche, if the concept of evolution is taken seriously, "we must develop a whole new set of specific ideals and values."

> The traditional aims inherited from Christendom cannot endure unchanged in the growing world of to-day. *We must advance beyond our past standards of good and evil*, and set about a complete revaluation of all values. (emphasis added)[5]

Randall explains that Nietzsche's "ideals are sufficiently in accord with the underlying spirit of the modern age . . . to be fraught with great significance" (CW, 584-5).

O'Connor was a regular book reviewer for the *Georgia Bulletin*, the periodical associated with the Catholic Diocese of Atlanta of which Milledgeville is a part. She reviewed *The Christian Opportunity*, by the Swiss scholar, Denis de Rougemont, writing that the author "examines the Nietzschean formula, God is dead (the gospel in reverse)." Whereas in previous centuries Western civilization has been plagued with various and sundry heresies, the appearance of nihilism in the late nineteenth century represents a philosophical threat of a new order of magnitude. In her review, O'Connor notes that for De Rougemont, this is a century when "the churches no longer find hostile doctrines in the world, but a doctrinal void that has no precedent."[6] O'Connor's perception of the unique nature of the nihilistic threat finds support in Gerhart Niemeyer's *Between Nothingness and Paradise*. Niemeyer describes nihilism as a "creatively destructive activism" that has as its aim the annihilation of "present reality," meaning that the nihilist is out to destroy God, creation, morality, and human nature! He urges the study of nihilism because of the pressing need for an "awareness of what it is that feeds the widespread disorder of our age."[7]

NIETZSCHE'S ANTIPATHY TOWARD CHRISTIANITY

Randall explains that Nietzsche's aim is "to pit himself against the whole moral tradition of the Western world, and to become, in the truest sense, the Anti-Christ."[8] When Randall uses the phrase "Anti-Christ" to explain Nietzsche's philosophy, he means it in the literal sense of the word, as Nietzsche himself meant it. Nietzsche's anti-Christ is not simply opposed to Christ; the anti-Christ is Christ's replacement. This is the biblical sense of the Greek *antichristos*, ("instead of Christ") and in this we better understand why nihilism, especially as promoted by Nietzsche, often takes on its own religious character: it is insufficient to destroy the Judeo–Christian tradition, it must also be replaced. But what it is that shall replace the Western tradition is not clear from Nietzsche's writings and was not entirely clear to him. But this uncertainty over the future does not temper Nietzsche's hostility toward Christianity. For example, in *Human, All-Too-Human* he mocks the religious tradition that consists of a "god who begets children with a mortal woman; a sage who bids men work no more, have no more courts, but look for the signs of the impending end of the worlds."[9] Christianity is a "sacrifice of all freedom, all pride, all self-confidence of the spirit; at the same time, enslavement and self-mockery, self-mutilation."[10] Prayer is for those people who have "no thoughts of their own," sin, a "Jewish invention."[11] In the last sane year of his life, Nietzsche's invective knew no bounds. In *The Antichrist*, he denounces the "Christian conception of God" as "one of the most corrupt conceptions of the divine ever attained on earth" and this conception is a "declaration of war against life, against nature, against the will to live!"[12]

In Nietzsche's philosophical novel *Thus Spake Zarathustra*, his eponymous protagonist explains that "tables of the law," such as the Ten Commandments, must be destroyed. "'I sit,' says Zarathustra, 'with old shattered tables of the law around me—and with new tables, too, half made out.'" The advance of the human race, Nietzsche believes, rests upon its admission that Christianity is a kind of "slave-morality, a code of submission and weakness and disease." For that reason, one must "abandon the meek and docile codes of the past."[13]

Nietzsche directs some of his most virulent attack at the idea of an afterlife, which, he argues, Christians have created as a panacea for human misery: "It was suffering and incapacity that created all afterworlds."[14]

Another motive for the Christian idea of eternal life is a crudely expressed desire for "revenge" against man's impotence to change his past. The pursuit of eternity is an escape from reality. Nietzsche argues, "A new pride my ego taught me, and this I teach men: no longer to bury one's head in the sand of heavenly things, but to bear it freely, an earthly head, which creates a meaning for the earth."[15]

As Nietzsche sees it, the consequence of the Christian idea of an afterworld has been the denigration of the human body in favor of the soul. He counters, though, that it is the physical body that holds man's creative power rather than the more vague notion of soul.

> It was the sick and decaying who despised body and earth and invented the heavenly realm and the redemptive drops of blood: but they took even these sweet and gloomy poisons from body and earth. They wanted to escape their own misery, and the stars were too far for them. So they sighed: "Would that there were heavenly ways to sneak into another state of being and happiness!"[16]

And so Zarathustra exhorts his followers to focus upon their body instead of a fictitious afterworld or an eternal soul. He preaches, "Behind your thoughts and feelings, my brothers, there stands a mighty ruler, an unknown sage—whose name is self. In your body he dwells: he is your body. There is more reason in your body than in your best reason."[17] As we will see in *Wise Blood*, O'Connor's nihilistic evangelist Hazel Motes uses similar language to dissuade his listeners from their preoccupation with their soul, although he is never able to convince himself that his own soul does not exist.

Nietzsche's radical depreciation of the transcendent renders his philosophy decisively materialistic. "Remain faithful to the earth, my brothers," admonishes Zarathustra.[18] But for all of Nietzsche's antipathy toward Christianity, he cannot suppress a certain metaphysical longing. This sentiment emerges in his doctrine of the "eternal recurrence." The eternal recurrence is the admittedly pessimistic idea that all life, every moment, will repeat itself perpetually. Eternal recurrence is a bold affirmation of life: indeed, how could one face life more courageously than to live it repeatedly? The concept, though, rests upon an underlying transcendental urge.

> "Have you ever said Yes to a single joy? O my friends, then you said Yes too to *all* woe. All things are entangled, ensnared, enamored; if ever you wanted one thing twice, if ever you said, 'You please me, happiness! Abide, moment!' then you wanted *all* back. All anew, then you *loved* the world. Eternal ones, love it eternally and evermore; and to woe too, you say: go, but return! *For all joy wants—eternity.*" Zarathustra challenges his followers to sing his hymn

to eternal recurrence. . . . "Now you yourselves sing me the song whose name is 'Once More' and whose meaning is 'into all eternity'—sing, you higher men, Zarathustra's round!"[19]

According to the Jesuit philosopher, Frederick Copleston, "in 1881 the idea of eternal recurrence came to Nietzsche . . . with the force of inspiration."[20] He also confirms that Nietzsche virtually forced this doctrine upon himself. Zarathustra only comes to accept it gradually, and even then it causes him fits of "nausea." Copleston explains,

> [T]he theory of the eternal recurrence was a test of strength, of Nietzsche's power to say "yes" to life. . . . Could he face the thought that his whole life, every moment of it, every suffering, every agony, every humiliation, would be repeated countless times throughout endless time? Could he face this thought and embrace it not only with stoical resignation but also with joy? If so, it was a sign of inner strength, of the triumph in Nietzsche himself of the yea-saying attitude of life.[21]

Nietzsche's metaphysical yearning also appears in his diatribe against the "spirit of gravity" which stands for all that would hold Zarathustra down in his evolutionary ascent. The spirit of gravity consists of "constraint, statute, necessity and consequence and purpose and will *and good and evil*." It is this spirit that restrains Zarathustra who is "impatient to fly, to fly off" (emphasis added).[22]

THE "LAST MAN" AND THE "OVERMAN"

As O'Connor well understood from her reading of Nietzsche, the waning of the Christian man of virtue and piety will allow the appearance of a new man, the "Übermensch," variously translated from Nietzsche's German as the "superman," or perhaps more aptly as the "overman," whose emergence constitutes the great evolutionary leap forward. These god-like individuals will be empowered by their irreverent courage and the exercise of their will, not constrained by obsolete notions of self-sacrifice. As Zarathustra proclaims, "I teach you the overman. Man is something that shall be overcome." Such individuals will be characterized by nothing if not their militancy, as Zarathustra explains, "I see many soldiers: would that I saw many warriors!"[23] These new men will be despised by the traditionally minded who will not accept the role the overman must play in human destiny.

> "Behold the good and the just! Whom do they hate most? The man who breaks their tables of values, the breaker, the lawbreaker; yet he is their creator.

"Behold the believers of all faiths! Whom do they hate most? The man who breaks their tables of values, the breaker, the lawbreaker; yet he is the creator."[24]

Coupled with Nietzsche's admiration for the overman is his disdain for those who are ineligible for such a status. "Of what concern to me are market and mob," he complains. It is "far from the market place" where great things occur; the "inventors of new values" have never mixed well with those more common than themselves. In Nietzsche's novel, Zarathustra comes to realize that he must not cling to the ideal of the equality of all men. He writes, "An insight has come to me: let Zarathustra speak not to the people but to companions. Zarathustra shall not become the shepherd and dog of a herd."[25] The Aristotelian–Thomistic system of virtue, consisting, for example, of the virtues of prudence, wisdom, temperance, and fortitude, is no better than an inducement to "sleep," the antithesis of daring heroic virtue. Sleep is "the master of the virtues" and sleep is the character of those who spend the day "chewing the cud" and who are "patient as a cow."[26]

Those above "the herd," the elite, will be justified in their "selfishness, . . . the wholesome, healthy selfishness that wells from a powerful soul;" selfishness will become their new "virtue."[27] The principle task of the overman will be to overturn Western moral values and create something new, something more fitting for a more advanced stage of humanity. But such creativity will first require destruction: As Zarathustra explains, "Change of values—that is a change of creators / Whoever must be a creator always annihilates." Nietzsche admonishes, "And if your hardness does not wish to flash and cut and cut through, how can you one day create with me? For all creators are hard. And it must seem blessedness to you to impress your hand on millennia as on wax." What must be "cut through" is the "old illusion, which is called good and evil."[28]

The overman will be driven by the force of his will, "his will to power" which is the source of his control.[29] He is subject to nothing and to no one. The will to power—the urge to dominate, conquer, and create anew—is, for Nietzsche, a primordial urge. It is not only an element of human nature, but also the force that drives the animate and inanimate universe itself. Although Nietzsche appreciated Darwin's evolutionary thesis, he rejected the mechanism of blind determinism; instead, he substituted the more visionary faculty of will to power as the propelling force of nature.

THE SEDUCTIVE AND DIONYSIAN CHARACTER OF NIHILISM

In several of her narratives, O'Connor exposes the seductive character of nihilism: "Nothingness" will seduce those who flirt with it. In one of her lesser-known short stories, "The Partridge Festival," a young man named Calhoun visits the rural home of his grandmother, not for the annual festival, but because a deranged inhabitant named Singleton has just been jailed for killing several of his fellow citizens. Calhoun, a man in his early twenties, works successfully as a salesman a few months out of each year to support his self-styled avocation as would-be novelist. He rejects the obvious evidence that the killer is simply insane; instead, he interviews various townspeople to develop his thesis that Singleton had been misunderstood and alienated by the townspeople and thereby driven to his crime. Calhoun unexpectedly finds a kindred spirit in a mysterious local girl far more advanced in her nihilistic beliefs than is Calhoun. Strangely resolute in her views, Mary Elizabeth calls Singleton a "Christ-figure." She challenges Calhoun to join her in visiting Singleton in the state institution so as to sympathize with the killer's role of town "scapegoat," and to seek "an existential encounter with his personality" (CW, 787-8). Calhoun is intimidated into making the visit.

When they arrive, the girl has brought a copy of Nietzsche's *Thus Spake Zarathustra* as a gift to Singleton. The visit, though, is an ugly debacle as the disturbed killer behaves like the lunatic he is. When he crudely exposes himself to Mary Elizabeth, she and Calhoun flee the obscene spectacle in a panic. Calhoun especially is devastated and finds that he has toyed with something more sinister than that for which he was prepared (CW, 796). The story teaches that the pursuit of nihilism will end in obscenity and that those who are drawn to its glamour will be outmatched. The seductiveness of nihilistic philosophy is also vividly depicted in several other works, most notably *Wise Blood* and "Good Country People."

Conspicuous in several of O'Connor's stories is the attention she gives to human sexuality. In her view, modern sexuality is the edge of the nihilistic blade, cutting its swath through traditional morality. O'Connor's judgment is confirmed by Nietzsche's teaching on the Dionysian dimension of the human personality, best elaborated in his first book *The Birth of Tragedy*, a study in the philosophical elements of the tragic art form. The book argues that the ancient Greeks' aesthetic life rested on the foundation of two pillars, the Apollonian and the Dionysian. The influence of Apollo in ancient Greek life is evident with the preoccupation with order, harmony, and discipline, and emblematic of this interest is Greek classical sculpture. The Dionysian impulse among the Greeks gave birth to the tragic art form; and, whereas the Apollonian is associated with the rational side of human nature, the Dionysian emanates from a different source, that part of the human being given to nonrational expressiveness, to abandon, and even to excess. Nietzsche further argues that the Dionysian influence is under appreciated by a world that gives undue attention to the

Apollonian, a obsession with order and reason promulgated by the fame of the Greek philosopher, Socrates.

History, Nietzsche maintains, is shaped by the interplay, indeed the tension, between these two forces, although the Dionysian urge has been neglected. The "death of God"—the waning authority of the Judeo–Christian tradition—has set the stage for a reemergence of the spirit of Dionysus. Apollo, the god associated with restraint, order and serenity, will recede so that the Dionysian man may greet life with abandon, embracing life in all its sublime beauty.[30]

Nietzsche redefines tragedy in such a way that it serves his philosophic argument. The classical view of tragedy, best explained in Aristotle's *Poetics*, involves protagonists who are quite ordinary, with the mixture of virtue and vice common to most people. They are neither very good nor very bad. When the tragic actor suffers the consequence of his weak character, the man or woman in the audience can identify with him and so experience a kind of vicarious pity or terror at seeing his misfortune. The audience is accordingly encouraged in their own growth in virtue and the mastery of their vices by the spectacle of the drama.[31]

But for Nietzsche, the tragic protagonist becomes a kind of hero because of his willingness to defy conventional norms of right and wrong, even if he does so inadvertently, as does Wagner's Siegfried. He suffers for his action, but does so heroically, as prototypical of all those who would push against the boundaries of convention. Thus Oedipus, as Sophocles portrays him, does not curb his curiosity as he should and so inadvertently commits, in one fell swoop, murder against his father and incest with his mother. But for Nietzsche, Oedipus is a hero because through his suffering he "spreads a magical power of blessing that remains effective even beyond his decease." Though the "moral world may perish through his actions, his actions also produce a higher magical circle of effects which found a new world on the ruins of the old one that has been overthrown." Through his unnatural incest, the "mother-marrying Oedipus" may "compel nature to surrender her secrets." And so man, "rising to Titanic stature, gains culture by his own efforts and forces the gods to enter into an alliance with him." Sophocles' Oedipus, as reinterpreted by Nietzsche, is "a prelude," a forerunner, of "the *holy man's* song of triumph." Apollonian attempts to restrain the Dionysian are a repulsive negation, a "nausea and disgust with life."[32] This explains why Nietzsche, at least at the earlier stages of his career, was so taken with Richard Wagner's *Tristan and Isolde*: the opera is a tragic celebration of uncontrollable adulterous love. This is also one reason why Nietzsche would have found Wagner's Siegfried exemplary, given that he is the offspring of an incestuous union.

In Euripides' *The Bacchae*, Dionysus comes to Thebes because the "city must learn its lesson," to respect and give proper homage to the god of wine whom it has ignored. The sign of his coming is that all the women of the town are suddenly scattered upon the hillsides, engaged in frenzied orgiastic pastimes. Although the wise Teiresias and Cadmus, even in their advanced age, are prepared to show proper piety to the god and join the festivities, they are blocked by the young headstrong Pentheus who is determined to "stop this obscene disorder."

Pentheus becomes the tragic figure of the play because he is crippled by his *amathía*—he is not only unwise, but also unteachable. He attempts to capture and imprison the women who have given themselves to "serve the lusts of men" and to lock Dionysus away as well. Dionysus, though, cannot be contained, so the god frees himself by creating an earthquake. But Pentheus is a slow learner and he brings about his own horrid dismemberment at the hands of the Bacchantes, Dionysus's frenzied females, when he persists in trying to imprison Dionysus: "I shall order every gate in every tower to be bolted tight." Nietzsche generalizes this myth and uses it as an indictment against the modern world if it, like Thebes, refuses to acknowledge that "there is no god greater than Dionysus," and that he cannot and should not be contained.[33]

Nietzsche, then, calls for a Dionysian pursuit of life, even if those who are so inspired shall suffer its consequences. In the *Birth of Tragedy*, he issues the invitation, "Yes, my friends, believe with me in Dionysian life and the rebirth of tragedy. The age of the Socratic man is over; put on wreaths of ivy. . . . Only dare to be tragic men. . . . Prepare yourselves for hard strife, but believe in the miracles of your god."[34] Such will be Nietzsche's "veritable hymn of impiety," sung in praise of "active sin."[35] To be sure, the Dionysian revolution will be socially destructive as sexuality becomes more of a strategy than a natural expression of human passion.

For Nietzsche, the traditional restraints upon excessive sexual expression are a denial of life itself, an opposition to "the triumphant Yes to . . . true life . . . through the mysteries of sexuality."[36] Those who teach the imposition of sexual constraints are "preachers of death" who find a ready audience because "the earth is full of those to whom one must preach renunciation of life." Although a restrained attitude toward sexuality may at times be appropriate for the masses, it is not so for the more sophisticated. Zarathustra advises, "Those for whom chastity is difficult should be counseled against it."[37] Dionysus becomes Nietzsche's tactic to break down the Judeo–Christian "resentment" against free sexual self-expression. As Copleston explains, "Dionysus is for Nietzsche the symbol of the stream of life itself, breaking down all barriers and ignoring all restraints."[38] Nietzsche boasts, "I abhor all those moralities which say: 'Do not do this!'"[39]

O'Connor's response to Nietzsche's elaborate theory of revolutionary sexuality is quite simple and straightforward; although, as later chapters will demonstrate, she repeats her response in artistically varied ways. For O'Connor, Nietzsche's romantic notion of history-changing Dionysian revelry is nothing more than illegitimate and crude sex. To be the work of a devout unmarried Catholic woman in the 1950s, this argument is made incisively though tastefully in, among other works, "The Partridge Festival," *Wise Blood*, and "Good Country People."

Nietzsche's view of suffering further develops his unique conception of tragedy. Unlike the existentialists, for whom suffering is no more than a confirmation of the absurdity of life, Nietzsche understands suffering as a creative opportunity. Zarathustra explains, "Creation—that is the great redemption from suffering and life's growing light. But that the creator may be, suffering is needed and much change. Indeed, there must be much bitter dying in your life, you creators."[40] Nietzsche's conception of suffering, however, is far removed from the Judeo–Christian doctrine of suffering. In the latter, an individual should submit himself to the divine purpose behind the tragedy; but for Nietzsche, suffering is an opportunity to challenge life, and if need be, to defy God himself. Even more startling is Nietzsche's opinion that genuine suffering may well be self-inflicted by means of Dionysian excess. Indeed, such willful suffering is "heroic."[41]

> Before tragedy, what is warlike in our soul celebrates its Saturnalia; whoever is used to suffering, *whoever seeks out suffering*, the heroic man praises his own being through tragedy—to him alone the tragedian presents this drink of sweetest cruelty.[42] (emphasis added)

Following her Catholic theology, O'Connor believes suffering to be a key mechanism in personal spiritual growth; but in her case, it is the opportunity to submit one's soul to God, not to blaspheme Him. She was confirmed in this opinion by her own personal experience of suffering, a suffering that was quite difficult and "unto death." By all accounts, she seems to have taken her own teaching to heart. A belief in the immense redemptive value of suffering is evident in her most intimate correspondence and in several of her stories, most of all in "The Artificial Nigger" and "The Displaced Person."

AQUINAS AND NIETZSCHE

The most notable philosophical influence on O'Connor's writing was the thought of St. Thomas Aquinas.[43] She wrote to friends, "At all the Methodist and Baptist institutions that I normally talk at around here, I quote St. Thomas prodigiously and as the audience is never too sure who he is, it is always much impressed."[44] O'Connor was a Thomist both because of her Catholic orthodoxy and by personal predilection; she once conceded that "for the life of me I cannot help loving St. Thomas." She further claimed, with tongue-in-cheek,

> I read [Aquinas's *Summa Theologica*] for about twenty minutes every night before I go to bed. If my mother were to come in during this process and say, "Turn off that light. It's late," I with lifted finger and broad bland beatific expression, would reply, "On the contrary, I answer that the light, being eternal and limitless, cannot be turned off." (HB, 93-4)[45]

O'Connor was quick to criticize Catholic contemporary writing for its sentimentality and for the inability of the average Catholic reader to understand good fiction. She writes, "Catholic readers are constantly being offended and scandalized by novels that they don't have the fundamental equipment to read in the first place." The problem may be their shallow spirituality; O'Connor argues that it is those whose faith is weak who often cannot appreciate "an honest fictional representation of life" (CW, 811).

Yet, O'Connor was just as quick to claim the beneficial influence of the Catholic Church on her own writing: "I feel that if I were not a Catholic, I would have no reason to write, no reason to see, no reason ever to feel horrified or even to enjoy anything." Despite the restrictions the Church occasionally puts on the intellectual inquiry of its members, she explains, "I have never had the sense that being a Catholic is a limit to the freedom of the writer, but just the reverse." Being a Catholic, she confessed, "has saved me a couple of thousand years in learning to write" (HB, 114). Indeed, she credited her Catholicism with her insight into the nihilistic threat and her ability to oppose it in her literature without succumbing to faithlessness. The Church, she explains, taught her "the necessity of fighting" nihilism, and was an institutional ally in her struggle.

She notes, "St. Thomas said that the artist is concerned with the good of that which is made." In the interest of expressing such goodness artistically, she cultivated a lifelong "habit of art," a phrase she drew from Jacques Maritain's writing. Such a habit "is a virtue of the practical intellect," meaning it is not theoretical but applied, and has as its basis "truth" (MM, 81, 65, 64). Since Thomistic aesthetics emphasizes "the good of that which is made," that which is comprehensible through the senses, her approach to writing fiction helps one to understand O'Connor's impatience with abstract theorizing. She learned from Thomas that the "beginning of human knowledge is through the senses, and the fiction writer begins where human perceptions begins. He appeals through the senses, and you cannot appeal to the senses with abstractions." The good fiction writer is not concerned primarily "with unfleshed ideas and emotions" (MM, 67).

She accordingly disapproved of the modern detached use of reason that ignores sensible experience, begins with unproven theories, and tries to remake the world accordingly, often with preposterous consequences. O'Connor learned from her Catholic philosophic heritage that once reason was detached from faith and experience, beginning with the French philosopher René Descartes, it was unable to bear the burden it was required to carry. When reason was separated from faith, it began a slow decline into a kind of pseudoreason, or sophistry, so that we now have "a radical deterioration in our conception of what it means to be reasonable."[46]

Such a faithless and distorted view of human reason eventually means a declining belief in the reality of the human soul (MM, 167). In a passage by Eric Voegelin that O'Connor has noted in pencil, the German philosopher anticipates the consequences of sophistry when he predicts, "The immediacy of order in the soul would be replaced by learned information," so that "[m]an would abdicate before the sophistic intellectual."[47] As O'Connor notes, "The supernatural is an embarrassment today even to many of the churches" (MM, 163). When this cynicism extends to a loss of the sense of sin, redemption, and judgment, O'Connor fears that such a superficial and colorless religion is in danger of suffering the "ultimate degradation" of becoming "fashionable" (MM, 166). G. K. Chesterton offers an incisive observation of what occurs when reason is separated from faith. He explains, "The madman is not the man who has lost his reason. The madman is the man who has lost everything except his reason."[48]

O'Connor believes that, aided by art, reason can recover its proper balance and encouragement in Thomistic philosophy. She approvingly quotes St. Thomas that art itself is "'reason in making.'" She characterizes this as "a very cold and very beautiful definition, and if it is unpopular today, this is because reason has lost ground among us." In the modern age, "imagination and reason have been separated, and this always means an end to art."

> The artist uses his reason to discover an answering reason in everything he sees. For him, to be reasonable is to find, in the object, in the situation, in the sequence, the spirit which makes it itself." (MM, 82)

"As a novelist," O'Connor explains, "the major part of my task is to make everything, even an ultimate concern, as solid, as concrete, as specific as possible." "The novelist," she continues, "begins his work where human knowledge begins—with the senses; he works through the limitations of matter" (MM, 155). With reference to St. Augustine, she argues "this physical, sensible world is good because it proceeds from a divine source" (MM, 157). By beginning with what is perceived rather than with abstract ideas, O'Connor contends that in penetrating "the concrete world" the novelist will "find at its depths the image of its source, the image of ultimate reality."

Flannery O'Connor sees Western civilization in the middle of a kind of cosmic struggle for its fate; a struggle that features, on one side, the menace of nihilism, the latest step in a long cultural decline that would eradicate the philosophy and religion of the past. Nietzsche justifies this act of destruction by a yearning for a new world. The nihilistic opportunity has been staged by the progression of Enlightenment philosophy that, once divorced from religion, promises the secular perfectibility of the human species. On the other side of the struggle is the Judeo–Christian tradition. O'Connor plays the role of a literary interpreter of this struggle and makes the contest intelligible by her fiction, prose, and correspondence. She is not an impartial commentator, though; she is, instead, a partisan advocate for the Thomistic worldview, infused as it is with his synthesis of Christian theology and classical philosophy.

Significant in her private library is the lecture "St. Thomas and Nietzsche," delivered by the Thomist philosopher Frederick Copleston.[49] Copleston notes that though "Nietzsche thought of himself as a creator . . . it is as dynamite, a destructive agent, that he will be remembered."[50] According to Copleston, one type of nihilist, the "passive" nihilist, is bent on destruction for its own sake and is content to watch, and even occasionally assist, the collapse of the existing order. Of even greater concern to Copleston—and to O'Connor—is the "active" nihilist, who will put his shoulder to the wall to assist its disintegration. He is likely to do so, not merely from hate or revenge, but in the interest of creating something new. Such men "hate the old order simply because it fetters in some way the unbridled expression of their own decadent and base lusts and passions." This kind of nihilist will also have a "disgust with the old order, with contemporary life and society, coupled with an urge to create, to create new values and a new society, it might be the product, not merely of man the destroyer but of man the creator, who sees the vision of a transfigured humanity arising on the debris of the old order."[51] Such a man is a "transvaluator of all values." Although Copleston writes against the backdrop of the Third Reich, his vision is broader: the contest is between Nihilism on the one hand and the absolute truth and values represented by St. Thomas on the other. This division, Copleston believes, "runs through all nations and peoples and classes."[52]

RETURN TO GOOD *THROUGH* EVIL

While the concept of goodness is prominent in O'Connor's works, the concept of evil is even more conspicuous. The corpus of her literature offers the argument that a recovery of goodness will be no more than dabbling in sentimentality and good intentions without an understanding of the equally important concept of evil. She explains that "just as it was Adam's task, on behalf of mankind, to name the animals and all the things that had been created before him," even so, "outside of the garden," the task of man "is still to name these things . . . which frequently gives him the added task of finding a name for evil." "This is something," O'Connor continues, "which necessitates a moral vision."[53]

So that the reader might acquire a meaningful appreciation of good, O'Connor spends considerable time leading her audience into encounters with evil. Her ideas closely follow those of Aquinas. One of the fascinating elements of his teaching is that evil, in itself, has no essence in the same way that good is an essential quality; rather, evil is the deprivation of good, the vacuum created by its absence. St. Thomas further teaches that a "principal cause of so much evil in the world" is so many misguided people trying to do good, "even though good and evil are opposites."[54] As O'Connor herself asserts, "I think evil is the defective use of good" (HB, 129).

In O'Connor's view the first attempt "beyond" good and evil is confusion over their meaning and this confusion consists of the contemporary reduction of goodness to mere "sentiment" and the outright denial of the reality of evil. O'Connor explores these ideas in several stories. For example, in "The Lame Shall Enter First," she demonstrates just how injurious the humanitarian impulse can be if it is divorced from the source of goodness, and if such altruism ignores the possibility of evil.

Nietzsche maintains that the paramount expression of man's "will to power" is his ability to create—or destroy—the concepts of good and evil. Zarathustra admits that he "found no greater power on earth than good and evil" but he maintains that good and evil are human inventions, expressions of man's will to power, and made for his own convenience.[55] Mimicking Jesus's manner of discourse, Zarathustra asserts, "Verily men gave themselves all their good and evil."

> Verily, they did not take it, they did not find it, nor did it come to them as a voice from heaven. Only man placed values in things to preserve himself—he alone created a meaning for things, a human meaning.[56]

The ultimate destructive and creative act, then, is the destruction of good and evil, mankind's arbitrary "values." As Zarathustra asserts, "Change of values—that is a change of creators. Whoever must be a creator always annihilates."[57]

One should ask, though, if Nietzsche succeeds in exhorting his readers beyond good and evil, or if he merely subverts the two concepts, preferring evil over good, or at least redefining evil as good. Zarathustra preaches, "For evil is man's best strength," and then, "Man must become better and more evil—thus *I* teach."[58] Nietzsche also suggests that Zarathustra identifies himself with Satan. In one instance, for example, Zarathustra reveals, "My foot is a cloven foot," and then confesses that his stomach craves "lamb" most of all.[59] O'Connor believes that an attempt to move away from good and evil is a movement toward evil. In *Wise Blood*, we will see that O'Connor's protagonist Hazel Motes attempts to "travel" beyond good and evil, but as he races toward the moral climax of his escapade, his behavior turns progressively more malevolent.

Nihilism's false promise is aptly expressed by an anonymous Russian parable. The citizens of a Russian village are delighted to learn that a new play will be performed soon in their community. Much anticipation and excitement among the townspeople precede the arrival of the troupe of actors. Finally, the evening arrives and the entire village files into the local hall at the scheduled time. On that winter evening, they find that they are required to check not only their hat and coat, but all of their clothes as well. They dutifully comply and take their seats facing the stage. Precisely on schedule the curtain rises, the stage is bathed in light—but it is completely empty and bare. The spectators stare at the stark stage until intermission and return after the interlude to the same experience. Nothing at all appears on the stage—no actors, no set, no music. The "performance" remains unchanged until the curtain falls to "conclude" the play. To their chagrin, all the villagers discover upon applying for their clothes, hats, and coats that all of their apparel has disappeared. They must then return to the frigid Siberian night with no clothing at all.

A final word is appropriate regarding Nietzsche's and O'Connor's symbolic use of theological concepts and practices. When Nietzsche pronounces God's death, he means the death, not just of the Judeo–Christian God, but the death of the entire Western tradition: of philosophy, of reason, and of the influence of Christianity. Even more, as Niemeyer suggests, the "destruction of God leads him to annihilate all existential social reality: the forms in which men have lived, acted, and striven." It means the "destruction of the moral order, including the radical depreciation of reason."[60] In a similarly symbolic way, when O'Connor uses the concepts of "Jesus" and "redemption," these theological ideas, usually presented with none of their idiosyncratic practices excused, mean more than rural, Protestant religion. Rather, in O'Connor's inimitable style, these practices are figurative of the broader sweep of the Judeo–Christian tradition. As oddly as they may be presented, they are symbols that O'Connor uses to argue for the restoration of a belief in virtue, of the divine reality that animates all of humanity, and of a modest rationality submissive to the inescapable mystery of human existence.

3

Modern Man as
Malgré Lui in *Wise Blood*

In reference to her novels, O'Connor confessed, "I do prefer to go where few choose to follow" (HB, 371). Her first novel, *Wise Blood*, is an unusual combination of the grotesque, the comical, and the philosophical. The novel is an allegory in which the story's protagonist Hazel Motes (usually shortened to Haze) illustrates the dangerous pursuit of nihilism through the rejection of God and traditional morality. The other characters of the story represent, each in their turn, important elements of this ill-advised endeavor. O'Connor explains this manner of writing fiction when she writes, "[A]ny character in a serious novel is supposed to carry a burden of meaning larger than himself" (MM, 167). Since the novel deals with such a disturbing phenomenon as the "death of God," it should not be surprising if the novel is troubling as well. The author wrote a friend, "I have finished my opus nauseous and expect it to be out one of these days. The name will be *Wise Blood*" (HB, 24).

One reviewer noted that "the best of [O'Connor's] work sounded like the Old Testament would sound if it were being written today" (HB, 109). If that is so, *Wise Blood* most resembles the story of Jonah, an allegory teaching the consequences of man's flight from God: if one should flee from God he will end up right where he began but only after spending three days, as it were, in the dark and dangerous belly of the whale.[1] It is not surprising, then, that O'Connor described *Wise Blood* as "a comic novel about a Christian *malgré lui*" (CW, 1265). A *malgré lui* is someone who does that which he is most trying to avoid, despite his best attempts to the contrary. So, too, Hazel Motes concludes his life by surrendering to the thing he has put all of his energy into destroying.

Wise Blood adapts the timeless notion of a *malgré lui* to the modern age by adding the contemporary innovation of nihilism. Hazel Motes's flight from God is expressed through his rank nihilistic pursuit and his manner of running from God is to deny his existence and to rush headlong into a defiant belief in "nothing." His arrogance consists of his assertion that he can believe in nothing and still avoid evil. O'Connor underscores Motes's shrill insistence that he does not believe in God, all the while he is being relentlessly drawn toward a final and costly encounter with Him. Motes illustrates, as Eric Voegelin explains, that man lives in an inescapable "tension" with the Divine, a tension that pulls all men toward himself.[2]

The nihilism of *Wise Blood* concludes with muted optimism. The novel offers a vision of the world that is guardedly hopeful by providing redemption to the protagonist, yet he returns to his philosophical senses only after suffering and loss. O'Connor explained to a correspondent that those who misinterpret her novel as a dark tale of despair err by drawing the wrong inference. She complained, "Everybody who has read *Wise Blood* thinks I'm a hillbilly nihilist, whereas I would like to create the impression . . . that I'm a hillbilly Thomist" (HB, 81). Although O'Connor was troubled by some of the reviews of this novel, she was grateful for one reviewer, Brainard Cheney, and she wrote him to express her appreciation. O'Connor's gratefulness sparked a friendship between the author and Cheney and his wife that continued until O'Connor's death. Cheney wrote that "no wiser blood [has] brooded and beat over the meaning of the grim rupture in our social fabric than that of this twenty-six-year-old Georgia girl in this, her first novel." The review continues,

> *Wise Blood* is about the persistent craving of the soul. . . . It is about man's inescapable need of his fearful, if blind, search for salvation. . . . Didactically stated her story seems over-simple: Hazel Motes, an hysterical fringe preacher, tries to found a church "Without Christ" and, progressively preaching nihilism, negates his way back to the cross. [3]

THE STORY

The story begins as Hazel Motes returns by train from military service to Eastrod, Tennessee (CW, 120). He is always described in severe terms, with special attention to his eyes. One of the passengers in his train car noted that

> He had a nose like a shrike's bill and a long vertical crease on either side of his mouth; his hair looked as if it had been permanently flattened under the

heavy hat, but his eyes were what held her attention longest. Their settings were so deep that they seemed . . . almost like passages leading somewhere and she leaned halfway across the space that separated the two seats, trying to see into them. (CW, 3-4)

Early in the story, O'Connor establishes Hazel Motes as both an allegorical figure and a caricature of man's denial of the transcendent. Motes asserts his disbelief in God, a position he angrily and desperately tries to maintain as the novel progresses. Part of the comedy of the novel consists of Motes making these unprovoked and unexpected assertions to anyone who happens to be nearby at the time of the outburst. For example, to a passenger he abruptly demands,

"Do you think I believe in Jesus?" he said, leaning toward her and speaking almost as if he were breathless. "Well I wouldn't even if He existed. Even if He was on this train."(CW, 7)

Hazel's grandfather "had been a circuit preacher, a waspish old man who had ridden over three counties with Jesus hidden in his head like a stinger" (CW, 9–10). He followed his itinerant route in a "Ford automobile" and "every fourth Saturday he had driven into Eastrod as if he were just in time to save them all from Hell, and he was shouting before he had the car door open" (CW, 10). As a boy, Hazel was infused with a sense of destiny that he, also, must become a preacher, and he was indoctrinated with an awareness of his need for "redemption." His grandfather, during the course of his jeremiads, would occasionally point to his grandson as a specific instance of someone in need of God's redemption and of the reality that, should he try to escape, "Jesus would have him in the end!" (CW, 11). The boy was also left with a curious "black wordless conviction in him that the way to avoid Jesus was to avoid sin" (CW, 11).

The reader must remember that O'Connor's description of Hazel's early moral and religious formation is drawn in cartoon-like style so as to catch the reader's attention; if not, one is likely to dismiss it as offensively idiosyncratic. Although his adolescent religious experience appears comic and exaggerated, it is meant to represent the Judeo–Christian heritage common to O'Connor's readership, at least her readership in the Western world. His "calling" to be a "preacher" is symbolic of every human being's calling to a supernatural vocation, union with God.

RESISTING EVIL, PURSUING GOOD

Motes is later drafted but he went into the service with "a strong confidence in his power to resist evil" (CW, 11). Even so, it is there that he abandons his religious heritage. He is invited by fellow soldiers to visit a brothel, but he rejoins that he is not going to have his soul "damned." They counter that "he didn't have no soul and left for their brothel." After they leave, he begins "to believe them because he wanted to believe them" (CW, 12).

He conceives of a way to abandon his faith without embracing corruption, "to be converted to *nothing* instead of to evil (CW, 12, emphasis added)." His subsequent army assignments, travel, and convalescence after a shrapnel wound afford Hazel with "all the time he could want to study his soul in and assure himself that it was not there" (CW, 12). He then decides, "this was something he had always known" and concludes that the "misery" he had experienced in his life was not a desire for "Jesus" but merely "a longing for home," for his hometown of Eastrod (CW, 13). This willful ignorance of his soul and revaluation of his inner longings is an early instance of Hazel's depreciation of the transcendent. If his deepest desires can be satisfied by no more than a return to a place in time, then he has taken a disquieting step toward a solely secular and materialistic existence.

One of the tensions running through the story is Motes's attempt to believe in "nothing" and still resist "evil." He fails pathetically as evil doggedly pursues him, and he lacks the moral clarity and fortitude to resist it. For example, when he steps into a bathroom in the nearby town of Taulkinham, he avoids the stalls with obscene pictures, but inadvertently steps into one that says, "WELCOME, followed by three exclamation points and *something that looked like a snake*" (CW, 15, emphasis added). Inside the stall he reads the address of a local prostitute

> Mrs. Leora Watts!
> 60 Buckley Road
> The friendliest bed in town! (CW, 16)

He exits the bathroom and takes a cab directly to her home. In the cab, the driver proposes that Motes must be a "preacher" because of his hat and "the look in your face somewheres." "'I ain't any preacher,' Haze said, frowning." As Hazel exits the cab, the exchange between the two is at once telling and comical. "Listen," Motes insists, "get this: I don't believe in anything." The driver pulls the cigar from his mouth: "Not in nothing at all?" The driver's incredulity underscores Motes's difficulty in escaping his heritage and the impossibility of his nihilistic adventure (CW, 17). As he arrives at Mrs. Watts's home, O'Connor's tawny description of the prostitute reinforces the cheapness and crudeness of Motes's easy capitulation to temptation:

Mrs. Watts was sitting alone in a white iron bed, cutting her toenails with a large pair of scissors. She was a big woman with very yellow hair and white skin that glistened with a greasy preparation. She had on a pink nightgown that would better have fit a smaller figure. (CW, 17)

Before culminating the relationship, Motes offers yet one more unsolicited assertion, "I'm no goddam preacher"—and he proceeds to prove it (CW, 18).

The reader might ask why it is important to Hazel that he should resist evil while simultaneously rejecting God. Why not embrace evil, if there is no one to condemn the indulgence? After all, if "God is dead" are not all things permissible, as Dostoyevsky suggests?[4] St. Thomas holds the answer. A pillar of Thomism is the natural law, a law emphatically stamped upon the human soul and conscience, from which imprint we derive many of our ethical inclinations. The most fundamental of all these intrinsic principles is that man is ineluctably inclined by nature so that "good is to be done and pursued, and evil is to be avoided."[5] Even though Hazel Motes might make some headway in rejecting his Maker, he cannot eradicate the principles of the natural law imprinted on his soul. There remains in Hazel an element of the natural law from which he cannot escape, however unconscious or inarticulate those inclinations might be. Eventually, Hazel's conscience becomes sufficiently seared so that the ideal of avoiding evil will become less important to him, but that will only be after he has, through a series of successive acts, done great harm to his moral inclinations.

But even if Haze instinctively resists evil, the reader might counter, why does he not pursue good as Aquinas indicates he should? The answer is that he does. As St. Thomas also teaches, man always pursues good even though his perception of the good may be grossly distorted. "Good," according to Aquinas, "is that which all things seek after." As a human being, he can do nothing more as the human will is so ordered that "every inclination is to something good," or at least that which is "apprehended" as an "apparent good."[6]

Even more to the point, every human being pursues his "perfection," and that *telos*, or goal, will prompt him to excel in moral and intellectual virtue and finally to seek union with God. Hazel Motes's manner of "seeking his perfection" might seem to make St. Thomas's thesis laughable; the joke, though, is not on Aquinas, but on Motes, because it is he who has so prostituted his natural moral tendencies that they are indeed ridiculous. They are ludicrous precisely because they are a distant and crude distortion of his true longings. Furthermore, the joke is on the reader given that Hazel Motes is a caricature of Everyman; accordingly,

O'Connor is suggesting the outlandish manner in which contemporary men and women try to satisfy their spiritual longings. O'Connor may have been familiar with the oft-cited quote, sometimes associated with G. K. Chesterton: "the young man who rings the bell at the brothel is unconsciously looking for God."[7]

The next day, after the episode with Mrs. Watts, Motes stumbles across several people important to his story. First are a blind street preacher, Asa Hawks, and his daughter Sabbath Hawks. When Motes first sees them they are giving out tracts and he takes his and angrily tears it into small pieces. Motes later discovers that Hawks is a mountebank and not really blind at all, but at this their initial encounter, Hawks grimly demands that Motes "Repent!" to which Haze insisted, "I'm as clean as you are." He then adds, "I don't believe in sin" and, finally, "Nothing matters but that Jesus don't exist" (CW, 29). Haze is simultaneously repelled by, and attracted to, Hawks and his daughter. He follows them and tries to sabotage their "ministry" announcing to the gathering crowd, "'Listen here,' he called, 'I'm going to preach a new church—the church of truth without Jesus Christ Crucified'" (CW, 31).

That night Haze visits Mrs. Watts again; afterward, "he was like something washed ashore on her." O'Connor reminds the reader of Hazel's impotence to resist evil, now that he has pursued "nothing." When Mrs. Watts looks at him, her "grin was as curved and sharp as *the blade of a sickle* (CW, 34, emphasis added). Her eyes "took everything in whole, like quicksand" suggesting that Haze will be impotent to her allure, no matter how hard he might struggle toward "nothingness."

Needing transportation, Haze buys a car for forty dollars, a car that plays an important emblematic role in his misadventure. It is an Essex described as "a high rat-colored machine with large thin wheels and bulging headlights," that had one door "tied on with a rope" (CW, 38). As the story unfolds, the pathetic car symbolizes Haze's confidence in his new religion of nothingness and will serve literally as his pulpit. O'Connor's description of it as "high and rat-colored" too closely resembles the term "hieratic," meaning "priestly," to be a coincidence.[8] The car is the most conspicuous feature of Mote's spiritual folly. Even in an odyssey as bleak and comic as Haze's attempt to destroy religion, he still cannot escape his spiritual yearnings. Though he may convince himself to the contrary, Haze is not so much destroying religion as creating a bastardized surrogate faith.

As if to reassure himself, Haze persistently asserts that the decrepit machine will take him anywhere he wants to go and so the automobile assumes fierce anti-Christian symbolism: "Nobody with a good car needs to be justified," he announces (CW, 64). With the car on the highway for the first time, Haze cannot avoid seeing a message painted on a boulder, "WOE TO THE BLASPHERMER AND WHOREMONGER! WILL HELL SWALLOW YOU UP?" Haze stops in the middle of the highway, troubled and transfixed. When an annoyed truck driver tries to get him to move on, Haze dismisses the crude highway theology by suggesting, just as Nietzsche does, that religion is a means of one social class subjugating the other: "Jesus is a trick on niggers." To the befuddled trucker, Haze adds, "I don't have to run from anything because I don't believe in anything" (CW, 43).

SEX, SABBATH, AND SEDUCTION

Hazel Motes' twisted relationship with Asa Hawks's daughter, Sabbath Hawks, illustrates an important theme in O'Connor's refutation of nihilism, a theme that is similarly illustrated in the short story "Good Country People." As a show of his superiority, the nihilist presumes his capacity to seduce those around him at will. This is an exercise of his "will to power" over those more mediocre than himself, those who still subscribe to conventional morality, and so this seduction has more to do with power than sex. O'Connor counters that those who follow the siren call of nihilism will be themselves the victims of seduction. Thus, although Hazel intends to seduce Sabbath, Sabbath will seduce Hazel.

> Haze had gone out in his car to think and he had decided that he would seduce Hawks' child. He thought that when the blind preacher saw his daughter ruined, he would realize that he was in earnest when he said he preached The Church Without Christ. (CW, 62)

Haze's interest in Sabbath's seduction is an act of moral defiance as "he felt that he should have a woman not for the sake of the pleasure in her, but to prove that he didn't believe in sin since he practiced what was called it." Her seduction would also be an audacious creative act in which he would lead her beyond good and evil, but Haze is naïve enough to equate her homeliness with innocence and vulnerability: "He wanted someone he could teach something to and he took it for granted that the blind man's child, since she was so homely, would also be innocent" (CW, 63). This is reminiscent of the defiant sexual act that Nietzsche advocates in *The Birth of Tragedy*, an act of fierce rebellion that has now become commonplace in modern culture. O'Connor's nihilistic characters employ their sexuality as a destructive and controlling act so that sexuality becomes a revolutionary weapon in her fiction. She foresaw with remarkable foresight the direction of modern culture, especially given the conservatism of the decade in which she was writing *Wise Blood*.

O'Connor was not loathe to chasten friends and colleagues when she thought they were themselves succumbing to the modern preoccupation with sex. She once kindly corrected William Sessions, a Georgia writer and devoted friend, who, in her view, saw *The Violent Bear It Away* through a lens of misapplied sexuality.

> I'm sorry the book didn't come off for you but I think it is no wonder it didn't since you see everything in terms of sex symbols. . . . Your criticism sounds to me as if you have read too many critical books and are too smart in an artificial, destructive, and very limited way. (CW, 1130–1)

She hoped that he would "get over the kind of thinking that sees in every door handle a phallic symbol," observing that the "Freudian technique can be applied to anything at all with equally ridiculous results." Sessions had apparently misinterpreted an innocuous descriptive detail, "a fork of the tree," so O'Connor's final exhortation is to exclaim, "The fork of the tree! My Lord, Billy, recover your simplicity. You ain't in Manhattan" (CW, 1131).

She once disclosed her reverence for the Christian attitude toward human sexuality when she wrote, "Purity is the twentieth centuries [sic] dirty word but it is the most mysterious of the virtues and not to be discussed in a light fashion even with one's own and surely not with strangers" (CW, 925). O'Connor's position was no mere abstractly-held philosophical concept: it constituted one of her most deeply held beliefs to which she subscribed even at personal loss. Although she was deeply gratified to have her work published in the *Kenyon Review*, she abruptly cut the literary relationship off when the journal illustrated her fifth story, "The Comforts of Home," with a small but salacious sketch of a naked woman. She wrote in protest to the editor, Robie McCauley, "I was pretty disappointed and sick when I saw the illustration you stuck in my story." She acidly continued, "It lowered the story and it lowered the Kenyon Review, which will not cease to be dull by becoming vulgar." She concluded, "I don't know what you've gained by it but you've lost a contributor." In closing, she admonished the editor to "quit trying to compete with PLAYBOY."[9]

Far from playing the role of tempter, it is Haze who is the victim of a conspiracy of seduction between the "fake blind man" and his daughter. Sabbath tells her father, "I want him and you ought to help and then you could go on off like you want to" (CW, 62). Sabbath's first attempt to seduce Haze is unsuccessful because he panics at her aggression. "'Git away!' he said, jumping violently" (CW, 70). This episode, though, demonstrates that her knowledge of good and evil surpasses his. Haze thinks he can dispense with these unfashionable moral ideas; she on the other hand, knows better. She proudly confesses that she and her father are shamelessly evil, not just "part way evil-seeming," but "[a]ll the way evil" (CW, 68). Eventually, Sabbath will seduce Haze, but not before the hapless preacher of nothingness is reduced to propping a chair against the inside of his boarding room door to try to keep her out. When Haze can resist no more, Sabbath climbs into his bed and brazenly asserts that she is "pure filthy right down to the guts." The only difference between the two of them is that "I like being that way, and I can teach you how to like it"(CW, 95).[10] In this way, O'Connor argues that the self-fashioned nihilist is guilty of the worst kind of naïveté by thinking that he can transcend good and evil by the rejection of those concepts. On the contrary, he only makes himself foolishly defenseless before evil.

ENOCH, THE "OVERMAN"

In a story full of peculiar characters, Haze meets the most peculiar character of the novel, Enoch Emery, who has been in town only a few months and works as a guard at the local zoo. Enoch experiences none of the religious conflicts with which Haze struggles. He is mentally feeble but clever. His is a driven, idiosyncratic manner and he will eventually become a kind of ludicrous high priest to Haze's gospel of nihilism.

As far as we know, Enoch is the only one that Haze inspires with his new "Church Without Christ" doctrine; it releases in him an urgent sense of destiny. After hearing Haze preach, Enoch is stirred to reveal to Haze his deepest and most mysterious secret. He leads the preacher into a wooded area of the zoo and as he pulls him along, he obsessively mutters, "'Muvseevum'" and "the strange word made him shiver." They arrive at a little building ensconced among the trees and "a concrete band was over the columns and the letters, MVSEVM, were cut into it. Enoch was afraid to pronounce the word again." They enter and Enoch pulls Haze across the room until they both stand before a glass case containing a bizarre object, an odd shrunken and mummified aboriginal man.

> He was about three feet long. He was naked and a dried yellow color and his eyes were drawn almost shut as if a giant block of steel were falling down on them. (CW, 56)

Haze is momentarily transfixed by the spectacle and then he bolts and runs from the building, as if, in seeing the relic, he has caught a glimpse of the extent of his own blasphemy. O'Connor explains in correspondence the significance of Haze's violent reaction. She writes

> That Haze rejects that mummy suggests everything. What he has been look-ing for with body and soul throughout the book is suddenly presented to him and he sees it has to be rejected, he sees it ain't really what he's looking for. (CW, 1130)

Enoch later confirms Haze's intuition when he hears Haze preaching that his "Church without Christ don't have a Jesus but it needs one! It needs a new jesus!" The new Church needs, Hazel explains, "one that don't look like any other man so you'll look at him!" He then demands, "Give me such a jesus, you people. Give me such a new jesus and you'll see how far the Church Without Christ can go!" He promises, "[y]ou'll see the truth . . . maybe somebody will bring us a new jesus and we'll all be saved by the sight of him!" (CW, 80–81). In response, Enoch fiercely whispers, "Lis-ten here, I got him! I mean I can get him! You know! Him! Him I shown you to. You seen him yourself!" (CW, 81).

Enoch races across the street in the grip of his obsession as cars screech to avoid him. He knows what he must do even though "he didn't even know yet how he would steal it out of the glass case" (CW, 81). Driven by a primordial impulse he cannot control or understand, and comically dis-guised in an obviously fake beard and heavy clothing, he steals the dwarfish mummy. He escapes with the "new jesus" stuffed in a sack and stops for a short while in his own apartment where he reverently lays his prize in the "tabernacle" he has prearranged in his room out of a wash-stand (CW, 74). After this devotional interlude, Enoch delivers the "new jesus" to Motes. Sabbath Hawks meets him at the door of Hazel's room and takes the package because, "My man is sick today and sleeping." (CW, 102) As soon as Enoch leaves, ignoring his instructions that Hazel alone can open it, she unwraps the bundle.

> Two days out of the glass case had not improved the new jesus' condition. One side of his face had been partly mashed in and on the other side, his eye-lid had split and a pale dust was seeping out of it. (CW, 104)

Sabbath affects a juvenile maternal solicitude for the bundle as she trills to him as to a baby. She asks soothingly, "Who's your momma and daddy?" O'Connor writes that an "answer came into her mind at once" and she coos to the ugly artifact, "Well, let's go give him a jolt." She immediately walks into the bedroom to present the corrupt infant jesus to Hazel. Hazel's reac-tion, though, is a violent rejection, since he is once again confronted with the logical conclusion of his sacrilege. He "lunged and snatched the shriveled body and threw it against the wall. The head popped and the trash inside sprayed out in a little cloud of dust" (CW, 106).

Enoch's prominence in this bizarre episode is meant to evoke nihilism's most salient promise, the creation of a race of "overmen," those individuals superior to the rest because of their rejection of bygone moral restraints, who by the courageous exercise of their will, lead everyone else into the promised land beyond good and evil. O'Connor's Enoch, however, gives teeth to Copleston's warning that Nietzsche's project of the overman might backfire. Copleston notes,

> Disgusted with mankind in general he called on those who had ears to hear to set themselves free from the slavery of the herd, from the standards and valuations of the all-too-many: he envisaged the coming of nature's aristocrats, who would raise the human type above the unheroic level of the bourgeois world and create the myth of the Superman, the personification of the intellectual talent and independence, physical perfection, of quality, bound by no slavery, deceived by no mirage, either of absolute truth and falsehood, beyond good and evil.[11]

But Copleston also notes that Nietzsche faced the possibility that his new man might be less than he had hoped for, that "to break through the accepted standards of mankind is a dangerous proceeding, that the man who does so may easily fall below those standards instead of rising above."[12] For this reason, even Nietzsche himself apprehensively depicts his evolutionary proposal as a hazardous one. He admits that his venture is as risky as the precarious activity of "a tightrope walker" who risks falling into the abyss: "Man is a rope, tied between beast and overman— a rope over an abyss. A dangerous across, a dangerous on the way, a dangerous looking-back, a dangerous shuddering and stopping."[13]

O'Connor believes that the Nietzschean pursuit of the overman will not be an evolutionary leap forward, but a long disastrous step backwards, and she illustrates this likelihood with her creation of Enoch, a parody of the overman. When Enoch is discussed in this novel, he is most often associated with animals. He is first introduced with a "fox-shaped face" and he works at the zoo (CW, 20).[14] O'Connor once explained that she could not have written *Wise Blood* without Enoch (HB, 353). Chapter 12 is especially important in understanding this eccentric character's significance. Enoch, O'Connor explains in the story, "was not a boy without ambition: he wanted to become something."

> He wanted to better his condition until it was the best. He wanted to be THE *young man of the future*, like the ones in the insurance ads. He wanted some day, to see a line of people waiting to shake his hand. (CW, 108; emphasis added)

To understand what O'Connor is trying to achieve, it is helpful to make reference again to the philosophy textbook she was assigned in her college class. Randall explains that the thrust of Nietzsche's philosophy is "to bring about higher types of life" and doing so requires that we "labor and fight for the future." So, not "to the past, not to the present, but to the future we must give whole-souled devotion." Randall's text also includes this excerpt from *Thus Spake Zarathustra*:

> I bring you a goal. I preach to you the Superman. Man is something to be overcome.

Zarathustra then chides his followers,

> What have you done to overcome him? All things before you have produced something beyond themselves, and would you be the ebb of this great flood? Would you rather go back to the animal than transcends man?

He then evokes the image of an evolutionary scale beginning with the ape, evolving to man, and then transcending man to the overman:

> What is the ape to man? A jest or a bitter shame. And just that shall man be to the Superman, a jest or a bitter shame. You have traveled the way from worm to man, and much in you is still worm.

He concludes,

> Lo I preach to you the Superman. The Superman is the meaning of the earth.[15]

So far from progressing toward the Superman, Enoch eventually becomes enamored of a local itinerant sideshow featuring a man in a gorilla suit billed as "GONGA! Giant Jungle Monarch and a Great Star! Here in Person!!!" who, for a small fee, shakes the hands of children (CW, 100). Enoch at first plans to insult the ape in some way, as he does the primates at the zoo: "To his mind, an opportunity to insult a successful ape came from the hand of Providence." This recalls Zarathustra's prediction that just as humans now visit the zoo and mock the apes, so will the overman, in time, laugh at human beings in the same way. But Enoch does the opposite. He becomes so mesmerized by the gorilla that a mental vision of his destiny unfolds in which he dreams of occupying the gorilla suit himself.

Before making his move, Enoch stops at the Paris Diner for "a bowl of split-pea soup and a chocolate malted milkshake" and there he warns the annoyed waitress:

"You may not see me again," he said, "—the way I am."
"Any way I don't see you will be all right with me," she said. (CW, 110)

Leaving the restaurant, he shadows Gonga's van until he finds the opportunity to slip in the back of the truck. The driver is oblivious to the mortal scuffle in the back and when the van slows, Enoch jumps out with the spoils of his lethal encounter and he "limped hurriedly off toward the woods." There he undresses and "folded each garment neatly after he had taken it off and then stacked it on top of the last thing he had removed" (CW, 111).

Why does O'Connor describe Enoch's disrobing in this way, whereby he abandons his clothes with such orderliness? The description of Enoch shedding his former identify for a new primate life is meant, possibly, to recall Jesus's resurrection, in which the apostle Peter finds Jesus's tomb empty. Yet, curiously, his grave clothes are not strewn about, nor do they trail toward the entrance of the tomb; instead, they are left in apparent order, "rolled up and in one place."[16]

In this way, Enoch's "transformation" may be an ironic allusion to the resurrection of Christ especially since much of Nietzsche's doctrine is an attempt not simply to imitate but to replace the Christian gospel. Whereas Christ was transformed into a higher being, Enoch, in following the anti-Christian Gospel of Nihilism, regresses toward his lower nature. The resurrection of Christ was a kind of Christian evolutionary step forward; but, the emergence of the "overman," Enoch, is a step backward, hence a parody of Nietzsche's promise. Enoch emerges from his "tomb"—the back of the truck—having come to life again, but this time as a monkey.

A certain biblical irony is already attached to Enoch's name just as it is with Sabbath Hawk's name. She represents, not the sacred contemplative "rest" promised in the book of Hebrews, but its antithesis—carnal indulgence. The Enoch of the book of Genesis "walked with God" for three hundred years after the birth of his son Methuselah. His name later appears in the Epistle to the Hebrews as an illustration of a life of faith because, as it is recorded earlier in Genesis, one day he ceased to exist in his mortal life, meaning that God presumably gave him a quick route to immortality. Enoch enjoyed such apparent intimacy with God that each day he grew progressively closer to Him until he simply "was not," suggesting that he took some kind of "short cut" into God's presence as a reward for his spiritual precocity. We might say then, borrowing Nietzsche's terminology, that the original Enoch is a kind of Old Testament overman in that he slipped ahead of the normal course of human progress toward God. Enoch Emery is just the opposite: having accepted Haze's nihilism unconditionally, he takes his own "short cut," but in reverse. The Enoch of *Wise Blood* walks not with God, but with the beasts.[17]

As Enoch changes his identify in the darkness of the woods, "he was burning with the intensest kind of happiness" (CW, 111).

> In the uncertain light, one of his lean white legs could be seen to disappear and then the other, one arm and then the other: a black heavier shaggier figure replaced his. For an instant, it had two heads, one light and one dark, but after a second, it pulled the dark black head over the other and corrected this. (CW, 111)

Thus clothed, and after standing still for a few moments, "it began to growl and beat its chest; it jumped up and down and flung its arms and thrust its head forward." The primeval sounds are tentative at first, but then grow in intensity, reaching a climax several decibels above where they began. O'Connor's last reference to Enoch in *Wise Blood* is an astonishingly artistic and philosophically striking portrait of contemporary man.

> No gorilla in existence, whether in the jungles of Africa *or California, or in New York City in the finest apartment in the world,* was happier at that moment than this one, whose god had finally rewarded it. (CW, 112; emphasis added)

O'Connor is associating the godless man of the modern era with Enoch, whether that godlessness is a consequence of West Coast cultural aberrations or East Coast affluence. Enoch is an allegory for mankind, who, despite his education, sophistication, success, or wealth, has by his denial of the Sacred, regressed down the evolutionary scale. Beneath his thin illusory layer of sophistication, he has become more ape-like than angelic. To borrow back Nietzsche's phrase, that he himself lifted from the Gospel: "Ecce Homo," behold the man, the nihilistic promise of the future. His name is Enoch Emery.

Although Nietzsche's Zarathustra had taught that man is a "bridge" between the ape and the overman, Enoch is infatuated with the lower part of his nature. He "is a moron," O'Connor once observed (MM, 116). Thomas Aquinas, following Aristotle, explains that the components of our personality range from the lower part of our nature that we share with the animals, and the higher part of our nature, our rationality, which makes us distinctly human. O'Connor demonstrates that nihilism leads us down the moral evolutionary scale, back toward the lower, animal-like part of our makeup. This is not an evolutionary step toward a kind of superman but a degeneration into bestiality.

Sabbath's reaction to Enoch's delivery of the new jesus underscores this point. The seductress found something "familiar about him." Sabbath discerned a universal quality to the pathetic museum relic and although she "had never known anyone who looked like him before, there was nonetheless "something . . . of everyone she had ever known, as if they had all been rolled into one person and killed and shrunk and dried" (CW, 104). What she sees in the relic is that to which Hazel has inadvertently appealed. It is the baser element of human nature, prone to celebrate and idolize human degeneracy, effectively symbolized by the subhuman, corrupted relic.

The importance of Enoch as Haze's first and only disciple cannot be overstated. Haze has not evangelized those whom Nietzsche would assume to be potential overmen, those of advanced education, rich talents, and intimidating intelligence. He has attracted a moron.[18]

TRUTH AND BLASPHEMY

O'Connor approvingly quoted a friend who asserted that the artist should "uncover the strangeness of truth," and she also observes, "The truth does not change according to our ability to stomach it emotionally" (HB, 100).[19] Hazel's encounter with the repulsive new jesus seems to deepen his despair and elicit a cry from deep within. "'I don't want nothing but the truth!' he shouted." Haze's preoccupation with the veracity or mendacity of religious doctrine, and his inability to ignore the concept of truth, is a dimension of his larger struggle with God. "The divine substance," explains St. Thomas, "is truth itself." Scripture confirms this idea, Aquinas argues, when it records Christ's words, "I am the way and the truth and the life."[20] It is logical, then, that Haze would find himself in a simultaneous struggle with God and with the concept of truth, since they are one and the same. Haze also illustrates Voegelin's assertion that "the search for truth . . . cannot be conducted without diagnosing the modes of existence in untruth." Stated conversely, Haze's consuming pursuit of the "untruth" of nihilism is indicative of his search for truth itself.[21]

To better understand Haze's confusion, it is helpful to note that Nietzsche struggles perhaps as fiercely with the idea of truth as he did with the concept of God. He rhetorically asks, "What, then is truth," and then offers his best response. Truth, he argues is a "mobile army of metaphors, metonyms, and anthropomorphisms" that have been "enhanced, transposed, and embellished poetically and rhetorically, and which after long use seem firm canonical, and obligatory to a people." Truths, he argues, are "illusions," the meaning of which has been long forgotten. Truths, he adds are "coins which have lost their pictures." But Nietzsche admits, "We still do not know where the urge for truth comes from; for as yet we have heard only of the obligation imposed by society that it should exist." He offers, with strained logic, that to be truthful, is "to lie."[22]

Haze's behavior suggests that the best the skeptic can do is either offer a competing conception of the truth or else rail against the truth that one despises. Haze does both: he insists that the "gospel" of his new church is "true," and he hurls invective against the tradition he opposes. The habit of blasphemy, though, is one that soon ensnares the blasphemer in a contradiction. Why blaspheme something if it is not true? Why is it worth the effort if it is false? In one place, Haze reveals just how convoluted his argument has become when he says, "Blasphemy is the way to the truth," he said, "and there's no other way whether you understand it or not!" (CW, 86). To his credit, Haze seems to recognize the rhetorical dead end into which he has wandered and he accordingly tries to amend his argument. He confesses to a gas station attendant that although he had previously believed "in blasphemy as the way to salvation," now he didn't because "then you were believing in something to blaspheme" (CW, 116). By this time, however, his personal moral collapse makes it impossible for him to maintain the abstract philosophy he has worked so hard to advance.

The nihilist must believe in "nothing" but at the same time try to annihilate what exists in order to prove his thesis of nihilism. Yet, in order to attack that which he denies, he must begrudgingly concede the merit and substance of what he assails—otherwise it wouldn't be worth the trouble to destroy it. According to Copleston, Nietzsche paints himself into this philosophical corner. On the one hand, he denies absolute truth, or at least "the attainability of absolute truth."

> [B]ut as we read his impassioned pages we can have little doubt that Nietzsche really did consider the values he asserted to be *objectively* superior to the values he disparaged. In theory he might deny this, but in practice he affirmed it.[23]

FRAILTY AND CONSCIENCE

Somewhat abruptly, Haze decides that he is going to another city to preach "The Church Without Christ." Yet his self-confidence is beginning to crack. He says, "'I got a car to get there in, I got . . .'"

> [b]ut he was stopped by a cough. It was not much of a cough—it sounded like a little yell for help at the bottom of a canyon—but the color and the ex-

pression drained out of his face until it was as straight and bland as the rain falling down behind him. (CW, 107)

This is a peculiar but significant passage. Hazel's nihilistic pursuit of "the truth" is beginning to fail him. He is stopped involuntarily in his hubristic reliance on his car by something quite insignificant, but very human, "a cough." Such an annoying incident, however minor, is a signal of the limitation of his humanity. As Pascal observes, our existence is so precarious, our state so fragile, that even with our rational faculty we are no better than a flimsy blade of aquatic grass, distinguished only by our intellect. He observes, "Man is only a reed, the weakest in nature, but he is a thinking reed." So far from being Nietzsche's heroic and iron-willed Übermensch, "[t]here is no need for the whole universe to take up arms to crush him: a vapour, a drop of water is enough to kill him."[24]

The strain wearing upon Haze is his conflicted conscience. Though he has worked hard to suppress it, its operation is involuntary, as when he reacts fearfully and violently to the "new jesus." For that reason, Haze has been preaching that the conscience must be pursued like a prey: one must "get it out in the open and hunt it down and kill it."

> "Who is that that says it's your conscience?" he cried, looking around with a constricted face as if he could smell the particular person who thought that. "Your conscience is a trick," he said, "it don't exist though you may think it does, and if you think it does, you had best get it out in the open and hunt it down and kill it, because it's no more than your face in the mirror is or your shadow behind you." (CW, 93–94)

Even later, Haze mutters absentmindedly to himself, "If you don't hunt it down and kill it, it'll hunt you down and kill you" (CW, 95).

According to St. Thomas, the function of the conscience is the application of one's reason to personal moral decisions. It operates retroactively, in respect to action taken; contemporaneously, when one is faced with an immediate choice; and proactively, in anticipation of imminent moral decisions. Without the conscience, good and evil are no more than abstract notions. The conscience takes these principles, and through its operation, turns them into concrete decisions and behavior.

Even more to the point, Hazel's militant campaign against his conscience is a tribute to the Thomistic conception of the same. Perhaps the most salient feature of the conscience is that it is *binding*, which is to say, it can only with great difficulty be escaped or ignored. Especially if one has religious and moral formation as Haze did as a child, the conscience will persist even if its owner willfully contradicts it. Haze is apparently plagued by his conscience; its operation has become so intense in response to his immoral choices that it is making him miserable. He is troubled by old-fashioned guilt that he can't dismiss into "nothingness." Haze's experience is similar to that of millions of men and women in the modern age who, for decades now, have tried to escape the experience of a guilty conscience with the help of any expert whose field of expertise seems even remotely relevant to one's distress. Many though, share Haze's experience in finding that the conscience is astonishingly resilient; even more, if one persists in exercising his will contrary to the dictates of his conscience, he may experience the same adverse psychological agitation with which Hazel is obsessed. The conscience must be accommodated, at least until such time that one has done such violence to it that it is weakened, a possibility that St. Thomas admits, but one that is only achieved after substantial effort and time.[25]

The conscience is so durable that it may be easier to redirect it than to extinguish it. In addition to Aquinas, O'Connor may have gained some of her insight on the nature of conscience from Hannah Arendt's arresting report of the trial of Nazi Adolf Eichmann. She wrote a friend, "I am reading *Eichmann in Jerusalem*. . . . Anything is credible after such a period of history. I've always been haunted by the boxcars, but they were actually the least of it. And old Hannah [Arendt] is as sharp as they come" (HB, 539). O'Connor was clearly enthused about both the book and its author. She wrote another friend, Cecil Dawkins, "Right now I'm reading *Eichmann in Jerusalem*. My what a book. I admire that old lady extremely" (HB, 540). Apparently on one occasion, she even heard Arendt speak in Atlanta, a trip undertaken at considerable personal effort given her physical limitations (HB, 578).

In her provocative book, Arendt gives notable attention to the difficult question of the conscience of those Nazis guilty of atrocities. Arendt does not describe Eichmann and others as having no conscience; rather, she suggests that their conscience was redirected, until they were imbued with such a sense of duty and loyalty that to contravene the demands of the Fuhrer would have been a *violation* of their conscience. She identifies Himmler as the official "most gifted at solving problems of conscience." He did so, in a sense, by reprogramming the conscience of his subordinates, coining and indoctrinating phrases such as "My Honor is my Loyalty." Even the moral judgment of the German people was redirected so that they might acquiesce in the extermination of the countrymen, collaborating in genocide in the interests of national security and well-being.[26] One of her most startling observations is that the moral re-direction of German officials was so efficient that *to murder* became a matter of conscience, even though those who carried out such atrocities might be "tempted" *not to murder*. Arendt writes, "And just as the law in civilized countries assumes that the voice of conscience tells everybody 'Thou shalt not kill,' even though man's natural desires and inclinations may at times be murderous, so the law of Hitler's land demanded that the voice of conscience tell everybody: 'Thou shalt kill.'"[27]

If Arendt's analysis is correct, then Haze's obsessed campaign to replace the existing church with the "Church of Jesus Christ Without Christ" is an undertaking propelled by a relentless conscience that demands satisfaction. He is driven by the very thing he claimed to be hunting in order to kill—his conscience.

4

Wise Blood and the
Difficult Return to God

O'Connor once revealed, "My audience are the people who think God is dead. At least these are the people I am conscious of writing for" (HB, 92). She demonstrates with her striking protagonist, Hazel Motes, that no matter how aggressively one might try to live as if God were dead, in the end he must acknowledge his existence and the divine demands that his existence imposes. Although the Catholic novelist Evelyn Waugh admitted that *Wise Blood* didn't suit his taste, he conceded, "If this is really the unaided work of a young lady, it is a remarkable product."[1] The book is indeed remarkable, but its meaning is not transparent. When O'Connor was anxiously awaiting news from Farrar, Straus and Giroux about the publication of the novel, she sent a note requesting an update on its progress. Robert Giroux responded, "I think you have done wonders, myself, but it is not an easy book or one that elicits easy publishing judgments."[2] After reading *Wise Blood*, Jacques Maritain wrote, "It seems to me that the critics have a poor understanding of her."[3]

EVIL AND GRACE

This story will end with Hazel Motes's "conversion." Two important events are catalysts for this transformation: the first occurs when Hazel murders a "prophet" who is competing with him on the streets, and the second is the loss of his car. The murder is by far the most sinister event of the book. The loss of his car, while significant, is accompanied by a measure of wry comic relief.

The murder shows that Hazel's attempt to avoid evil while denying faith has utterly failed: not only does he kill, but he also does so in a cruel fashion. The victim has been working alongside another charlatan to make money, and on the night of the murder, the two have just raked in "fifteen dollars and thirty-five cents," three dollars of which went to the prophet, Solace Layfield, who had "consumption and a wife and six children and being a Prophet was as much work as he wanted to do." O'Connor adds, "It never occurred to him that it might be a dangerous job" (CW, 113).

Hazel follows Layfield out of town until they are on a stretch of rural highway at which time Hazel accelerates and rams the Prophet's car. When Layfield steps out, Hazel rams the car again and knocks it off the road into the ditch. He demands that Layfield take off his hat and suit. "'You ain't true,' Haze said. 'You believe in Jesus.'" Still in the Essex, Hazel chases Layfield down the highway as the man tries to undress while also trying to escape. Free of his coat, shirt, and trousers, and still running, Layfield grabs for his shoes just as Hazel savagely runs over the unfortunate man; he then backs over the body again. Hazel steps out and kicks Layfield in the side as he lay bleeding and writhing spasmodically. He accuses Layfield: "'Two things I can't stand . . . a man that ain't true and one that mocks what is.'" In making this accusation, Haze is guilty of rank hypocrisy since he himself had earlier railed against the possibility of truth. This suggests the significance of his name, an allusion to the famous scriptural admonition against hypocrisy that asks "how wilt thou say to thy brother, Let me pull the *mote* out of thine eye; and, behold, a beam is in thine eye" (emphasis added).[4]

Through "a kind of bubbling in his throat," Layfield attempts a crude confession: "Give my mother a lot of trouble. . . . Never giver no rest. Stole theter car. Never told the truth to my daddy." But Hazel denies the pathetic dying figure even the bare opportunity to unburden himself of his sin. He tells Layfield several times to shut up, and when he will not, "Haze gave him a hard slap on the back and he was quiet" (CW, 115). The reader should note that for a writer as devoutly Catholic as O'Connor, Haze's interference with Layfield's attempt at absolution would be an especially impious finale to Haze's already profane odyssey.

Motes follows the nihilistic rubric: Nietzsche argued, as O'Connor's philosophy textbook explains, that a serious pursuit of nihilism means "we must abandon all pity and all compassion." The first nihilistic principle of humanity teaches that the "weak and ineffective must go under." "[M]ore harmful than any vice" is "pity for the condition of the ineffective and weak—Christianity."[5]

Hazel's moral collapse is now complete. Having replaced mercy with cruelty, and compassion with contempt, he has perpetrated a heinous murder motivated by nothing more than angry envy; and, he has done so sacrilegiously by denying Layfield a final confession. Haze is no longer satisfied in destroying doctrine; he must now annihilate those who persist in beliefs with which he disagrees.

As he races out of town, he notes a sign that says, "'Jesus Died for YOU,' which he saw and deliberately did not read." Despite his haste, Hazel "had the sense that the road was really slipping back under him." O'Connor's next sentence is remarkable:

> He had known all along that there was no more country but he didn't know that there was not another city. (CW, 117)

Hazel cannot escape—there is no place for him to go.

But what is the *philosophical sense* of this passage—where is Haze trying to go? All along, his pursuit of nothingness has been an attempt to follow Nietzsche "beyond good and evil." Both the fact and the manner of Layfield's murder is a nihilistic challenge to the very boundary of evil, and by that challenge an attempt to move across the frontier. But there is nothing beyond the "nothingness," nothing beyond good and evil. Although Haze knows that he is, in a sense, leaving his homeland behind, he had anticipated that there would still be another dwelling place, another city in which he might take up his philosophical and theological residence. In describing Hazel's journey in such a way, O'Connor means to say that the destructive journey of the modern world will find as its destination a spiritual "no-man's-land," a place in which it is impossible to dwell because it does not philosophically exist. Later in his boarding house, when his landlady warns him that he will not find a better arrangement than the one he has with her, he confirms the lesson that he had learned on the highway: "There's no other house nor no other city" (CW, 129).

The proximate instrument of grace that stops Hazel's flight is announced by "a siren" and appears in the shape of "black patrol car." O'Connor writes, "The patrolman had a red pleasant face and eyes the color of clear fresh ice" (CW, 117). O'Connor uses the same technique here that she uses in her story "The Enduring Chill," discussed in chapter 7, in which the Holy Spirit is symbolized by ice, rather than the more traditional metaphor of fire. The patrolman's demeanor is a reminder that O'Connor's instances of intervening grace rarely meet theological stereotypes of tenderness: the policeman told Haze that he stopped him because "'I don't like your face.'" The patrolmen asks for his license, which Hazel doesn't own. The patrolmen responds, "'I don't reckon *you* need one'" (CW, 117).

He invites Hazel to drive his car to the top of the next hill because, "I want you to see the view from up there, puttiest view you ever did see." Hazel shrugs but obeys, and then gets out of the car because the patrolmen explains he can't see the view if he doesn't.

> The patrolman got behind the Essex and pushed it over the embankment. . . . The car landed on its top, with the three wheels that stayed on, spinning. The motor bounced out and rolled some distance away and various odd pieces scattered this way and that. (CW, 118)

"'Them that don't have a car, don't need a license,' the patrolman observed, dusting his hands on his pants." Haze is shocked. For the first time in the story, he has lost his angry self-assurance; his fragile pride has been shattered. His gaze turns outward to the horizon, a vista that O'Connor uses to announce a turning point in the story.

> Haze stood for a few minutes, looking over at the scene. His face seemed to reflect the entire distance across the clearing and on beyond, the entire distance that extended from his eyes to the blank gray sky that went on, depth after depth, into space. His knees bent under him and he sat down on the edge of the embankment with his feet hanging over. (CW, 118)

Haze had earlier indicated the car's prominence in his nihilism when he asserted, "Nobody with a good car needs to be justified" (CW, 64). The loss of the car is so significant for the plot and so critical for Haze's conversion that O'Connor once admitted the seriousness with which she arranged it: "The Lord's dispatchers are mighty equivocal these days anyhow. I only knew I had to get rid of that automobile some way and having the patrolman push it over and then say the things he did seemed right to me . . . when he pushed that car over, he was an angel of light."[6]

After the car is destroyed, Hazel seems to concentrate "on space" for a long time and he quietly declines a ride back into town with the patrolman. The return trip takes him three hours and then he stops "at a supply store and bought a tin bucket and a sack of quicklime." He proceeds to his boarding house, mixes the lime with water in the bucket, goes to his room—and blinds himself with the solution.

This act signifies Hazel's conversion. Asa Hawks, the bogus blind man, had supplied the inspiration for Haze's unnerving act of self-mutilation; but unlike Hawks, Haze does not merely threaten to blind himself. In reference to Haze's troubling deed, O'Connor admitted the possibility of her being inspired by the tragedy of Oedipus because for both the king and Haze, self-inflicted blindness is associated with awful moral revelation. She explains,

Of course Hazel Motes is not an Oedipus figure but there are obvious resemblances. At the time I was writing the last of the book, I was living in Connecticut with the Robert Fitzgeralds. Robert Fitzgerald translated the Theban cycle with Dudley Fitts, and their translation of the Oedipus Rex had just come out and I was much taken with it. . . . I am not an authority on such things but I think it must be the best, and it is certainly very beautiful. Anyway, all I can say is, I did a lot of thinking about Oedipus." (HB, 68)

MRS. FLOOD

At this point of the story, we are introduced to a most important character: *ourselves*. O'Connor creates a conspicuous shift in the point-of-view of the story as the reader now sees Hazel through the eyes of his landlady, Mrs. Flood. She represents all those in need of "The Flood" of Genesis, chapters 6 through 9 in which the incessant forty-day rain wiped out all of mankind except Noah and his family. Thus, this woman stands for all of those in need of judgment and redemption—the entire human race. Haze now becomes a kind of pioneer who is emerging from his long dark night of nihilism and is, by the sheer grace of God and the effort of his penance, walking the long slow road of reconciliation with the Divine. The reader should identify with Mrs. Flood, not only in her self-righteous complacency, but also in the incipient and unsettling recognition of her spiritual poverty. Haze, albeit in comic, exaggerated fashion, demonstrates the difficult path of return.

Mrs. Flood is a narrow, self-righteous woman who will not hesitate to take pecuniary advantage of a tenant, even a blind one. Yet the appearance of the enigmatic Hazel Motes unsettles her. Her priggish self-assurance begins to slip away, because she comes to understand that the sightless Hazel sees something she does not. Although "the mess he had made in his eye sockets" repulses her, she finds herself involuntarily "leaning forward, staring into his face as if she expected to see something she hadn't seen before" (CW, 120).

At first her cynicism disposes her to think, as she habitually did, that if she doesn't understand something, she is probably being cheated in some way, and "what provoked her most was the thought that there might be something valuable hidden near her, something she couldn't see" (CW, 120). The irony is that she is correct, although her estimation of value is a material calculation, whereas the wealth close at hand belongs to the province of the soul. She notices that "[h]is face had a peculiar pushing look as if it were going forward after something it could just distinguish in the distance" (CW, 120-121). He seems to be "straining toward something."

This perplexes and unsettles his landlady because "she knew he was to-
tally blind" (CW, 121). Although Hazel has no vision, she is the one who is
confounded.

> She didn't understand it. She didn't like the thought that something was be-
> ing put over her head. She liked the clear light of day. She liked to see things.
> (CW, 123)

She wonders, "How would he know if time was going backwards or forwards or if he was going with it?" (CW, 123). Hazel is indifferent to everything around him. He always appears preoccupied, eating without comment whatever Mrs. Flood serves. He is equally indifferent to her: he sits
for hours on the front porch with Mrs. Flood, yet barely acknowledges her
compulsive chatter.

Mrs. Flood's problem is that she can only "see" what is material; she
has no sight for the spiritual. Hazel, by this time, does see beyond the material and this is what she doesn't understand but cannot dismiss. The
landlady begins to imagine that Hazel sees no more than "a pinpoint of
light" (CW, 123). At first she interprets this as indicative of his desperate
blind state, but this image persists and takes on a new meaning for her as
if there is something in the distance to which he has access but she does
not. Still, Mrs. Flood tries to justify her persistent disbelief, but in so doing, she reveals the self-doubt rooted in her deepening spiritual insecurity. "'I'm as good, Mr. Motes,' she said, 'not believing in Jesus as a many
a one that does.'" Hazel's response is ironic: "You're better," he said, leaning forward suddenly. "If you believed in Jesus, you wouldn't be so
good." (CW, 125)

This irony recalls an earlier assertion of the unregenerate Haze when
he was sitting at a soda fountain counter with Enoch. Then he angrily
tells the flirtatious waitress behind the counter, "I AM clean," but then
admits, "If Jesus existed, I wouldn't be clean" (CW, 52). In the present exchange, Haze agrees with Mrs. Flood, but not in the way she understands. What he means is that, by not "believing in Jesus," Mrs. Flood
will not be convicted of her true miserable state; she will not see herself
as she is. She will not, as Pascal says, know that she is "miserable." For
this reason, she is "better," at least in her own mind, by "not believing."
Not surprisingly, the point is lost on Mrs. Flood: "He had never paid her
a compliment before!" She is so flattered that she suggests he should begin preaching again, to which he responds enigmatically, "'I don't have
time'" (CW, 125).

He doesn't have time because his time is spent in penance. As his landlady discovers, he fills his shoes with rocks until his gait is so painful that
he limps. This is a practice he had once engaged in as a child, after

furtively visiting an obscene exhibit at the fair. She is repulsed and asks him why he does it.

> "To pay," he said in a harsh voice.
> "Pay for what?"
> "It don't make any difference for what," he said. "I'm paying."
> "But what have you got to show that you're paying for?" she persisted.
> "Mind your business," he said rudely. "You can't see." (CW, 123)

His answer seems callous, yet he is correct. Unless Mrs. Flood can change, his purpose will remain an enigma. Yet, when she discovers him wearing barbed wire under his shirt, because "I'm not clean," as he explains, her repulsion is not enough to prevent her attraction to him. Although "her first plan had been to marry him and then have him committed to the state institution for the insane" so as to get his welfare check, her plan evolves into an aspiration of marriage, because "she wanted to penetrate the darkness behind [his face] and see for herself what was there" (CW, 127). Her anxiety to do so grows as he succumbs to influenza and weakens. So, in her own way, she proposes. Her manner of doing so reveals the emptiness of her existence: "'[I]f we don't help each other, Mr. Motes, there's nobody to help us,' she said. 'Nobody. The world is a empty place'" (CW, 128). Hazel declines to respond and instead goes outside for a walk. O'Connor's remarkable description of the weather conditions suggests that his demise is near: he enters a "driving icy rain" and a wintry wind that "slashed at the house from every angle, making a sound like sharp knives swirling in the air" (CW, 127-9).

Mrs. Flood anxiously awaits him, and when he does not return, she falls back upon her raw instinct to manipulate her tenant and reports him to the police as having left in default of his rent so that they will forcibly return him. Two policemen discover him lying in a drainage ditch. He is still alive, but the two officers so brutalize him that he dies in the back of the squad car, though they are ignorant of his passing. They carry him into Mrs. Flood's kitchen and prop him in a chair. His landlady, ignorant of his condition, chides him while she welcomes him home again. It is then she notices that his face is "composed and she grabbed his hand and held it to her heart" (CW, 131). O'Connor closes the novel with a description of their final encounter that dramatizes the contrast between Mrs. Flood's dissatisfied emptiness and Hazel's fulfillment. O'Connor suggests the pitiable landlady's deepening longing to follow where he has gone. As if in imitation of Haze's blindness, she "shut her eyes" in order to "see" better:

> The outline of a skull was plain under his skin and the deep burned eye sockets seemed to lead into the dark tunnel where he had disappeared. . . . She

shut her eyes and saw the pin point of light but so far away that she could not hold it steady in her mind. She felt as if she were blocked at the entrance of something. She sat staring with her eyes shut, into his eyes, and felt as if she had finally got to the beginning of something she couldn't begin, and she saw him moving farther and farther away, farther and farther into the darkness until he was the pin point of light. (CW, 131)

LEISURE AND THE BEGINNING OF CONTEMPLATION

The unconverted and defiant Hazel had insisted that it "was not right to believe anything you couldn't see or hold in your hands or test with your teeth" (CW, 116). One of the important thrusts of nihilistic doctrine is materialism and the condemnation of those who would cast their gaze toward the transcendent. "'Remain faithful to the earth,'" Zarathustra demands.[7] Before his conversion, Haze Motes preached that there was no reality beyond the material and he encouraged his scattered listeners to limit their vision to the most material object of all, their own bodies. In this instance, O'Connor again reveals her prescience as she anticipates the cult of the human body that has marked the turn of the millennium. Haze argues for radical materialism in contrast to the Christian doctrines of sin, redemption, judgment, and eternal life:

> "Nothing outside you can give you a place," he said. "You needn't to look at the sky because it's not going to open up and show no place behind it. . . . In yourself right now is all the place you've got. If there was a Fall, look there, if there was a Redemption, look there, and if you expect any Judgment, look there, because they all three will have to be in your time and your body and where in your time and your body can they be?" (CW, 93)

In *The Violent Bear It Away*, the sinister but unseen stranger with the "sibilant" voice coarsely suggests to Tarwater that the metaphysical longing he feels inside "comes from you, not the Lord. When you were a child you had worms. As likely as not you have them again" (CW, 430).

For the nihilist, the only thing behind the nothingness that he so aggressively pursues is materialism. To the extent that the nihilist has been successful in purging himself of appreciation for the transcendent, he will be left with no more than the materialistic and a preoccupation with the physical body that is made crass by its idolization. Haze, on the other hand, has begun to reject the material by his indifference to any money beyond his immediate needs. When Mrs. Flood finds his leftover cash in the wastebasket she asks "How did you make that mistake?" He explains that it was no mistake: "'It was left over,' he said. 'I didn't need it'" (CW,

124). By contrast, "When she found a stream of wealth, she followed it to its source and before long, it was not distinguishable from her own" (CW, 120).

Mrs. Flood's attitude toward the leisure that his blindness affords differs markedly from Haze's use of his free time. Whereas he finds in it an opportunity to sit quietly, if Mrs. Flood had been blind, "she would have sat by the radio all day, eating cake and ice cream, and soaking her feet" (CW, 122). In O'Connor's economical writing, she has in this short passage suggested the contemporary misuse of leisure time. Classical philosophy divides human activity into "work," "play," and "leisure," but this conception of leisure is largely unknown today. Whereas we equate it with play or recreation, the word's etymology reveals the ancient teaching: the Greek word is *schole*, and like our ideal of liberal education, leisure is the time spent in personal improvement—moral, intellectual, and spiritual. Work is performed to provide opportunity for leisure and we engage in play for the sake of relief from work.[8] O'Connor marked in her edition of one of Voegelin's works a passage that begins, "Leisure is not playtime." For that reason, Voegelin continues, "[e]ducation must . . . equip a man with knowledge and train him in intellectual pursuits," for leisure is the time to be spent in activities that serve no other end than to shape the "man of excellence."[9]

But Mrs. Flood's hypothetical use of leisure symbolizes the worst in the experience of contemporary men and women. Her first priority would be to sit by the radio. In this, O'Connor points to the Western infatuation with passive entertainment, a trend identified in postwar Europe and America by Josef Pieper in his important work *Leisure, the Basis of Culture*, and a phenomenon incisively diagnosed by Neil Postman in his precocious *Amusing Ourselves to Death: Public Discourse in the Age of Show Business*.[10] Such a passive attitude to free time and entertainment promotes Mrs. Flood's second and third priorities, interests that cater only to her sensuality—to eat, and soak her feet.

Pascal notes that man's greatest problem is his inability to use his free time quietly and reflectively. He writes, "I have discovered that all the unhappiness of men arises from one single fact, that they cannot stay quietly in their own chamber." Instead, Pascal observes, a man must surround himself with all sorts of "diversions" just to keep at arm's length the opportunity for reflection because he is likely to find such meditative opportunities horribly depressing when confronted with the truth of his condition.[11] In the O'Connor short story "Judgment Day," Tanner's daughter is conflicted between her duty to her aged father, and the allure of a more superficial, less thoughtful life. She succumbs to the latter when she admonishes the old man that his trouble is sitting "in front of that window all the time where there's nothing to look out at." In her diagnosis, he needs "some inspiration and an outlet," and so she advises, "If you would let me pull your chair around to look at the TV, you would quit thinking about morbid stuff, and death and hell and judgment" (CW, 685–6).

The loss of Hazel Motes's car prepares him for a better use of his leisure. Whereas the car has been a source of pride and distraction, when the policeman pushes it over the embankment, the loss has the effect of leaving Haze receptive to a more contemplative experience. Hence, O'Connor describes his view as nothing more than a "blank gray sky," as if his personal horizon were an empty screen or palette now prepared for better use (CW, 118).

After Haze blinds himself, Mrs. Flood "observed his habits carefully." Despite the decline in his health, "he walked out every day." From downstairs, she could tell that he "got up early in the morning and walked in his room," and "then he went out and walked before breakfast and after breakfast, he went out again and walked until midday." She determines by following him that he "knew the four or five blocks around the house and he didn't go any farther than those." She thinks, "He could have been dead and get all he got out of life but the exercise" (CW, 122-3).

Mrs. Flood concludes, "He might as well be one of them monks," living in a "monkery." O'Connor observes, "She didn't understand it" (CW, 123). Indeed she did not and she urges him to *do something*, learn to strum a guitar, or take up preaching again. Mrs. Flood is certain that Haze is "out of connection" with the "real world." Of course, in a sense he is.

Engagement in leisure, in the classical sense, may at times look like idleness. Because he rarely speaks, Mrs. Flood is often annoyed at him. He mystifies her. She does not understand Pieper's explanation that, "Leisure is a form of silence, of that silence which is the prerequisite of the apprehension of reality: only the silent hear and those who do not remain silent do not hear." Leisure, Pieper continues, is antithetical to an anxious grasping for control as "there is a certain serenity in leisure."

> That serenity springs precisely from our inability to understand, from our recognition of the mysterious nature of the universe; it springs from the courage of deep confidence, so that we are content to let things take their course.[12]

In his *Reflections on America*, Jacques Maritain observes that that the "American attitude toward time" is such that there is "a certain horror of any span of time which a man might have at his own disposal in order to do nothing. The great value and efficacy of standing idle, and lingering over one's dream, is little appreciated in this country." He notes that Americans squander leisurely opportunities by a "sort of stupefying passivity that is more often than not developed by movies or television." Leisure offers opportunities "to experience the joys of knowledge, of art and poetry, of devotion to great human causes, of communicating with others in the dreams and anxieties of the mind, of silently conversing with himself and silently conversing with God." Maritain adds that the very best use of time is "contemplative activity. *Be still, and know that I am God.*"[13] Rather than taking an escape in thoughtless diversion, Haze's eye has offended him and so he has "plucked it out," an act that has prepared him for a proper use of leisure.[14]

CONTEMPLATION AND DARKNESS

Noted in the previous chapter is Haze's fundamental impulse to obey the natural law impulses of right and wrong resident in his soul, however puny and undernourished his soul has been. He now finds opportunity in his affliction to follow that urging more directly. That longing for moral completion leads Haze to the contemplation of "truth," which in turn will urge him toward a contemplation of God himself. Therefore, when the policeman tells Haze, "I want you to see the view from up there, puttiest view you ever did see," his promise is an augur of the enlarged vision Haze is about to acquire. To apply Aquinas's teaching, Haze's final happiness cannot be found in anything "exterior," nor in "the body" and so it remains for him to discover that the "final happiness of man consists in the contemplation of truth" and such contemplation has no further motivation but "is sought for its own sake, and is directed to no other end beyond itself."[15] But in the interest of truth, nothing less than "the vision of the Divine Essence" will suffice because "a man is not perfectly happy so long as something remains for him to desire and seek."[16]

The "pinpoint of light" that Haze follows and that Mrs. Flood finds so alluring, represents the beginning of contemplation, a state to which Haze arrives through the penance that facilitates redemptive grace. O'Connor once tried to straighten out her former philosophy professor on the meaning of *Wise Blood*:

> The theme of this book is expiation and the form of life in it is penance. The light Haze is traveling toward is the light of Bethlehem by way of the cross. To my mind, tenderness, beauty, and love are contained within his suffering, and as much absolution as the writer, not being God, can give.[17]

She reinforces this point by revealing that Hazel Motes "was a mystic" (HB, 116). She once expressed mild concern that the grotesque element of

Wise Blood may have been overdone and for that reason, the connection with mysticism overlooked by the reader. If there were a failure to the novel it seemed "to be that he is not believable enough as a human being to make his blinding himself believable for the reasons he did it" (HB, 116).

In light of this emphasis upon contemplation, it is fair to ask if O'Connor herself pursued some measure of contemplative practice. It appears that she did. She prized the spiritual teachings of the great Spanish contemplatives St. John of the Cross and St. Teresa of Avila and she offers the teaching of both as an antidote to "false mysticism" (HB, 113). In respect to the teaching authority of her Church, she explains, "For me a dogma is only a gateway to contemplation and is an instrument of freedom and not of restriction." O'Connor's contemplative opportunity, moreover, was most likely the Eucharist, which she attended often, even though it may have been difficult physically to do so. For St. John of the Cross, the Eucharist was "all his glory, all his happiness, and for him far surpassed all the things of the earth."[18] Likewise, O'Connor revealed in correspondence that the Eucharist "is the center of existence for me; all the rest of life is expendable" (HB, 125). Undoubtedly, her reading of the University of Munich philosopher and theologian Romano Guardini deepened her devotion to the Eucharist. She wrote Sally Fitzgerald, "I am reading everything I can" of Guardini and she reviewed at least six of his books for her diocesan periodical (HB, 74). In her review of his *Meditations Before Mass*, she includes his contention that "the words spoken at the consecration are 'the equals of those which once brought the universe into existence.'"[19]

Since O'Connor was familiar with St. John's teaching, and recommended it to friends, it is reasonable to suppose the mystic's metaphors could inform her narrative of Hazel Motes. She also reveals an interest in St. John when she calls Edith Stein, the brilliant philosopher and scholar of the Spanish mystic, one of "the two 20th—century women who interest me most" (HB, 93).[20] In her review of Stein's book on St. John of the Cross, *The Science of the Cross*, O'Connor describes the saint in a manner that suggests the difficulty Mrs. Flood experiences in trying to understand Haze: "As for St. John of the Cross, his life was lived so very near eternal realities that it seems an impossible life to understand."[21]

St. John writes a great deal about darkness. He describes the journey to God as consisting of two important experiences, the "dark night of the senses" and the "dark night of the soul." This "first night of purgation," concerns the sensory part of the soul. He depicts it poetically in the first stanza of his famous "Dark Night of the Soul," in which his "senses" have been darkened, and his "house," that is his soul, is "stilled."

> One dark night,
> Fired with love's urgent longings
> —ah, the sheer grace!—
> I went out unseen,
> My house being now all stilled.[22]

This darkness is not an end in itself, but the beginning of the process of contemplation, described symbolically as his "secret ladder." The second darkness is that which facilitates a more intimate encounter with the divine presence.[23] It is described in the second stanza of his poem:

> In darkness and secure,
> By the secret ladder, disguised,
> —ah, the sheer grace!—
> in darkness and concealment,
> my house being now all stilled.[24]

As St. John himself describes the sequence of these two events, "The first night is the lot of beginners, at the time God commences to introduce them into the state of contemplation. . . . The second night or purification takes place in those who are already proficients, at the time God desires to lead them into the state of divine union." Perhaps Hazel Motes, by his self-inflicted blindness, has entered the first "night," in which "the sensory part" of his being has been "stilled" and is "asleep." This promotes a kind of stillness in his soul. The "pin point of light" suggests that he is approaching the second dark night in which true contemplation begins.[25] As he begins to enter into this darkness, his progress rouses something in his landlady: "Watching his face had become a habit with her; she wanted to penetrate the darkness behind it and see for herself what was there" (CW, 127).

Since the first night is a kind of "point of departure," it also involves the voluntary deprivation of the craving "for worldly possessions." It is not the possessions themselves that must be forsaken; it is the distracting materialistic appetite, the longing for such possessions that must be put away. Accordingly, St. John refers to "the denudation of the soul's appetites and gratifications," a process suggested by Haze Motes's endeavors when he discards his leftover cash and pursues a harsh penance with broken glass and barbed wire.

At this point, it is important to reiterate the significance of O'Connor's use of the grotesque. The reader must neither be distracted by the repulsive nature of Haze's mystical pursuits, nor even by his self-mutilation. These extremes are a part of O'Connor's literary technique, meant to jolt the reader and to capture his attention. If the reader is so offended by these events so as to turn away from the novel, he will have allowed himself to be "scandalized"; that is, he will have been ensnared or "tripped up" before reaching the understanding to which O'Connor wishes to lead him.

ST. JOHN ON BLINDNESS

St. John even offers a fascinating discussion of the concept of spiritual "blindness," describing, in fact, two types of blindness. The first is a "spiritual blindness" imposed by inordinate sensuality that leaves one separated from God. He laments, "Oh, if people but knew what a treasure of divine light this blindness caused by their affections and appetites takes from them and the number of misfortunes and evils these appetites occasion each day when left unmortified!" His concern arises from his belief that "these appetites weaken and blind."[26]

> We have felt our way along the wall as though blind, we have groped as if without eyes, and our blindness has reached the point that we stumble along in broad daylight as though walking in the dark. For this is a characteristic of those who are blinded by their appetites; when they are in the midst of the truth and of what is suitable for them, they no more see it than if they were in the dark.[27]

Eventually, though, the believer must experience another kind of blindness, a condition that, if not self-imposed, is at least willingly embraced. This is a blindness to everything that might distract one from God, and it is requisite to mature faith.

> Faith, manifestly, is a dark night for souls, but in this way it gives them light. The more darkness it brings on them, the more light it sheds. For by blinding, it illumines them, according to those words of Isaiah that if you do not believe you will not understand; that is, you will not have light.[28]

This blindness comes about because one's journey toward God eventually requires that faith—as well as hope and charity—have no other support than God himself. This austerity of belief leads one into an "abyss of faith." To advance in this spiritual manner means that at times those who long for God must, like Hazel Motes, "darken and blind themselves."[29]

At first, Mrs. Flood cannot imagine, "[W]hat possible reason could a person have for wanting to destroy their sight?" O'Connor's prose drips with irony when she reveals the landlady's reaction to Haze's self-inflicted traumatic loss: "A woman like her, who was so clear-sighted, could never stand to be blind." But even at this early juncture, Haze's radical act unsettles her self-righteousness when she "recalled the phrase, 'eternal death,' that preachers used, but she cleared it out of her mind immediately, with no more change of expression than the cat" (CW, 119).

Mrs. Flood, though, begins to sense there is something to this state of blindness that she does not understand. One night at dinner she asks, "Do you think, Mr. Motes, that when you're dead, you're blind?" He answers, "I hope so" (CW, 125–6).

> "Why?" She asked, staring at him.
> After a while he said, "If there's no bottom in your eyes, they hold more."
> The landlady stared for a long time, seeing nothing at all. (CW, 126)

When he says, "If there's no bottom in your eyes, they hold more," Haze means that in spiritual blindness one can see more, than if one has sight. St. John explains that those who have not undertaken this self-inflicted blindness, like Mrs. Flood, see "nothing at all." Shortly before Haze's death, his landlady concludes that her tenant can see and she cannot—at least in matters of the soul. As she admits to herself that she is in the dusk of her own life, she concludes that she should ally herself with Haze because, "If she was going to be blind when she was dead, who better to guide her than a blind man?" (CW, 130).

A stanza from one of St. John's lesser-known poems might have provided a fitting epitaph for Haze Motes.

> And though I suffer darknesses
> In this mortal life,
> That is not so hard a thing;
> For even if I have no light
> I have the life of heaven.
> For the blinder love is
> The more it gives such life,
> Holding the soul surrendered,
> *Living without light in darkness.*[30]

Given this analysis of O'Connor's antinihilistic novel, another of St. John's insights is startling and ironic: the man or woman of faith must pursue a kind of sanctifying nihilism, a state of being that St. John usually designates by the Spanish *nada*. His nothingness, however, is a kind of self-denial or even self-annihilation that serves as a means to greater intimacy, indeed union with God. Nietzsche's *nada*, by contrast, is a means of "destroying" the memory and possibility of intimacy with God, thus eliminating man's opportunity for reunion. For St. John, *nada* means one has so emptied himself of resistance to God, that there is nothing that may oppose his progress toward divine union. He writes, "These impediments of contrary attachments and appetites are more opposed and resistant to God than nothingness, for nothingness does not resist."[31]

The fate of Hazel Motes suggests that O'Connor is holding out a melancholy hope for the modern world. Although Haze returns to God, his return comes only after suffering irreparable loss. O'Connor explains,

> It's hard to believe always but more so in the world we live in now. There are some of us who have to pay for our faith every step of the way and who have to work out dramatically what it would be like without it and if being without it would be ultimately possible or not. I can't allow any of my characters, in a novel anyway, to stop in some halfway position. This doubtless comes of a Catholic education and a Catholic sense of history—everything works toward its true end or away from it, everything is ultimately saved or lost. (HB, 349-350)

O'Connor leaves the reader no middle ground just as she does not leave her characters in a "halfway position." This attitude comes from the Aristotelian–Thomistic doctrine of the *telos* of human life. To stop short is to leave oneself in an untenable state of incompletion. Haze "is saved by virtue of having wise blood," the instinct and strength of character that prevents him from quitting before he has discovered his spiritual destiny. In that sense, O'Connor's reader will be saved or damned by his own "wise blood," that is, his willingness to recognize his spiritual instincts, and the integrity to pursue those instincts to their proper conclusion (HB, 350; MM, 115). The "Misfit" of O'Connor's short story "A Good Man is Hard to Find" spoke for her when he said, "He thrown everything off balance and it's nothing for you to do but follow Him or find some meanness" (HB, 227). In correspondence, O'Connor connects the choice facing both the Misfit and Haze. She writes, "Haze knows what the choice is and the Misfit knows what the choice is—either throw away everything and follow Him or enjoy yourself by doing some meanness to somebody, and in the end there's no real pleasure in life, not even in meanness" (HB, 350). O'Connor understood, as did T. S. Eliot, that one of the diseases of the modern age is the flippant lack of resolution in matters of consequence: "Time for you and time for me, / And time yet for a hundred indecisions, / And for a hundred visions and revisions, / Before the taking of a toast and tea."[32]

O'CONNOR ON CHARITY

The reader may ask: "If Haze is on a path leading to union with God, why does he not act more charitably to Mrs. Flood as opposed to his stern, even rude behavior?" That is to say, should he not make Mrs. Flood feel better? This question, though, reveals the confusion between sentiment and love against which O'Connor warns. Haze, by his manner and disposition, unsettles his landlady, causing her to question the premise of her life, and ultimately, provoking her to examine her eternal future. This, O'Connor would argue, is true charity. She explains, "Charity is hard and endures;" indeed, "there is nothing harder or less sentimental than Christian realism" (HB, 308, 90). In her view, one of the "worst sins" in fiction is "sentimentality;" she believes it as serious an error as the gratuitous sexuality in modern novels (HB, 142).

O'Connor once noted to a friend, "You are right that *enjoy* is not exactly the right word for our talking about religion. As far as I know, it hurts like nothing else" (HB, 341). O'Connor liked Edith Stein because, as she explained, "If she is ever canonized, she will be one saint that I don't think they can sweeten up on holy cards and write a lot of 'pious pap' about" (HB, 173). O'Connor found Guardini's writing attractive for a similar reason. For example, in her review of his *Prayer in Practice*, she explains, "He speaks of having a 'sense of honor' in prayer, a sense which will be offended by the mawkish, sentimental and exaggerated." Regarding Guardini's *Jesus Christus*, she observes, "This book avoids the treacly and exaggerated presentations that we are accustomed to receive in sermons."[33] O'Connor criticized what she called "The Pious Style" in religious writing (HB, 369). She objected to the devotional style of the eighteenth-century theologian St. Alphonsus Liguori because she felt he imposed his own subjective emotional style on the reader. She complained that "the emotion is somebody else's fever-pitch emotion—particularly in the Stations of the Cross, the ones of St. Whatshisname Liguori—you are stuck with *his* emotion, and it's something you can't live up to." She reports reading the Thomistic philosopher Etienne Gilson and happily recalls "I don't believe the word emotion even came up in it" (HB, 279).

O'Connor was much taken with Guardini's highly acclaimed *The Lord*; she called it "very fine" and in 1955 wrote, "In my opinion, there is nothing like [*The Lord*] anywhere, certainly not in this country" (HB, 74, 99). Reading Guardini, one is struck with the similarity between his observations of contemporary man and O'Connor's description of Hazel Motes. Guardini comments upon the amazing modern spectacle of God's creation declaring that God, the creator, does not exist: "[I]t is . . . possible for God, the one Reality, to exist, and for man, his own creature to declare: God is dead!" Guardini notes that although man's "vital soul" is that which defines his existence as man, it is also possible for "man . . . to insist that he is soulless." Though "serious contemplation" is a "vital" process, man's "capacity for negation is illimitable."[34]

5

"Good Country People"
and the Seduction of Nihilism

In her short story "Good Country People," Flannery O'Connor gives the fable of the farmer's daughter an acutely philosophical and sinister turn. In doing so, she offers her most concise response to the threat of nihilism, making two distinct and important points about the nature of that philosophy. She suggests, as did her literary compatriot Walker Percy, that its roots are to be found in the ground made fertile by the French philosopher René Descartes, and she reiterates her warning in *Wise Blood*, but this time more emphatically, that nihilism is malevolently seductive and is likely to consume those naïve enough to think they can embrace and contain it.

O'Connor seemed to realize, upon writing this short story, that she had written something especially important, a story unique for its significance even among her other stories. She wrote to her publisher Robert Giroux, "I have just written a story called 'Good Country People' that [my friends] Allen and Caroline both say is the best thing I have written." (HB, 75) She acceded to uncharacteristic braggadocio in writing to her intimates, the Fitzgeralds, "I trust Giroux will be sending you a copy of the book soon. I wrote a very hot story at the last minute called 'Good Country People.'" But if she allowed herself a bit of bragging, it was quickly tempered with self-deprecation when she noted to another friend, "A lady in Macon told me that she read me under the dryer. I was gratified" (HB, 78). Although she occasionally suffered criticism from fellow Christians who were scandalized by her subject matter and style, she predicted that those offended by this story might be nonbelievers. With this prediction, O'Connor indicates the theologically apologetic nature of the story. She suggests, "If I could be of any assistance in providing an answer to any complaints you might get about 'Good Country People,' I'll be glad to; but perhaps the complaints this time will be from pious atheists and not from irate Catholics" (HB, 86). Whereas O'Connor usually wrote at a snail's pace, she reported that she wrote "Good Country People" very quickly—"in about four days"—suggesting she enjoyed a uncommon inspiration in the task: "[I] just sat down and wrote it" (HB, 160). Even at that quick pace, she was barely able to include it in her first collection of short stories. The publisher, though, was impressed enough to undertake the difficulty of incorporating it at the last minute. He wrote, "'Good Country People' is a marvelous story and I'm glad there was just time to include it in the book."[1]

THE STORY

The protagonist of this story is a young woman named Hulga who lives with her mother, Mrs. Hopewell. Hulga is "a large blond girl" with an artificial leg. She is thirty-two and "highly educated" and the artificial leg is the consequence of a hunting accident when Hulga was ten. Her name originally had been "Joy," but she changed it to Hulga, a change invoking the Nietzschean imperative to create in the crucible of suffering. Hulga, we are told, considers her name change to be "her highest creative act." Turning herself into Hulga was "her major triumph." She identifies herself, O'Connor writes, with Vulcan, the god of the forge, who was reportedly far and away the ugliest of the gods, but who commanded authority because of his stewardship over fire, because of his artistry, and because of his influence over the goddess Athena.[2]

> She had arrived at it first purely on the basis of its ugly sound and then the full genius of its fitness had struck her. She had a vision of the name working like that ugly sweating Vulcan who stayed in the furnace and to whom, presumably, the goddess had to come when called. (CW, 267)

Ubiquitous in Mrs. Hopewell's kitchen is her hired help, Mrs. Freeman. Mrs. Hopewell and Mrs. Freeman are, in O'Connor's phrase, "good country people." Mrs. Hopewell especially admires such people, and it is on the basis of this appreciation that she will admit into her home a devious Bible salesman, who describes himself as "good country people" but who drives the story to its distressing dénouement. Hulga holds "good country people" in contempt in much the way that Nietzsche was contemptuous of the democratic masses, of "the herd." More accurately, she holds such people in disdain until she needs them, and she will need them when the bible salesman humiliates and subjugates her.

For reasons unknown to the reader, Mrs. Hopewell has divorced her husband years before, but she remains responsible and hard working. She and Mrs. Freeman are idiosyncratic in a common sort of way, and their foibles are maddening to someone of Hulga's education, given the cynicism with which she has been equipped by the university. Mrs. Freeman often eats with Mrs. Hopewell and her daughter, and the two older women pass platitudes back and forth across the table, an activity Hulga can barely digest:

> "Everybody is different," Mrs. Hopewell said.
> "Yes, most people is," Mrs. Freeman said.
> "It takes all kinds to make the world."
> "I always said it did myself." (CW, 265)

Mrs. Freeman is as stubborn as a mule, and, "the nosiest woman to walk the face of the earth," according to her former employer (CW, 264). Even worse, she derives a perverse pleasure from calling Hulga by her given name Joy, knowing that the habit infuriates the maimed girl. She seems to detect Hulga's insecurity, even though the older woman has comparatively no education. The woman's habit imperils the protective philosophic shell in which Hulga dwells and threatens her cynical self-assurance with boorish but penetrating insight: "Mrs. Freeman's relish for using the name only irritated her. It was as if Mrs. Freeman's beady steel-pointed eyes had penetrated far enough behind her face to reach some secret fact" (CW, 267).

Mrs. Hopewell is flawed like the rest of her little social group, but O'Connor wryly notes that having "no bad qualities of her own . . . she was able to use other people's in such a constructive way that she never felt the lack" (CW, 264). Mrs. Hopewell does not understand her daughter, especially her daughter's unrelieved sour attitude toward life and her disdain for the "good country people" with whom she lives. Although she doesn't pretend Hulga is a beauty, she believes, "There was nothing wrong with her face that a pleasant expression wouldn't help" (CW, 267). She also does not understand her daughter's "constant outrage": Hulga has "the look of someone who has achieved blindness by an act of will and means to keep it" (CW, 265). Her mother prefers to still think of her "as a child because it tore her heart to think instead of the poor stout girl in her thirties who had never danced a step or had any *normal* good times" (CW, 266). She is certain that Joy changed her name into the ugliest sounding substitute she could find. Mrs. Hopewell, as her name implies—though no Pollyanna—is inclined to see the positive in life and wishes her daughter would do the same. O'Connor writes, "Mrs. Hopewell said that people who looked on the bright side of things would be beautiful even if they were not" (CW, 267). She "could not understand deliberate rudeness, although she lived with it, and she felt she had always to overflow with hospitality to make up for Joy's lack of courtesy" (CW, 272). This, of course, encourages Hulga's rudeness to all visitors.

Mrs. Hopewell is at a loss to understand why her daughter has taken a Ph.D. in philosophy and finds it socially embarrassing—"You could not say, 'My daughter is a philosopher.'" She can't quite discern the effect that the advanced degree has had upon her, though she suspects she has not absorbed it well. Mrs. Hopewell "could not help but feel that it would have been better if the child had not taken the Ph.D." (CW, 267). Hulga spends all her time reading, doesn't "like dogs or cats or birds or flowers or nature," and "she looked at nice young men as if she could smell their stupidity" (CW, 268). Her general assessment of her daughter is that she "is brilliant" but doesn't "have a grain of sense" (CW, 268).

MANLEY POINTER

This story takes a dark turn with the arrival of Manley Pointer, "a tall gaunt hatless youth" who calls at the Hopewell home selling bibles. He is skilled at what he does, in a crude rural sort of way: he presumes an acquaintance with the needs of the family, noting that although they are good Christians, they have no family bible. Mrs. Hopewell though, "never liked to be taken for a fool," and declines his offer by explaining, "My daughter is an atheist and won't let me keep the Bible in the parlor" (CW, 270). Pointer cries, "People like you don't like to fool with country people like me!" He adds that he is working because he has a heart condition, not because he aspires to attend college as other young salesman might. Mrs. Hopewell is stunned that he would have an ailment similar to Hulga's ("He and Joy had the same condition!") and hastily invites him to dinner (CW, 271).

Pointer's uncanny knack for identifying himself with little known and intimate family secrets implies that he possesses an unearthly nature and, by this and other characterizations, O'Connor hints that Manley Pointer is something more than human. Indeed, whereas Hulga is a self-fashioned nihilist, Pointer represents the essence of nihilism itself, a concentrated and rarefied sample of the philosophy made incarnate. It is as if Hulga's persistent flirtation with nihilism, by word and behavior, has conjured up the spirit of nihilism itself and it has come to claim its own. This implies a parallel with Dr. Faust and Mephistopheles in which the latter comes at last to claim what is rightfully his, namely Faust's soul. In Hulga's case, her commitment to nihilism is not so absolute as to give Pointer such an unqualified claim, though, as the story demonstrates, she has flirted with a force she does not understand and which is competent to violate her soul in a most obscene manner, thus exposing its emptiness.

At dinner, Pointer reveals that when he was eight years old, he lost his father when a felled tree crushed the elder; now his ambition is to "be a missionary because he thought that was the way you could do most for people" (CW, 272). Ironically, he is a kind of missionary, but not the kind that his hosts would infer. Joy is predictably cold to the guest although "the boy would dart a keen appraising glance at the girl as if he were try-ing to attract her attention" (CW 272). Pointer sells no Bible to the family though he secures an invitation from Mrs. Hopewell to visit again. But as he leaves, he comes upon Joy on the drive leading to the house and they walk to the gate together. Mrs. Hopewell can't imagine what they might have said to each other, "and she had not yet dared to ask" (CW, 273).

What she doesn't know is that Joy has arranged to meet the Bible salesman at ten o'clock the next morning. The agreement began for Hulga as a "great joke" but as she lay in bed half the night thinking about it, "she had begun to see profound implications in it" as she imagined conversa-tions between the two of them that could reach "below to depths that no Bible salesman would be aware of" (CW, 275). Hulga begins to anticipate their tryst as a kind of philosophical project in which she imagines that she will seduce and then master Pointer by condescending mercifully to help her hapless victim deal with his remorse. In so doing, she will replace his backwoods religiosity with an enlightened view of existence. She knows that "[t]rue genius can get an idea across even to an inferior mind." She will take "his remorse in hand" and "change it into a deeper under-standing of life." What Hulga does not know is that it is she who will be seduced by the shrewd Pointer (CW, 276).

THE LOSS OF HULGA'S PRESUMPTION

The remainder of the story is a study in manipulation, seduction, and sub-jugation, with Pointer as the teacher. Hulga will prove vulnerable because of the empty and wounded state of her psyche. As Allen Tate perceptively observed, "It is without exception the most terrible and powerful story of Maimed Souls I have ever read."[3] In commentary on "Good Country People," O'Connor herself observes that Hulga "is spiritually as well as physically crippled" as there is "a wooden part of her soul that corresponds to her wooden leg" (MM, 99).

The next day, before they even meet, Hulga is unsettled, finding herself alone at their designated meeting place on the highway—"She had the furious feeling that she had been tricked" (CW, 277). Pointer suddenly stands up behind the bush where he had been hiding and says, "'I knew you'd come!' The girl wondered acidly how he had known this" (CW, 277). He has the valise he uses to carry his Bibles but it "did not seem to be heavy today; he even swung it." Pointer upsets her equilibrium again when "he asks softly, 'Where does your wooden leg join on?'" to which she turns an "ugly red" (CW, 277). He surprises her yet again with a heavy kiss, and as they walk across the pasture, she works to maintain her equanimity.

> Even before he released her, her mind, clear and detached and ironic anyway, was regarding him from a great distance, with amusement but with pity. She had never been kissed before and she was pleased to discover that it was an unexceptional experience and all a matter of mind's control. (CW, 278)

When he asks if they might sit down somewhere, she suggests the barn. In response to his doubtful look that she could ascend to the loft, she "gave him a contemptuous look, and putting both hands on the ladder . . . pulled herself expertly through the opening." Pointer feigns admiration, though his attitude is more of mockery than of esteem (CW, 279). Once in the hayloft, Hulga lays back and through the opening of the barn can see outdoors: she turns her head and gazes at the "two pink-speckled hillsides" that "lay back against a dark ridge of woods. The sky was cloudless and cold blue" (CW, 279).

Manley Pointer continues setting the pace of their encounter by insisting that Hulga express her love for him. O'Connor interjects that Hulga "was always careful how she committed herself" but, she writes this ironically, because the girl has no idea how vulnerable she has become. Hulga responds with adolescent self-assurance, employing the jargon of the nihilist: "'In a sense,' she began, 'if you use the word [love] loosely, you might say that. But it's not a word I use. I don't have illusions. I'm one of those people who see *through* to nothing'" (CW, 280). "'We are all damned,' she teaches Pointer, "'but some of us have taken off our blindfolds and see that there's nothing to see. It's a kind of salvation'" (CW, 280). Responding to more insistence from Pointer, Hulga casually offers that she "loves" him, treating him, though, with maternal condescension.

> "Yes," she said and added, "in a sense. But I must tell you something. There mustn't be anything dishonest between us." She lifted his head and looked him in the eye. "I am thirty years old," she said. "I have a number of degrees." (CW, 280)

Pointer has been playing along, letting Hulga enjoy her false confidence, but at this point things take an unexpected turn, a turn in a direction in which her control slips away, slowly at first, and then all at once. In response to Hulga's emotionless admission of love, Pointer demands: "Prove it." Hulga, thinking she understands, smiled and looks "dreamily out on the *shifty* landscape" (emphasis added). O'Connor's use of the unusual adjective "shifty" for a line of trees and sky is undoubtedly a reference both to Pointer's character as well as to the unstable philosophical grounding on which Hulga has based her life and which now Pointer is about to upset. Hulga concludes that she "had seduced him without even making up her mind to try." He shocks her, though, when, as a proof of her "love" he whispers, "Show me where you wooden leg joins on" (CW, 280). Hulga is unnerved. She utters "a sharp little cry and her face instantly drained of color," as the increasingly sinister Pointer expertly exposes the locus of her vulnerability.

The leg, in a perverse sort of way, is the source of Hulga's hubristic self-confidence as well as a commentary on the wounded state of her soul. O'Connor explains "she was as sensitive about the artificial leg as a peacock about his tail. No one ever touched it but her. She took care of it as someone else would his soul, in private and almost with her own eyes turned away"(CW, 281). Still, Hulga retains an illusion of self-control, but by this time, she had fallen completely under Manley's domination.

> She decided that for the first time in her life she was face to face with real innocence. This boy, with an instinct that came from beyond wisdom, had touched the truth about her. When after a minute, she said in a hoarse high voice, "All right," it was like surrendering to him completely. It was like losing her own life and finding it again, miraculously, in his.

In so doing, a Ph.D. in philosophy quickly and completely falls under the control of a barely literate and uncultured itinerant salesman. As Pointer practices removing and reattaching the leg with a child's delight, the seduction continues and Hulga has by now wholly lost her intellectual and psychological bearings. She is "thinking that she would run away with him and that every night he would take the leg off and every morning put it back on again" (CW, 281).

But when she asks him to replace it, he murmurs "Not yet. . . . Leave it off for a while. You got me instead." Hulga gives a "little cry of alarm but he pushed her down and began to kiss her again. Without the leg she felt entirely dependent on him." O'Connor explains, "Her brain seemed to have stopped thinking altogether and to be about some other function that it not very good at." Keeping O'Connor's symbolism in mind, Hulga is now in danger not only of losing her leg to Pointer, but also of

losing her soul to the dangerous philosophy with which she has so per-
ilously toyed. As she often does, O'Connor now uses a description of the
human eye, in this instance to indicate the nature of Hulga's captivity:
"Every now and then the boy, his eyes like two steel spikes, would glance
behind him where the leg stood" (CW, 282).

Pointer refuses another plea from Hulga to restore her leg and instead
opens his suitcase to reveal only two Bibles, a flask of whiskey, a pack of
cards with obscene pictures, and a small blue box with printing on it. It
reads "THIS PRODUCT TO BE USED ONLY FOR THE PREVENTION OF
DISEASE." He "laid these out in front of her one at a time in an evenly-
spaced row, like one presenting offerings at the shrine of a goddess, putting the blue box in her hand." Hulga sat as if "mesmerized" "'Aren't
you,' she murmured, 'aren't you just good country people?'" (CW, 282).
This pathetic query indicates just how hypocritical has been Hulga's contempt for common, everyday life. It only takes the distress of her
predicament to expose her need for that which formerly only disgusted
her, and this crisis further suggests that she is no more superior to ordinary folk than her mother or her hired help Mrs. Freeman. They accept the
limitations of their mortality and can, in contrast to Hulga, live with a
salutary everyday hope, as her mother's name implies, and enjoy the dignity of being a "free man," as Mrs. Freeman's name suggests, even though
Hulga has mocked them as pitiful prisoners to their parochial attitudes
and preferences. Heretofore, Hulga has only shown disdain for "good
country people," but now she appeals to the reliability inherent in those
who can enjoy the predictability and safety of an ordinary life. So far from
being Nietzsche's Übermensch, she is reduced to the status of a helpless
little girl.

Like a fly caught in the web of a spider, but not yet devoured, Hulga
suddenly understands the conquest. "'Give me my leg!' she screamed and
tried to lunge for it but he pushed her down easily." Pointer mocks her,
"You just a while ago said you didn't believe in nothing. I thought you
was some girl!" Hulga vainly tries to save herself by appeal to a religion
in which she does not believe: "'You're a fine Christian!' she hissed.
'You're a fine Christian! You're just like them all—say one thing and do
another.'" Pointer disarms her with his angry reply: "I hope you don't
think . . . that I believe in that crap! I may sell Bibles but I know which end
is up and I wasn't born yesterday and I know where I'm going!" She
grows more desperate: "'Give me back my leg!' she screeched." But she
watches in horror as he "jumped up so quickly that she barely saw him
sweep the cards and the blue box back into the valise." Helplessly, she
"saw him grab the leg and then she saw it for an instant slanted forlornly
across the inside of the suitcase with a Bible at either side of its opposite

ends. He slammed the lid shut and snatched up the valise and swung it down the hole and then stepped through himself." Before his head disappears down the ladder, he turns back to Hulga and says, "You ain't so smart. I been believing in nothing ever since I was born!" (CW, 282-283).

HULGA'S SEDUCTION

In *Wise Blood*, O'Connor uses Sabbath Hawks to illustrate the seductive nature of the nihilism that Hazel Motes pursues; "Good Country People" reintroduces her argument. Two Old Testament proverbs are helpful in following her reasoning. The first warns, "Can a man take hot coals into his bosom and not be burned?" In typically Semitic style the second proverb affirms the meaning of its predecessor: "Can a man walk on hot coals and not be scorched?"[4] He who would pursue the modern spirit of nihilism will find that that which he has pursued will turn back to devour him. This calamity occurs more easily because of the naiveté by which one presumes to be capable of playing with such danger.

Compared with Manley Pointer, Hulga is a dilettante in nihilism, an amateur in "nothingness." She knows and believes just enough about nihilism to get herself in serious trouble. Pointer, by contrast, is an expert. But for O'Connor he is more than an expert: he represents something extra-human, the spirit of nihilism himself, a force that no man or woman can master, a power only safely dealt with by its avoidance. Indicative of Hulga's comparatively childish philosophical dabbling is Pointer's contemptuous use of her name, the proud symbol of her own nihilistic creativity. O'Connor explains that he speaks "the name as if he didn't think much of it" (CW, 282). Thus, her nihilism is a playful diversion compared with Pointer's lethal implementation of the same.

Whereas O'Connor was disturbed over nihilism, the Russian novelist Fyodor Dostoyevsky agonized over it in his novels. In *The Brothers Karamazov* he, like O'Connor, exposes its seductive character. Walker Percy once admitted that Dostoyevsky "is nearly always my model" and added, "I think maybe the greatest novel of all time is *The Brothers Karamazov*, which, written in the latter part of the nineteenth century, almost prophesies and prefigures everything—all the bloody mess and issues of the 20th century."[5]

One of the dramatic episodes in Dostoyevsky's great work occurs when the Devil, in the guise of a "Russian gentlemen," visits the distraught Ivan Fyodorovich Karamazov. The visit is possibly illusory, induced by Ivan's weakened mental state, but it reveals the truth of the philosophic enterprise in which he has been engaged. Ivan has just realized that due to his nihilistic misadventures, he may have been inadvertently complicit in his own father's murder, and his atheism leaves him groundless in this moral crisis. As the satanic visitor wittily but cruelly teases him as a cat would its prey, Ivan grows aware that by embracing nihilism he has, in a sense, "waded over his head," not understanding the implications of his intellectual pursuit. The Devil first tells the alarmed young intellectual that he, the devil, really does exist, even though Ivan, in keeping with his faddish ideas, resists such an outmoded notion. The Devil explains to Ivan that since he and his companions have had no more objective than "to negate," they have not perceived where their destructiveness will lead.[6] The Devil startles Ivan with his frightening vision:

> Oh, I love the dreams of my young and ardent friends a-tremble with the thirst for life! 'Those new men . . . they think they can destroy everything. . . . In my view it is not necessary to destroy anything, all that need be destroyed in mankind is the idea of God, that is what one must proceed from! . . . Once mankind, each and individually, has repudiated God . . . the whole of the former morality, will collapse, and all will begin anew. . . . Man will exalt himself with a spirit of divine, titanic pride, and the man-god will appear.[7]

This is all too much for the young intellectual who sits "with his hands pressed to his ears and looked at the floor, but began to tremble in all his body." He becomes even more agitated as the Devil explains that this episode of destruction and recreation may take "one thousand years." In the meantime, man will become a law unto himself—he will effectively have to manage a lawless society after the death of God until a new era emerges. As Ivan sees exactly what it is that he has undertaken, he physically strikes out at his sinister visitor until his nightmare is cut short by the arrival of his brother Alyosha.[8]

An important element in the process of seduction is the elimination of the sense of modesty and shame. In regard to Hulga, O'Connor explains, "As a child she had sometimes been subject to feelings of shame but education had removed the last traces of that as a good surgeon scrapes for cancer" (CW, 281). In George Bernard Shaw's play, *Man and Superman*, the revolutionary nihilist John Tanner explains how annoyingly pernicious the cultural sense of shame has become, and he passionately argues that it must be destroyed. He employs an *argumentum ad absurdum* to trivialize the human experience of shame and thereby discredit its importance.

> We live in an atmosphere of shame. We are shamed of everything that is real about us; ashamed of ourselves, of our relatives, of our incomes, of our accents, of our opinions, of our experience, just as we are ashamed of our naked skins. Good Lord . . . we are ashamed to walk, ashamed to ride in an om-

nibus, ashamed to hire a hansom instead of keeping a carriage, ashamed of keeping one horse instead of two and a groom-gardener instead of a coach-man and footman.[9]

Later in this play, the Devil appears, as he does in *The Brothers*. Here he proclaims, "Man measures his strength by his destructiveness."[10] In the appendix to the book, we find John Tanner's "Maxims for Revolutionar-ies" in which he explains, "Self-sacrifice enables us to sacrifice other peo-ple without blushing."[11]

Nietzsche himself, through his protagonist Zarathustra, argues against that same moral quality that involves "blushing,"

> To him who has knowledge, man himself is "the animal with red cheeks." How did this come about? Is it not because man has had to be ashamed too often? O my friends! Thus speaks he who has knowledge: shame, shame, shame—that is the history of man. And that is why he who is noble bids him-self not to shame."[12]

St. Thomas Aquinas teaches that both the phenomenon of shame and the virtue of modesty are integral to upright moral behavior, giving cre-dence to the insight of both O'Connor and Shaw that these qualities are obstacles to the Nietzschean call to destructive sexual impropriety. Closely associated with virtuous behavior, shame is a passion that causes one to recoil against what is disgraceful. It fortifies an individual in re-sisting improper, immodest choices. Shame can be weakened if not exter-minated: if one were to immerse himself repeatedly in wrongful behavior, shame would lose its force. Shame employs the emotion of fear specifi-cally, "the fear of something base, namely of that which is disgraceful." It is the "fear of doing a disgraceful deed or of a disgraceful deed."[13] Hulga, having lost her sense of shame at the university, was all the more vulner-able to Manley Pointer, whose name is redolent of the sexual methods he so expertly uses.

Continuing with Aquinas's teaching, a habit of modesty is a virtue that supports moderate behavior. It has to do with both an inner attitude and with the outward behavior that flows from that internal disposition. Modesty restrains a person from capitulating to impulsive, excessive be-havior and is reflected in one's action, speech, and attire.[14] Modesty in-volves humility that provides further help in avoiding arrogance and immodesty. As the scholastic philosopher notes, it is derived from the Greek *metrioteis*, the word etymologically related to terms of measure-ment. Modesty thus denotes a "measured" attitude and behavior, an idea repulsive to Nietzsche who associated such restraint with weakness and lack of vision; indeed, the whole of Nietzsche's system embodies the pride that St. Thomas emphatically condemns.[15] Without modesty, Hulga was the more easily victimized by unrestrained sexual indulgence. O'Connor owned a copy of C. S. Lewis's *The Problem of Pain* in which he notes that "even Pagan society has usually recognized 'shamelessness' as the nadir of the soul." For that reason, Lewis maintains, "In trying to extirpate Shame we have broken down one of the ramparts of the human spirit, madly exulting in the work as the Trojans exulted when they broke their walls and pulled the Horse into Troy."[16] In her personal copy of Eric Voegelin's *The World of the Polis*, O'Connor has notated the author's discussion of Aristotle's classic work of moral philosophy, the *Nichomachean Ethics*. In that passage, Voegelin explains that for the ancient Greeks, "aidos," alternately translated as shame or modesty, is "the condition of a good society."[17]

O'CONNOR'S CONCERN WITH CARTESIANISM

Sometimes, Mrs. Hopewell finds Hulga's behavior inscrutable. The handicapped girl once stood up in the middle of a meal with "her mouth half full" and exclaimed:

> "Woman! Do you ever look inside? Do you ever look inside and see what you are *not*? God!" she had cried sinking down again and staring at her plate, "Malebranche was right: we are not our own light. We are not our own light." (CW, 268)

The reference to Malebranche, the seventeenth-century Cartesian philosopher and theologian, may appear to be no more than rhetorical flourish, but O'Connor's choice of philosophers is quite strategic. It reveals her opinion that the troubles of the modern world find their origin in the philosophical revolution introduced by the mathematician and philosopher René Descartes. Although Descartes was not as flagrantly hostile to tradition as later philosophers of the Enlightenment would be for O'Connor, his method of doubting and ascertaining "truth," the Cartesian method, is the spring from which nihilism eventually flowed centuries later. She shared this opinion with the novelist Walker Percy who attributed to Descartes "many of the troubles of the modern world."[18] O'Connor's college philosophy textbook explains that the Cartesian revolution introduced a world view conspicuous for the absence of religion's mystery, and notable for its reduction, of not just science but moral philosophy, to mechanics. Descartes promoted "a conception of the universe governed throughout by natural mechanical laws, all stripped of the magic and mystical symbolism that before his day had led men to seek not sober description but divine perfection and purpose."[19] Descartes was the "great formulator of the new world view," and beginning with his *Discourse on Method* (1637), he sought to take the enthusiasm for science and mathematics and apply its methodology to all experience. He hoped to unlock not only the conundrums of mathematics but the mysteries of human existence by applying quantitative measurement and analysis to life itself. As Descartes explains, "I took especially great pleasure in mathematics because of the certainty and the evidence of its arguments. But I did not yet notice its true usefulness and, thinking that it seemed useful only to the mechanical arts, I was astonished that, because its foundations were so solid and firm, no one had built anything more noble upon them." So, Descartes decided that "I could not do better than to try once and for all to get all the beliefs I had accepted from birth out of my mind, so that once I have reconciled them with reason I might again set up . . . other, better ones or even the same ones." Accordingly, he adopted the attitude that he would only accept that which could be held with absolute certainty: "I took to be virtually false everything that was merely probable."[20]

As O'Connor's textbook explains, Descartes conceived of the world entirely in material terms, amenable to scientific investigation. Hence the entire universe, with all its mystery, was nothing more than a giant physics problem resolvable by the disciplined use of the scientific method.[21]

> To Descartes . . . space or extension became the fundamental reality in the world, motion the source of all change, and mathematics the only relation between its parts. . . . He had made of nature a machine and nothing but a machine; purposes and spiritual significance had alike been banished. . . . Intoxicated by his vision and his success, he boasted, "Give me extension and motion, and I will construct the universe."[22]

Unfortunately, as Randall observes, "The Cartesian world had exempted two things from its all-embracing mechanical sweep, God the creator, and the soul of man."[23] As O'Connor would have argued to Descartes, both the concept of God and that of man's soul will always remain in the shadow of mystery; this means that they will always be shaded by doubt. For Descartes to assume the rigid position that, "I reject as absolutely false everything in which I could imagine the least doubt," then he would necessarily have to reject anything obscured by mystery. As O'Connor saw it, Descartes set a tone for modern philosophy in which the most important things with which philosophers should be concerned must all be rejected peremptorily before they might be probed.[24]

O'Connor further learned from her textbook that there were two responses to Descartes's method in France; one camp was "primarily interested in natural science," and the other camp, that included Malebranche, was interested in "establishing tottering religious ideas upon the firm Cartesian foundation of the method of reason." Malebranche "particularly attempted to prove by reason the truth of the religious tradition." There was then, for O'Connor, a fundamental contradiction in Malebranche's endeavor because he seeks to use Descartes to remedy the damage Descartes has already inflicted on the Classical-Judeo–Christian heritage. Malebranche was opposed by Pascal, among others, who realized that much of the mystery of human nature was simply not amenable to rational resolution in the manner in which a problem of physics might yield to analysis. Thus, under Malebranche's stewardship, faith would be stripped of much of its meaning. Randall writes, "Malebranche's attempt might just as easily have established Mohammedanism or Judaism;—might better have done so, in fact, since they contained fewer 'mysteries' than orthodox Christianity."[25]

Malebranche advocates that which O'Connor most opposes, the unlawful divorce of theory from actual experience. Malebranche maintains that sensation and even imagination are produced, not by the everyday objects with which we have contact, but directly by God himself. He argues, just as Descartes had, that ideas are the only genuine substance of the world. Malebranche promotes Descartes's divorce of mind and matter, and though he does so under the cover of religion, he is still fundamentally at odds with the Aristotelian—Thomistic system that never allows theory to ignore common experience. O'Connor finds Malebranche's rationalization of religion at the expense of its mystery an unacceptable transaction.

But O'Connor's concern over forcing life and religion to be "reasonable" is no depreciation of reason itself. In Randall's, Jacques Maritain's, and O'Connor's view, it is the impossible role that Descartes assigned to reason that spawned the utopian promise of curing life of all misery, which in turn deteriorated into a loss of confidence in reason itself. When Descartes announced that "what pleased me the most" about his new methodology was that he "was assured of using my reason in everything," he failed to appreciate the naiveté of his endeavor, and that he was assigning a role to reason that would prove its undoing because of the impossibility of its demands.[26]

O'Connor learned from Maritain's *The Range of Reason*, that to recover the essential but balanced use of reason, it must be put "in the proper perspective, where it serves and not substitutes for revelation." In her review of his work, she further notes,

The age of Enlightenment substituted reason for revelation, with the result that confidence in reason has gradually decayed until in the present age, which doubts also fact and value, reason finds few supporters outside of Neo-Thomist philosophy.[27]

She was attracted to Maritain's writing because he "has been one of the major voices in modern philosophy to reassert the primacy of reason."

When confidence is lost in reason, as has happened in recent decades, an overreliance is placed upon "feeling." As T. S. Eliot has suggested, though our heads may be stuffed with "straw," we are "trembling with tenderness."[28] In the absence of faith and reason, all that is left is unstructured emotion and because of its isolation, "compassion" is prone to become ugly and abusive. Though the path may be paved with good intentions, the modern "virtue" of "tenderness," when it "is detached from the source of tenderness" and deprived of the guiding hand of reason, will end logically in "terror" in the Nietzsche-inspired "forced labor camps and in the fumes of the gas chamber" (CW, 636, 830-1).

The Cartesian revolution has also opened a doorway to "scientism," the unauthorized dominance of science in all human affairs that has introduced the unquestioned reign of "the expert," a credentialed elite who exercise a dubious rule over all human activity, not merely in the properly narrow sphere of their expertise. O'Connor's opinion of these technical mandarins is like Mrs. Hopewell's opinion of her daughter, who is "brilliant," but doesn't "have a grain of sense" (CW, 268).

To carry this analysis a step further and expose its link to Nietzsche, confusion over the source and exercise of authority is a prelude to the emergence of the undemocratic rule of Nietzsche's overman, especially since ordinary common sense is scorned as ignorant and irrelevant. In the "Revolutionary's Handbook," George Bernard Shaw's Tanner urges the rise of the "Superman" who is essential to man's improvement and without whom progress will be no more than a broken promise. If the Superman is to emerge, however, the average citizen who is too shortsighted or cowardly to permit his preeminence must not limit him: "We must eliminate the Yahoo, or his vote will wreck the commonwealth."[29]

On one other occasion, Mrs. Hopewell picked up one of Hulga's books and found the following underlined passage.

Science, on the other hand, has to assert its soberness and seriousness afresh and declare that it is concerned solely with what-is. Nothing—how can it be for science anything but a horror and a phantasm? If science is right, then one thing stands firm: science wishes to know nothing of nothing. Such is after all the strictly scientific approach to Nothing. We know it by wishing to know nothing of Nothing. (CW, 269)

Although Mrs. Hopewell doesn't understand what she has read, the words worked on her "like some evil incantation in gibberish." She subsequently "shut the book quickly and went out of the room as if she were having a chill." (CW, 269)

O'Connor's quote from the existentialist philosopher and Nietzsche scholar Martin Heidegger surely is meant to demonstrate the bankruptcy of reason to which Descartes led philosophy. Even in science, where reason rightly should dominate, Heidegger introduces an irrational nihilistic impulse as he was preoccupied, not with science, but with the "nothingness" that lay behind it. More specifically, the reference is from Heidegger's essay "What is Metaphysics?" in which the author proposes that metaphysics, the concern with "being" itself and with the first principles of existence, ought not to exclude the study of "nothing," the opposite of being.[30] He asks, "Why is there any Being at all—why not far rather Nothing?"[31] Heidegger argues that we should not limit ourselves to rational inquiry but pay closer attention to our "feelings" and "moods," and specifically to the vague emotion of "dread." Dread, by its very ambiguity and fear of the unknown, is an indication of, and a possible channel to, "nothing." In other words, in response to Heidegger's question, "Where will we find nothing?" he himself answers, "Dread reveals Nothing."[32] Taking this route constitutes a kind of "leap" that involves "letting ourselves go into Nothing, that is to say, freeing oneself from the idols we have and to which we are wont to go cringing." Reason, if it is to support such a proposition, must be redefined, as must logic itself. Heidegger argues, "If this thesis is correct then the very possibility of negation as an act of reason, and consequently reason itself, are somehow dependent on Nothing."[33]

Heidegger proposes a pursuit of Nothing through dread by redefining reason. For O'Connor, Heidegger's proposal may well represent the nadir of the deterioration of rationality begun with Descartes. In contrast to Heidegger, O'Connor believes that the recovery and right use of reason as traditionally understood are vital for man's well-being. As St. Thomas explains in the "Treatise on Happiness," because one's happiness is ultimately a *rational* activity, happiness is most fundamentally a function of the intellect. It is the apprehension of truth and of God. Accordingly, and again as O'Connor had learned from St. Thomas and Maritain, reason's proper function is crucial to one's ability to live an ethical and contented life. As Aquinas explains, "If reason does not occupy a place of dominion over one's 'emotions,' 'feelings,' and 'moods;' and if life is not lived logically with respect to the principles and assumption upon which good behavior is based, then men and women cannot possibly be happy and free."[34]

HULGA, O'CONNOR, AND FAITH

O'Connor explains in another letter to her friend Betty Hester, "She (Hulga) is full of contempt for the Bible salesman until she finds he is full of contempt for her."[35] Hulga realizes "in the end that she ain't so smart. It's not said that she has never had any faith but it is implied that her fine education has got rid of it for her, that purity has been overridden by pride of intellect through her fine education." This is not just any education; O'Connor was of course well educated herself, much of that education being self-taught. O'Connor here is condemning a modern and emphatically secular education, one without respect for tradition and religion, and one that fails to discriminate between the province of science and the excessive and misapplied claims of the scientific method.

O'Connor continues in her letter, "Further it's not said that she's never loved anybody, only that she's never been kissed by anybody—a very different thing. And of course I have thrown you off myself by informing you that Hulga is like me" (HB, 170). O'Connor's admission that she is like Hulga suggests several mutually compatible meanings. Like Hulga, O'Connor was well educated, especially so for a woman in the 1950s. While not asocial, O'Connor did not pursue the public life typical of some young women of her day. Even though she was attractive, she did not regularly date as a few of her contemporaries might: her writing, study, and the pursuit and defense of her Catholic faith were reportedly her priorities.[36] Later, after the success of her first novel, O'Connor found it increasingly difficult to avoid social invitations: "I am having a terrible time getting out of parties. . . . I have to be very stealthy, all eyes and ears" (HB, 33). Like Hulga, O'Connor even changed her name—from Mary Flannery O'Connor to Flannery O'Connor—though not for the same cynical reasons. O'Connor did so for literary advantage; she thought her given name would be truncated to the nondescript and easily ignored "Mary O'Connor."

O'Connor never abandoned her faith but she did hint that it had been tested. After a talk to a class at Emory University in 1962, a young poet, Alfred Corn, wrote O'Connor. He received in reply instructions on resisting the pull toward faithlessness in higher education and encouragement on turning challenges to his faith into opportunities to strengthen it. She writes, "As a freshman in college you are bombarded with new ideas, or rather pieces of ideas, new frames of reference, an activation of the intellectual life which is only beginning, but which is already running ahead of your lived experience. You are just beginning to realize how difficult it is to have faith." She recommends the "prayer of faith" of St. Peter: "Lord,

I believe. Help my unbelief." She also recommended Corn read Pierre Teilhard de Chardin's *The Phenomenon of Man* to see how the Christian paleontologist was able to think broadly about issues of faith and reason in the face of intellectual perplexities. Also included on her booklist were Etienne Gilson's *The Unity of Philosophical Experience* and John Henry Newman's systematic analysis of the intellectual process of belief, *The Grammar of Assent* (HB, 477). She admits, "At one time, the clash of the different world religions was a difficulty for me," but then she learned not to expect "absolute solutions" to important and difficult questions (HB, 477). O'Connor also faced the challenge of reconciling education and personal tragedy with Christian faith. O'Connor adored her father but lost him when she was fifteen years old. Maintaining vibrant faith in the face of personal loss is difficult for anyone, but the very intelligent sometimes find the paradoxical tension especially tough to resolve.

Most of all, she warned Corn to expect "intellectual difficulties" in the university, but her recommendation is to cultivate what she called "Christian skepticism." She explained, "It will keep you free—not free to do anything you please, but free to be formed by something larger than your own intellect or the intellects of those around you" (HB, 478).

Hulga's problem, and ours, has been developing for centuries. It began with a demand for certitude that asked of science and reason the impossible—to cure all human misery—and to do so by means of a method that discredited or denied the transcendent. The result has been the diminished authority of reason itself, in favor of an irrational pursuit of "nothingness." And whereas the persistence of human suffering in a technological age should temper the Cartesian hubris, for some it becomes an excuse for cynicism or it provides the pretext for radical Nietzschean pretension expressed in the kind of moral "creativity" that Hulga pursued in her "Vulcan's forge."

O'Connor's story also teaches that a belief in nihilism is something less than a clear, rational choice; it is more likely an example of seduction. And contrary to what one may believe, the one who chooses the moral void of "nothingness" will not so much exercise his freedom as he will suffer a victim's fate. Whatever decision he makes, the message of "Good Country People" seems clear: roll in the hay with a nihilist and you'll be left without a leg to stand on.

6

The Nature of Evil in "The Lame Shall Enter First"

O'Connor notes, "Conrad wrote that the artist descends within himself and in that region of stress and strife—if he be deserving and fortunate—he finds the terms of his appeal."[1] In a similar manner, and in perhaps her most disturbing short story, O'Connor seems to have reached deep within her own reservoir of wisdom and talent to teach something about one of the most difficult of philosophical and theological truths—the nature of evil. In O'Connor's personal library one finds *The Devil's Share*, in which the French philosopher Denis de Rougement argues for the usefulness of "myth" in exposing truths otherwise difficult to uncover, especially for the modern rationalist mind. Rougement explains, "A myth alone, by personifying or anthropomorphizing Evil," can uncover its meaning. He continues, "It is my conviction that the figures of myth guide us more surely than modern experiment and the analysis of reason."[2] As if on cue, O'Connor offers this short story to awaken the spiritual consciousness of a world consumed by rationalist thought.

THE STORY AND SHEPPARD'S INADEQUACY

"The Lame Shall Enter First" involves just three characters identified by name. Sheppard is the Recreational Director for the unidentified city in which he lives. It is not his vocation, though, with which the story is concerned, but his self-styled avocation. Sheppard works pro bono as a counselor at the reformatory. It is there that he encounters Rufus Johnson, a delinquent from a broken home whose father died before he was born, whose mother is in the penitentiary, and whose grandfather beat him.

Sheppard's own son Norton is eleven years old and the pair lives alone, having been deprived of their wife and mother by her untimely death. Sheppard is impatient with his own son's selfishness and inability to put his grief aside after a year. Seeing a greater challenge in the rehabilitation of an intelligent delinquent than the nurturing of his own mediocre off-spring, Sheppard coaxes Rufus Johnson into living with him and Norton. His motivation for doing so is twofold: he plans to "save" Johnson and at the same time, teach Norton to be unselfish and distract him from his self-indulgent mourning.

After meeting with Sheppard on several occasions, Rufus Johnson accepts Sheppard's offer to move in though he regards the amateur counselor with amused contempt. Sheppard gives Johnson a house key as an enticement to join the small family. Johnson arrives unannounced one afternoon, entering with the key and consequently frightening Norton. He mocks Sheppard in his absence: "You're his kid all right," he said. "You got the same stupid face." He further traumatizes Norton by invading the sacred space of his mother's vacant bedroom, dressing in her clothes, and dancing about the house in a macabre insult to her memory (CW, 602–6).

Sheppard's name is ironic because he is the worst of all possible shepherds; the misspelling of the word "shepherd" reinforces this idea. He is a secular shepherd, ignorant of the spiritual dimension of moral life; one might say that his rod consists of overweening confidence in his meager talents and his staff is a dogged reliance on a wholly rationalistic world-view. Most importantly, he doesn't recognize that Norton or Rufus Johnson have a soul. Norton has a soul that is fractured and needy because of the death of his mother; yet, Sheppard attends only to his intellect. He reasons with Norton to put his grief aside, advising Norton not to be self-ish. "Almost any fault," Sheppard brooded, "would be "preferable to selfishness" (CW, 596).

> Sheppard sat helpless and miserable, like a man lashed by some elemental force of nature. This was not a normal grief. It was all part of his selfishness. She had been dead for over a year and a child's grief should not last so long. "You're going on eleven years old," he said reproachfully. (CW, 597)

Sheppard further counsels his son, "If you stop thinking about yourself and think what you can do for somebody else . . . then you'll stop missing your mother" (CW, 597).

Just as Sheppard's appreciation of human nature is so defective that he does not understand the normal process of grief, neither does he understand that Rufus Johnson has a soul; although, in Rufus's case, his soul is so badly damaged as to be deformed, a deformation symbolized by his repulsive club foot. But Sheppard is oblivious to Johnson's inner deformity. In Sheppard's unidimensional analysis, Johnson is "the most deprived" child he has ever met; yet, he is "the most intelligent" and it is this latter index that most encourages Sheppard. Johnson's IQ of 140, though, should terrify rather than excite him because of the harm of which a brilliant juvenile delinquent is capable (CW, 597, 599).

Sheppard makes invidious comparisons between his own son and Johnson. In his view, Johnson has more potential because of his superior intelligence: Johnson has a capacity for real development, having been deprived of everything from birth. Norton, by contrast, possesses average intelligence or below and has enjoyed every advantage (CW, 599). Sheppard supposes that by explaining his problem to him, Johnson will naturally choose to behave differently. He explains to the delinquent, "'Rufus,' he said, 'you've got into a lot of senseless trouble but I think when you understand why you do these things, you'll be less inclined to do them. . . . There are a lot of things about yourself that I think I can explain to you.'" Rufus counters, "Satan . . . has me in his power." Sheppard's counterresponse exposes his contempt for religion: "'Rubbish!' he snorted. 'We're living in the space age! You're too smart to give me an answer like that'" (CW, 600).

Sheppard's plans to reform Johnson by feeding his intellect. He buys a telescope and sets it up in his attic, pictured as a "large unfinished room with exposed beams and no electric light." On several occasions, O'Connor eerily describes the room as consisting of a "jungle of shadows" and it is here that the horrid denouement of the story will occur. Johnson initially is taken with the instrument. Seeing him so absorbed, Sheppard's

> face was flushed with pleasure. This much of his dream was a reality. Within a week he had made it possible for the boy's vision to pass through a slender channel to the stars. He looked at Johnson's bent back with complete satisfaction. (CW, 609)

At first, Norton shows no interest in the telescope. "Don't you want to get up and look through the telescope, Norton?" Sheppard admonishes. He is annoyed because "the child shows no intellectual curiosity whatsoever." He warns, "Rufus is going to be way ahead of you" (CW, 610).

Blinded by his temporal psychology, Sheppard cannot perceive Rufus's true nature. But, no matter how malicious the delinquent behaves, Sheppard is not dismayed.

Sheppard was amused by these sudden turns of perversity. The boy resisted whatever he suspected was meant for his improvement and contrived when he was vitally interested in something to leave the impression he was bored. Sheppard was not deceived. Secretly Johnson was learning what he wanted him to learn—that his benefactor was impervious to insult and that there were no cracks in his armor of kindness and patience where a successful shaft could be driven (CW, 611).

As the story progresses, however, Johnson begins to exert a sorcerer's influence over Norton. This influence is especially disconcerting to Sheppard because Johnson employs what Sheppard finds most contemptuous—religious rhetoric and imagery. In the first instance, Johnson speaks of his own sure destiny for hell. Sheppard tries to divert the talk by stimulating both boys with the best science has to offer—the possibility of going to the moon. Johnson retorts, "I ain't going to the moon; . . . when I die I'm going to hell" (CW, 611). Exasperated, Sheppard tries a different tactic: he decides to "handle this kind of thing . . . with gentle ridicule." The moon, he explains, is visible to the senses. "We know it's there." By contrast, he adds, "Nobody has given any reliable evidence there's a hell" (CW, 611).

Thus begins a theological dialogue between Rufus and Sheppard. Rufus, with his unsophisticated fundamentalism, consistently gains the upper hand, however malevolent his use of religion may be. Norton, starved as he is for spiritual comfort, falls progressively under Johnson's influence. At first Norton seeks assurance from Rufus that his mother is not resigned to hell. He becomes a willing proselyte because Rufus offers him a way to think about his mother, a way of thinking denied to him by his father, who can only feebly respond, "Rufus is mistaken. Your mother isn't anywhere. She's not unhappy. She just isn't." However sophisticated Sheppard's position might seem to the adult, it does not address Norton's neediness, so his son naturally turns to Rufus who offers him an enlarged vision in which he can massage the memory of his mother, whose absence is still quite reasonably painful. When Sheppard tries to reason with Norton he "wrenched himself away and caught Johnson by the sleeve. 'Is she there, Rufus?' he said. 'Is she there, burning up?'" (CW, 612). Johnson, with an air of theological omniscience that further enhances his reputation with the younger boy, matter-of-factly asks if she were "evil" and a "whore." Sheppard sharply interjects that she was not but "[h]e had the sensation of driving a car without brakes" (CW, 612). After ascertaining from Norton that his mother believed in Jesus, Johnson confidently assures Norton that his mother is "on high," which he explains is "in the sky somewhere . . . but you got to be dead to get there" (CW, 612). The careful reader discerns at this point that something sinister and conclusive has just occurred in Rufus's influence over Norton. After Norton has advised Norton that only in death would he see his mother, O'Connor's description of Johnson's behavior is notable: "There was a narrow gleam in [Johnson's] eyes now like a beam holding steady on its target" (CW, 612).

From this point on in the story, Rufus and Norton are inseparable and Sheppard often glimpses secret communication between the two. On one occasion, when Sheppard attempts to intrude into their intimacy at a ball game, the "hiss of Johnson's voice stopped as he approached." Norton also becomes interested in the telescope and Sheppard often finds him in the attic "hunched over, looking intently through the instrument" (CW, 614).

Additionally, allegations begin to emerge of fresh violence and misbehavior on Rufus Johnson's part. The police visit the home on several occasions with reports of violent vandalism in nearby homes but Johnson always has a plausible alibi. Sheppard loses more of his tactical advantage as he is torn between the police accusations and Rufus's strong protestations of innocence. He is further divided as Rufus expertly manipulates him, daring him to believe the police and thus prove that Sheppard's benevolence and confidence in him are shallow and hypocritical.

Sheppard then continues to do no more than what he has already done—attempt to reach Rufus through his twisted intellect.

> After this he redoubled his efforts. Since Johnson had lost interest in the telescope, he bought a microscope and a box of prepared slides. If he couldn't impress the boy with immensity, he would try the infinitesimal. For two nights Johnson appeared absorbed in the new instrument, then he abruptly lost interest in it, but he seemed content to sit in the living room in the evening and read the encyclopedia. He devoured the encyclopedia as he devoured his dinner, steadily and without dint to his appetite. (CW, 617)

There is no problem with Rufus's mind; it is his soul that is dysfunctional. O'Connor's language here is carefully chosen and ominous: "each subject appeared to enter his head, *be ravaged*, and thrown out" (CW, 617). But Sheppard is content to see the boy intellectually stimulated and so "his confidence returned. He knew that some day he would be proud of Johnson" (CW, 617).

Until the next Thursday night, that is, when the police visit the home again. "A house on the corner of Shelton and Mills," one of the officers explained. "It looks like a train run through it" (CW, 617). Johnson vehemently denies culpability, blaming instead "some nigger." Though the officers warn Sheppard he is being duped, he defends Johnson just as adamantly as Johnson defends himself and suggests that the police are making a "mistake" again (CW, 617). "It ain't our funeral," one of them ominously warns (CW, 618). After they leave, Sheppard dares to question Rufus and he is punished for the effort.

> "You make out like you got all this confidence in me!" a sudden outraged voice cried, "and you ain't got any! You don't trust me no more now than you did then!" The voice, disembodied, seemed to come more surely from the depths of Johnson than when his face was visible. It was a cry of reproach, edged slightly with contempt." (CW, 618)

Sheppard is so cowed by the juvenile that he doesn't even dare to ask his son to substantiate Rufus' alibi for fear that Rufus will notice. Each day Rufus extends his control, not only over Rufus, but also over Sheppard. In one instance, O'Connor explains, "In the middle of the room [Rufus] turned and jerked his arm at Sheppard and Sheppard jumped up and followed him as if the boy had yanked an invisible leash" (CW, 616).

LOSING THE BATTLE, LOSING THE WAR

More police allegations will come, and as they do, Sheppard will eventually realize Rufus Johnson's guilt, but only when Johnson, with a sneer, tells him himself how he has outwitted the police. Sheppard's failure is symbolized by his vain attempt to equip Johnson with a new, modern, well-fitting shoe that promises to all but remedy the boy's awkward gait. The new shoe represents Sheppard's presumptuous but terribly naïve aspiration of "saving" Rufus Johnson. He has Johnson fitted for a replacement for Rufus' worn, tattered shoe, but when it arrives, it has been badly fabricated and does not fit. After a second order, the shoe fits perfectly, but Johnson refuses it; Sheppard is emotionally crushed and psychologically devastated.

Like a general who loses a decisive battle that makes the loss of the war inevitable, Sheppard has to accept his own failure when Johnson rejects the replacement shoe that Sheppard believed would so elevate his self-esteem that his life would be forever improved. The shoe symbolizes Sheppard's baseless confidence in the secular salvation he had designed for Rufus Johnson. When Sheppard takes Johnson to the brace shop to pick up the newly designed shoe, "[t]here was an excited flush on Sheppard's face; his heart was beating unnaturally fast" (CW, 620). The clerk exudes the same excitement, even if it was not as deeply felt as that of Sheppard. "'With this shoe,' the clerk said, 'you won't know you're walking. You'll think you're riding'" (CW, 619)!

But when Johnson's deformity is uncovered, both the clerk and Sheppard are repulsed and shaken, as if they had encountered a measure of evil for which they are unprepared. O'Connor describes Rufus's foot alternately as grotesque and lethal as the disfigurement is "unsheathed." The clerk

> bent his bright pink bald head and began gingerly to unlace the twine. He removed the old shoe as if he were skinning an animal still half alive. His expression was strained. The unsheathed mass of foot in the dirty sock made Sheppard feel queasy. He turned his eyes away until the new shoe was on. (CW, 620)

The clerk recovers his composure, and then winks at Sheppard as he tells Johnson to "stand up and walk around . . . and see if that ain't power glide." For his part, "Sheppard's face was bright with pleasure." Johnson walks across the room in the shoe and, indeed, his gait and posture are straightened, as if Sheppard "had given the boy a new spine" (CW, 621). But

> Johnson turned around. His mouth was set in a thin icy line. He came back to the seat and removed the shoe. He put his foot in the old one and began lacing it up. (CW, 621)

"I ain't going to wear it." Johnson announces. The clerk and Sheppard are stunned. Rufus tells Sheppard he doesn't need it and, besides, if he does, he can get one himself. The clerk "rose glumly . . . and asked Sheppard what he wanted done with the shoe, which he dangled dispiritedly by the lace." Sheppard's face was a "dark angry red" (CW, 621).

> "Wrap it up," Sheppard muttered. He turned his eyes to Johnson. "He's not mature enough for it yet," he said. "I had thought he was less of a child."
> The boy leered. "You been wrong before." (CW, 621)

After this devastation, Sheppard never recovers his confidence. That night at home in the living room, in a mood of troubled pensiveness, he tries to rationalize Rufus's behavior. As if he were pathetically trying to re-join the fragments of a broken vase, he attempts to piece together a new psychological profile of the delinquent that will explain Rufus's behavior in some reasonable way, keeping the reprobate amenable to his amateurish psychology. Yet, as soon as he arrives at a new tentative diagnosis of the troubled boy, the police visit again with yet another allegation, this time of voyeurism. As the police again have no hard evidence, Sheppard stands in a forced solidarity with Rufus, defending him against the police accusations, although the officers are even more certain of Rufus's guilt. When they leave, however, Rufus, with an expression described as "predatory" and "openly leering," implies that Sheppard has been defending the delinquent's guilt, not his innocence. Sheppard is completely broken:

> He dropped down on the sofa and gazed at the rug beneath his feet. The boy's clubfoot was set within the circle of his vision. The pieced-together shoe appeared to grin at him with Johnson's own face. He caught hold of the edge of the sofa cushion and his knuckles turned white. A chill of hatred shook him. He hated the shoe, hated the foot, hated the boy. He face paled. Hatred choked him. He was aghast at himself. (CW, 624)

Like a fallen man who is mortally wounded and tries to rise from his deathbed, Sheppard "caught the boy's shoulder and gripped it fiercely as if to keep himself from falling. 'Listen,' he said, 'you looked in that window to embarrass me. . . . [B]ut my resolve isn't shaken. . . . I'm stronger than you are and I'm going to save you. The good will triumph.'" But Johnson is in possession of more discernment than Sheppard. As if he were striking the reeling man again, Johnson perceptively retorts, "Not when it ain't true. . . . Not when it ain't right" (CW, 624) Then, in foreboding language, O'Connor describes Rufus's second retort, and in doing so, reveals the philosophical and theological truth of the encounter: "'Save yourself,' he hissed. 'Nobody can save me but Jesus'" (CW, 624). Rufus's tactical advantage over Sheppard consists in Rufus's belief in evil while Sheppard is a skeptic. Accordingly, the delinquent possesses freedom of aggression in a theater of operations that Sheppard doesn't even believe exists.

All that remains is the tragic conclusion of the story. Johnson's mastery over Sheppard and his son is complete. Sheppard, though, is so spiritually barren and devastated that he doesn't even possess the manliness to kick Johnson out of the house. He only weakly and passively hopes that he will leave of his own accord, or that he might become angry enough, for some reason, to abandon the small family. For Sheppard to act more assertively would be a public acknowledgment of what is already apparent—the collapse of his worldview and his unwarranted confidence in human nature.

> Why not simply tell the boy to go? Admit defeat. The thought of facing Johnson again sickened him. The boy looked at him as if he were the guilty one, as if he were the moral leper. (CW, 625-626)

Sheppard tries to console himself with the only source of consolation he knows, an assurance of his own goodness. O'Connor writes, "He knew without conceit that he was a good man, that he had nothing to reproach himself with" (CW, 631). Sheppard's traumatic experience seems to bring him to the verge of self-knowledge and a more sensible view of human nature as he "longed for the time when there would be no one but himself and Norton in the house, when the child's simple selfishness would be all he had to contend with" (CW, 626).

But Johnson does not leave. His influence over Norton seems complete and he begins to taunt Sheppard by more frequent references from a Bible he and Norton have stolen from "a ten cent store" and, by telling Sheppard that, "Satan has you in his power." Johnson announces that, though Satan also has him in his power, he could repent if he chose and "become a preacher." This prompts Norton to shout, with a "glitter of wild pleasure in his eyes," that he is going to become a "space man" (CW, 626-627).

The story rapidly draws to a dreadful close that evening. Johnson, unbeknown to Sheppard, slips out of the house. Norton meanwhile turns fanatical while using the telescope in the attic. Sheppard finds him peering through the instrument while waving wildly but pathetically to the sky, crying out that he has found his mother. "'She's there!' he cried, not turning around from the telescope. 'She waved at me!'" Sheppard, by this time seared of emotion, can only wearily order his son to bed (CW, 629). Within moments, though, he hears a siren. This time Rufus is caught red-handed by the police, yet as the police bring him in, accompanied by a news reporter, the delinquent begins to accuse Sheppard of atheism and abuse: "The Devil has him in his power." He adds portentously, "He made suggestions to me!"

> Sheppard's face blanched. He caught hold of the door facing.
> "Suggestions?" the reporter said eagerly, "what kind of suggestions?"
> "Immor'l suggestions!" Johnson said. "What kind of suggestions do you think? But I ain't having none of it, I'm a Christian." (CW, 630)

The police take Rufus to the awaiting patrol car as the reporter runs alongside with more questions about Sheppard's behavior. Watching them leave, "Sheppard remained there, bent slightly like a man who has been shot but continues to stand," repeating softly, "'I have nothing to reproach myself with'" until his self-justification sounded "dry and harsh" (CW, 631).

Suddenly the belated revelation of his own emptiness, inadequacy, and misdeeds descends upon him as he realizes that he has abused his own son through neglect while attending to Johnson with his misguided altruism. "Slowly his face drained of color. . . . His mouth twisted and he closed his eyes against the revelation" as he is afflicted with a vision of

Norton's face "empty" and "forlorn." He is seized with sudden repentance. His "heart constricted with a repulsion of himself so clear and intense that he gasped for breath." (CW, 632) He is overwhelmed with remorse and tenderness for Norton as a "rush of agonizing love for the child rushed over him" and he "groaned with joy." He resolves at that moment to "make everything up to him" to "never let him suffer again" as he pledges to "be mother and father." O'Connor writes the last dreadful lines of the story,

> He jumped up and ran to his room, to kiss him, to tell him that he loved him, that he would never fail him again.
> The light was on in Norton's room but the bed was empty. He turned and dashed up the attic stairs and at the top reeled back like a man on the edge of a pit. The tripod had fallen and the telescope lay on the floor. A few feet over it, the child hung in the jungle of shadows, just below the beam from which he had launched his flight into space. (CW, 632)

ST. THOMAS AQUINAS AND MISGUIDED HUMANITARIANISM

Although in "The Lame Shall Enter First," the theme of evil is palpable, the reflective reader should ask whether O'Connor, with Aquinas as her inspiration, is merely using Johnson as an instance of evil behavior, or if her thesis asks a more profound question: is Sheppard himself malevolently complicit in this tragedy? Upon a closer analysis, it becomes evident that Johnson is not the cause of evil; rather, he only takes advantage of a situation already prepared for evil by the absence of faith and sound reason. In the *Summa Theologica*, St. Thomas Aquinas's teaching on the concept of evil is filled with the language of deficiency, privation, and incompleteness. Evil is the consequence of a kind of deficiency and "can only proceed from a deficient cause." Evil, moreover is not a substance per se, it is a privation of good. He writes, "Evil is the absence of the good."[3]

Aquinas's teaching is an elaboration of St. Augustine's conception of evil in which the latter explains, "evil has no positive nature; what we call evil is merely the lack of something that is good." Evil is an evil in so far as it is "defective," as blindness in an eye.[4] In his *Confessions*, St. Augustine explains the nature of evil as the deprivation of goodness. After several years of flirtation with the heresy of Manicheanism, which teaches that evil is a separate and contrary substance from good, St. Augustine announces his discovery in a prayerful acknowledgement before God: "To You, then, evil utterly is not."[5]

Seen from a different angle, evil has as its purpose the interruption of something en route to its final cause, to its telos.[6] Thomas explains that evil is the result of a defect in the principles by which we act; or, evil is the result of the person's defect in his endeavor toward some conception of the good. In some cases, as O'Connor's story illustrates, evil may be the consequence of both flawed principles and a flawed agent. Johnson's principles of life are more sophisticated than Sheppard's because Johnson acknowledges the spiritual. In this story both Sheppard and Johnson are both personally flawed, but Sheppard doubles the defect by acting upon flawed principles. Sheppard's morally bankrupt philosophy, coupled with his own hollow soul, is sufficient to corrupt his well-meaning but injurious humanitarianism.[7]

For Shepherd since there is no transcendent dimension beyond the material, there are no fixed principles of life beyond a rationalistic hubris in human progress. Indeed, "the very nature of evil is against the idea of a first principle."[8] His conception of human nature is fundamentally flawed. His is a one-dimensional picture of humanity that gives rise to flawed remedies for the alleviation of personal suffering. Not perceiving the divine, he misunderstands the human. Sheppard's debacle demonstrates that if one does not believe in the possibility of divine goodness, he is equally oblivious and vulnerable to the reality of malevolent evil. For that reason, his best efforts at beneficence are prone to disaster.

O'Connor further suggests that Sheppard, having rejected the possibility of a deity, can only look to himself as a replacement. He is introduced in the first paragraph of the story as "a young man whose hair . . . stood up like a narrow brush *halo* over his pink sensitive face" (CW, 595; emphasis added). In the closing lines of the story, as the crushing revelation of his own inadequacy falls down upon him, O'Connor explains, "Slowly his face drained of color. It became almost grey beneath the white *halo* of his hair" (CW, 632; emphasis added). Early in the story, Sheppard subtly reveals his secularism and contempt for things religious when he thinks that his "credentials were less dubious than a priest's; he had been trained for what he was doing" (CW, 599). Another time, Johnson complains to Norton of his father's intrusiveness. His complaint, though, is not mere peevishness; it is a perceptive analysis of Sheppard's self-perception.

"God, kid," Johnson said in a cracked voice, "how do you stand it?" His face was stiff with outrage. "He thinks he's Jesus Christ!" (CW, 609)

To be sure, Sheppard does not pursue evil, he chases after something good. He explains to Norton, "If I can help a person, all I want is to do it. I'm above and beyond simple pettiness" (CW, 609). St. Thomas explains in the *Summa* that no one pursues evil as such, it is impossible to do so, as we saw with Hazel Motes in *Wise Blood*. Rather one stumbles into evil inadvertently by chasing after something good to which the evil is attached. He says, "since evil is opposed to good, it is impossible that any evil, as such, should be sought." Yet, Aquinas adds that "evil may be sought accidentally, so far as it accompanies a good."[9] The mistake may occur from the best of motives, yet those motives may be misguided due to naiveté. This is exactly what occurs with Shepherd; he does not pursue evil; he seeks good.[10] O'Connor herself once explained, "I think evil is the defective use of good" (HB, 129). She emphasizes elsewhere, "Catholics believe that all creation is good and that evil is the wrong use of good" (HB, 144).

However, because Sheppard doesn't allow for the nonmaterial—the supernatural—he cannot possibly understand the nature of the evil with which he is entangled. Thus, his pursuit of what is good is as prone to generate evil, as it is likely to foster good. Thomas teaches emphatically that evil does not arise in itself, that there is no independent source of evil. He writes "there is no one first principle of evil, as there is one first principle of good."[11] Ultimately its occurrence may be traced back to the good: "Hence it is true that evil in no way has any but an accidental cause."

In a profoundly ironic way, then, good can be the cause of evil, especially if one's pursuit of the good proceeds from a deficiency of faith and is based upon sentimentalism and good intentions rather than being rooted in the transcendent. Although good works might be undertaken below the banner of humanitarianism, they may be no more than shallow, ineffectual, and potentially damaging "do-good-ism."

It is for this reason that O'Connor describes Rufus Johnson's new shoe, the one he so emphatically rejects, in such troubling and eerie terms. "It was a black slick shapeless object, shining hideously. It looked like a blunt weapon, highly polished" (CW, 620). One would not expect that an instrument of rehabilitation, however misguided its use might be, to be treated with such scorn by the author. She does so, however, to underline Thomas's teaching that attempts at doing good, especially in difficult circumstances and against challenging perplexing odds, if disconnected from faith, may result in something evil, however unintended the consequence. Sheppard illustrates that without spiritual guidance, one may well produce an evil result worse than the original wrong in need of correction.

There is another reason why Sheppard's faithless benevolence is sure to fail: it is his attempt of trying to fill his own need, the void in his own soul left by his rejection of the spiritual. O'Connor explained to a friend, "If Sheppard represents anything here, it is, as he realizes at the end of the story, the empty man who fills up his emptiness with good works" (CW, 1174). For this reason, his behavior is more selfish than benevolent. O'Connor explains this indirectly but unmistakably. When he is trying to convince Johnson to stay despite Norton's objections, Sheppard's anxiety and desperation is palpable. Although his pretext is Norton's need to learn to share, this is hardly plausible. He practically begs the juvenile delinquent to remain in his home. His motive, though, is not so much to rehabilitate the reprobate, but to fill his own spiritual emptiness by pursuing Johnson's "salvation."

> "Listen," Sheppard said, "we need another boy in the house." There was a genuine desperation in his voice. "Norton here has never had to divide anything in his life. He doesn't know what it means to share. And I need somebody to teach him. How about helping me out? Stay here for a while with us, Rufus. I need your help." The excitement in his voice made it thin. (CW, 608)

Later, as Sheppard's grand aspirations for Johnson's rehabilitation begin to unravel, his judgment is still crippled by his own spiritual need. Considering the possibility that Johnson may have to leave, Sheppard is distraught at by the prospect: "Oh my God, he thought. He could not bring it to that" (CW, 614). Even in the final scene of the drama when he is stunned by ugly self-revelation, that self-knowledge is incomplete as Sheppard merely switches the focus of his own salvation from Rufus to Norton. His reawakening to the possibilities of life with his own son "rushed over him like a transfusion of life. The little boy's face appeared to him transformed; the image of his salvation; all light" (CW, 632). Sheppard though is incapable of selfless giving. Had Norton survived and Sheppard clung to his stubborn materialism, his relationship with Norton likely would have been as dysfunctional as his tortured relationship with Rufus.

O'Connor once explained that "The Lame Shall Enter First" was "about one of Tarwater's terrible cousins, a lad named Rufus Johnson" (CW, 456). Young Francis Marion Tarwater is the protagonist of her second novel, *The Violent Bear It Away*. When his grandfather dies, the boy's uncle Rayber the schoolteacher takes young Francis Marion in order to raise him in a more "normal" environment than the one Tarwater experienced with his grandfather. Rayber's self-confidence is reminiscent of Sheppard's. Rayber scoffs at his religious-minded neighbors: "All such people have in life," he said, "is the conviction they'll rise again" (CW, 399). Rayber's general attitude toward life is the same as Sheppard's—rank rationalism of the worst sort. In his own secular way, he "preaches" to his nephew:

> "The great dignity of man," his uncle said, "is his ability to say: I am born once and no more. What I can see and do for myself and my fellowman in

this life is all of my portion and I'm content with it. It's enough to be a man."
(CW, 437)

But since Rayber is a skeptic like Sheppard, his benevolence is a response to his own neediness; he needs to help Tarwater to remedy his
own problems. He asserts to the boy, "Now I can make up for all the time
we've lost. I can help correct what he's done to you, help you to correct it
yourself." But O'Connor reveals that his true if unconscious motive has as
much to do with meeting his own need as helping his nephew: "'This is
our problem together,' he said, seeing himself so clearly in the face before
him *that he might have been beseeching his own image*" (CW, 395, emphasis
added). Consequently, his altruism is as empty and tragic as is that of
Sheppard. When Tarwater drowns Rayber's retarded son, Rayber's acquiescence and his neglect of his own longing for "mystical love" makes
the event possible. For that reason, according to O'Connor, Rayber
"makes the Satanic choice" (HB, 484). So, it is not what Rayber did that
was evil, it is what he did not do that allowed evil to take place.

O'Connor, then, shows that humanitarianism without faith may be the
cruelest kind of kindness; but, benevolence inspired by the transcendent
is goodness indeed. O'Connor's spirituality is not a detached faith irrelevant to human need or insensitive to the evil of the human condition. To
the contrary, she warns the reader against a faithless humanitarianism, a
confidence in human progress alone that ignores the spiritual reality of
human life.

THE HUMAN SOUL

If the altruist denies that men and women have a soul, as did Sheppard,
he is capable only of a kind of inept benevolence as likely to multiply evil
and aggravate suffering as to supply its remedy. Modernity's rejection of
the conception of the soul represents hubris at its worst. The term has
been dropped from the modern lexicon, in part, because it can't be fully
studied or understood; yet, it touches upon the deepest mysteries of life.
Aristotle concedes that "in all ways, it is one of the hardest of things to
gain any conviction about the soul."[12] Yet, such mysteries, O'Connor once
noted, can't be measured easily. St Augustine avers, nonetheless, that the
soul's resistance to quantification in no way diminishes its "greatness."[13]

St. Thomas explains in his "Treatise on Man" that our understanding of
the human and the divine is hinged on our recognition of the soul. It is the
soul that bridges the two dimensions of our existence. The soul is the "life
principle" of the body, the composite of the intellect and will that outlives

the body; it is our "spiritual substance." The "spiritual soul, substantially joined with matter . . . constitutes an existing human being." Aristotle explains, "knowledge of the soul is . . . held to make a great contribution to the complete understanding of truth."[14]

Thus, an understanding of what constitutes a human being is indispensable to fruitful humanitarian effort.[15] As the essayist Montaigne explains, in order to cultivate virtue and attenuate vice, one must acknowledge that the "true seat of virtue" is found in the "workings of the soul."[16] Aristotle teaches that the study of the soul is a prerequisite to study in ethics and politics, which is to say, one cannot properly address moral deficiencies in another, nor prescribe remedies, without an understanding of the soul.[17] To do so would be to act as a surgeon who attempts to heal without knowledge of human anatomy.

7

Social Change in
"The Enduring Chill"

In "The Enduring Chill," O'Connor employs some of her wittiest writing in what may be her most morally incisive story. Walker Percy called it "witty . . . almost a masterpiece."[1] But judging by her own comments, achieving her goal in this story was a challenge. She wrote to Betty Hester in November of 1957,

> I announce with wild pleasure that I have finished the story once through as of today and that when I go over it about three more times, I think I will have done it; another month, I guess. Right now I am highly satisfied with all its possibilities and all that's already in it.

She mischievously adds, "Nobody appreciates my work the way I do" (HB, 256). A few days later she admitted to more uncertainty over whether she had completed her task:

> I have a few things to do to the story yet but you will see it shortly. I go from liking it to not liking it. When I am in the liking-it stage I am tempted to send it to you, but when I am in the not-liking-it stage I decide to keep it a while longer. (HB, 256)

She confessed to Hester a month later, "I have torn the story up and am doing it over or at least a good deal of it over" (HB, 259). A month later she wrote her editor at Farrar, Straus and Giroux, asking her to substitute several new pages for the old, explaining, "I have made some significant changes in it, improved it greatly" (CW, 264).

Perhaps O'Connor's difficulty came from the challenge of weaving varied strands of material together to fashion her story. She casts her protagonist in the guise of James Joyce's suffering artist to illustrate her recurrent theme of the need for self-knowledge, often violently supplied through grace. In this case, O'Connor's character, in his mean-spirited attempt to "improve" the lot of his mother's hired Negroes, is arrogant to the point of hubris, and his violent pride must be tamed. The story teaches that those who are driven by anger and pride are unlikely to possess the humility and modesty that should safeguard the delicate task of social reform.

O'Connor's attitude toward social reform is perhaps the most important element of her political philosophy and it consists of the importance of respecting social manners when undertaking social reform. But, the necessity of prudential public change, imaginatively taught in "The Enduring Chill," must be understood in light of her belief in the basic equality of all men as it is rooted in their mortality. This belief is most evident in her short story, "Revelation," which will be introduced later in this chapter. Such equality, in which all men are made equal by their common dependence on God, is unaffected by social status or even by the wide variation in intelligence or talent found in the human species. Everyone is equally mortal before an immortal God.

In "The Enduring Chill," O'Connor's protagonist Asbury appears as a parody of James Joyce's Stephen Dedalus in *Portrait of the Artist as a Young Man*. O'Connor may have chosen Joyce in part because she perceived in the Irish writer's prose an inescapable longing for transcendence and truth. She wrote that she sometimes tired of reading Catholic authors like Léon Bloy, Georges Bernanos, and François Mauriac because at some point their didacticism reached a point of diminishing returns.[2] Sometimes, she noted, "you get more benefit reading someone like Hemingway, where there is apparently a hunger for a Catholic completeness in life, or Joyce who can't get rid of it no matter what he does" (HB, 130).

Asbury, driven by his own anger and unhappiness, tries to remake his mother's southern milieu according to more "progressive views" on race. For Asbury, a life of tradition that hands outworn rural values from one calloused hand to another, is a life of corruption. His reckless and arrogant attempt to foist social change, however, only leads to his misfortune. O'Connor once insisted, "Southern writers are not lonely, suffering artists gasping for purer air" (MM, 53); and so, she uses the persona of the suffering artist as an opportunity to condemn the modern misuse of the imagination, as Asbury tries to refashion the foibles and injustices of his hometown according to untested abstractions. As Asbury himself put it, he had gone to New York "to escape the slave's atmosphere of home . . . to find freedom, to liberate my imagination" (CW, 554). But Asbury's contempt for his own homestead deprives him of the grounding in prudence, common sense, and goodwill that O'Connor insists is necessary to bring about lasting social improvement. More specifically, he fails to recognize the importance of the collective "manners" that furnish the intangible infrastructure holding any society together. For O'Connor, should change occur, it must transpire with respect to this social framework. Thus, in "The Enduring Chill," O'Connor reiterates her firmly held belief that a sense of place and region, while not an excuse to avoid reform, is a safeguard against silly and even dangerous social engineering. Regional grounding is an aid to prudence in that it helps one preserve a balance between principle and practical action. In O'Connor's view, the rootless imagination is easily confused by theory (MM, 53-4).

ASBURY'S RETURN AND "DEMISE"

The story begins with the twenty-five-year-old Asbury stepping off the train that has just returned him from New York to his rural Southern hometown. He has come home because he is sick: he has suffered for some months from recurrent chills and fever, a dissipation of energy, and "inconsistent aches and headaches." Having lost his part-time job at a bookstore and depleted his savings, he had no choice but to abandon the beatnik two-room hovel that had been his glory and come home. He rudely greets his mother with "'I don't feel like talking'" and he is distressed at helplessly watching the train disappear and leave him in "this collapsing country junction." Asbury "had become entirely accustomed to the thought of death, but he had not become accustomed to the thought of death *here*" (CW, 548).

Asbury is tormented by the conjunction of his belief that the creative artist is a superior species and his self-assessment that he is not one of them. Thus, he is simultaneously contemptuous of those with whom he interacts while full of self-loathing for his own inadequacy, a failing for which he blames his mother in the absence of anyone else to indict. Given his lack of creative genius, Asbury despairs that he might be no more than one of the despised Nietzschean "herd." While his mother is driving him home from the train station, she vainly tries to interest him in developments on the family farm. When she stops the car to comment on the health of the cows, Asbury deliberately looks the other way, "but there a small walleyed Guernsey was watching him steadily as if she sensed some bond between them" (CW, 552).

His mother Mrs. Fox, as her name suggests, holds a shrewd if disappointed opinion of her son and of his sister Mary George, a local elementary school teacher. They are both smart, but it is their intelligence that ruins their character. She thinks, "When people think they are smart—even when they are smart—there is nothing anybody else can do to make them see things straight, and with Asbury, the trouble was that in addition to being smart, he had an artistic temperament" (CW, 551). After the death of her husband, Mrs. Fox had managed to get the two children through college, "but she had observed that the more education they got, the less they could do. Their father had gone to a one-room schoolhouse through the eighth grade and he could do anything" (CW, 552).

Upon arriving at the farmhouse, Asbury falls asleep in his room staring at the water stains on his ceiling. They form a pattern that he remembers interpreting from his childhood and this picture will become the imaginary instrument of his redemptive "enduring chill."

> Descending from the top molding, long icicle shapes had been etched by leaks and, directly over his bed on the ceiling, another leak had made a fierce bird with spread wings. It had an icicle crosswise in its beak and there were smaller icicles depending from its wings and tail. (CW, 555)

The image, Asbury remembers, "had always irritated him and sometimes had frightened him. He had often had the illusion that it was in motion and about to descend mysteriously and set the icicle on his head" (CW, 556).

Asbury awakens that afternoon staring into the face of Dr. Block the town doctor who possesses none of the sophistication to which Asbury has come to think he is entitled. "What's wrong with me is way beyond Block," he protests (CW, 549). As the doctor thumps, prods, and draws blood, all under Asbury's impudent gaze, the younger man meanly says, "I didn't send for you. I'm not answering any questions. You're not my doctor. What's wrong with me is way beyond you" (CW, 557). But Block plays a role opposite Asbury, similar to the role Mrs. Freeman played against the self-styled nihilist Hulga in "Good Country People." Block possesses unsettling insight into Asbury's character and he provides a counterweight to Asbury's pseudo-intellectual snobbery.

> "Most things are beyond me," Block said. "I ain't found anything yet that I thoroughly understood," and he sighed and got up. His eyes seemed to glitter at Asbury as if from a great distance. (CW, 557)

Over the next few days, Asbury's health continues to decline. His mother insists he sit on the porch each afternoon, "and as resistance was too much of a struggle" he would drag himself out wrapped in an afghan and gaze at the distance. As he does so, he reminisces about his previous visit home, when he had taken a special interest in the male Negro help, Morgan and Randall, undertaking to write a play about their life instead of helping out around the dairy farm. He had spent time with them trying to understand "how they really felt about their condition," but the two were generally uncooperative and tended to look at him askance. On one occasion he had encouraged them to share a cigarette in the barn as an act of communal defiance. For Asbury it was a creatively iconoclastic moment, "one of those moments of communion when the difference between black and white is absorbed into nothing" (CW, 558). Two cans of milk were ruined in the process, having absorbed the tobacco, "but the experience had so exhilarated him that he had been determined to repeat it in some other way" (CW, 559).

The next afternoon he had found his opportunity. He picked up a glass, filled it out of the cans of fresh unpasteurized milk in the barn, and drained it. Randall stopped in the middle of pouring a can and watched him. "She don't 'low that," he said. "That *the* thing she don't 'low." Both Randall and Morgan refused his repeated offers—"She don't 'low noner us to drink noner this her milk." Asbury drank several glasses even though he hated milk. After this episode, he became bored again as the "insufferableness of life at home had overcome him and he had returned to New York two days early" (CW, 560).

The next day, Asbury awakens to the sound of Block's car arriving at the house. He hears the doctor and his mother rush up the stairs and his mother's voice "broke in on him with the force of a gunshot." "Guess what you've got, Sugarpie!" Block broadcasts the news with uncharacteristic swagger: "Found theter ol' bug, did ol' Block." Mrs. Fox explains that he had "undulant fever. It'll keep coming back but it won't kill you!" The country doctor adds, "Undulant fever ain't so bad, Azzberry. . . . It's the same as Bang's in a cow." Asbury is shocked into immobility, as "Block's gaze seemed to reach down like a steel pin and hold whatever it was until the life was out of it." His mother adds an observation drenched in inadvertent irony, "He must have drunk some unpasteurized milk up there" (CW, 571-2).

O'Connor concludes this story with an artful account of Asbury's culminating experience of grace. Asbury's eyes are "shocked clean as if they had been prepared for some awful vision about to come down on him." Asbury realizes that, in a sense, his life is over: "The old life in him was exhausted. He awaited the coming of the new," which he felt as a kind of "chill" and "[h]is breath came short." The strange image of the bird on the ceiling, all at once, becomes a waiting Deity who has been patiently orchestrating the events of Asbury's life, even while Asbury had imagined that he controlled his own destiny. He is immobile before "[t]he fierce bird which through the years of his childhood and the days of his illness had been poised over his head, waiting mysteriously, appearing all at once to be in motion."

> He saw that for the rest of his days, frail, racked, but enduring, he would live in the face of a purifying terror. A feeble cry, a last impossible protest escaped him. But the Holy Ghost, emblazoned in ice instead of fire, continued, implacable, to descend. (CW, 572)

THE PROBLEM OF HUMAN PRETENSION

To her informal literary critic Caroline Gordon Tate, O'Connor wrote, "I'm busy with the Holy Ghost. He is going to be a waterstain—very obvious but the only thing possible" (CW, 257). In a letter to Maryat Lee, O'Connor explained writing the final scene: "The problem was to have the Holy Ghost descend by degrees throughout the story but unrecognized, but at the end recognized, coming down, implacable, with ice instead of fire." She added, "I see no reason to limit the Holy Ghost to fire. He's full of surprises" (HB, 293). In associating the Holy Spirit with ice instead of fire, O'Connor was in good company: T. S. Eliot did the same in his poem "East Coker." He wrote in this semi-autobiographical account of the spiritual life, "If to be warmed, then I must freeze / And quake in frigid purgatorial fires."[3]

In the beginning of this story, as Asbury descends from the train, O'Connor offers a description of the horizon that metaphorically introduces Asbury: "[T]he sky was a chill gray and a startling white-gold sun, like some strange potentate from the east, was rising beyond the black woods that surrounded Timberboro" (CW, 547). It is as if Asbury, full of angry contempt for his rural homeland, were fashioning himself to be nothing less than the sun itself, this "strange potentate from the east." It is not until the end of the story, when Asbury has been humiliated through the work of the Holy Spirit, that O'Connor is able to correct the hubristic and unjust association of Asbury with the sun. Then, the author frames Asbury's moral revelation with a second description of the horizon. This time the tree line symbolizes Asbury's prideful character, and the sun, more appropriately, stands for God himself. The majestic "blinding red-gold sun" moved "serenely" from under a "purple cloud" against a tree-line that forms "a brittle wall, standing as if it were the frail defense he had set up in his mind to protect him from what was coming" (CW, 572).

To be sure, O'Connor states explicitly that Asbury's final experience is all about "humility." She explains, "So I have let it be known that he undeniably realizes that he's going to live with the new knowledge that he knows nothing." She continues in explaining that he has not yet reached the point of faith; first he must learn humility through the only means that will break through his pride—humiliation. "Faith can come later," O'Connor added (HB, 261).

O' Connor once referred to "terrible radical human pride" (HB, 307). Apparently, she felt that nothing less powerful than the Holy Spirit could break through Asbury's arrogance. Throughout her literary career, O'Connor divided human pride and pretension. This concern illuminates, in part, her attraction to Joseph Conrad's writing. She explained when she began reading in earnest in graduate school that, "I became a great admirer of Conrad and have read almost all his fiction" (HB, 99). O'Connor wrote in 1953, "I have read just about everything [Conrad] wrote by now. . . . I keep reading them hoping they'll affect my writing without my being bothered knowing how" (HB, 63).

In Conrad's powerful novel *Nostromo* the author explodes the human pretentiousness that would resolve life's complexities through audacious political solutions. Charles Gould, the cold master of the San Tomé mine, is said to be "calmness personified . . . extremely sure of himself." The peculiar but perceptive Dr. Monygham wryly observes, "If that's all he is sure of, then he is sure of nothing. . . . It is the last thing a man ought to be sure of."[4]

O'CONNOR, LEE, AND JACQUES MARITAIN ON RACIAL JUSTICE

Although Asbury's personal transforming experience may be the most conspicuous event in this story, the political implications of "The Enduring Chill" are important. Walker Percy noted the significance of this story in respect to the race problem of the South.[5] Indeed, for O'Connor, Asbury's lesson in humility and the social challenges of the South are closely related, because it is Asbury's arrogance that propels his foolish conduct; and that arrogance must be chastened so that he might learn more prudential behavior. Asbury's ill-starred and rash adventure in forcing a change in the customs and manners of race relations on the farm seem to be a literary comment on racial reform in the South in particular, and on social reform more generally. To be sure, O'Connor recognized that change must come and she was impatient, and sometimes disgusted, with ludicrous and sometimes violent attempts to preserve racial segregation. She most often corresponded on issues of racial justice with Maryat Lee. For example, she sent Lee an update on Southern politics when she wrote to her on the Georgia gubernatorial elections of 1958. "We are about to elect us a governor. We have a choice of three segregationists: 1) the present lieutenant governor whose only visible merit is good looks, 2) a hillybilly singer, Leroy the Boy Abernathy, and 3) a rabid preacher, who claims to be backed by the Bible" (HB, 293-4).[6]

Sally Fitzgerald explains that O'Connor placed her hopes not in "the activist and immediate [activities] to which Maryat Lee was devoting her generous energies" rather, "Flannery's hope lay in a slower process." O'Connor herself once explained that the Southerner's "social situation demands more of him than elsewhere in the country." Because the South is divided between black and white, and because of its troubled history, social change can't occur "without a code of manners based on mutual charity. . . . The South has to evolve a way of life in which the two races can live together with mutual forbearance." This cannot be done by forming "a committee to do this or pass a resolution; both races have to work it out the hard way" (HB, 193-4). Lee once remarked that although she and O'Connor debated the best means to rectify the South's social problems, "I could only believe that she shared with me the sense of frustration and betrayal and impotency over the dilemma of the white South" (HB, 193).

O'Connor's correspondence with Maryat Lee has been one of the sources of ill-conceived charges that O'Connor was tainted by racism. Friends who knew both women maintain that their correspondence can only properly be understood in the context of their relationship, and in light of Lee's fairly outlandish personality, often displayed in her dress and public manners. The two often adopted nonsensical nicknames each for the other. Lee's behavior was at times so outrageous as to embarrass even her most liberally minded friends and family. O'Connor appreciated Lee's intelligence and friendship but felt Lee could be simpleminded about complex social problems, especially the racial problems of the South. So, O'Connor occasionally took delight in "baiting" Lee with her exaggerated language.[7] O'Connor's social views, though, were humane and charitable and she disapproved of racial meanness.

In one letter, O'Connor describes the complex and distasteful mix of prejudice, politics, and education during Guy Wells's tenure as president of Georgia State School for Women.

> Once about ten years ago while Dr. Wells was president, there was an education meeting held here at which two Negro teachers or superintendents or something attended. The story goes that every thing was as separate and

equal as possible, even down to two Coca Cola machines, white and colored; but that night a cross was burned on Dr. Wells' side lawn. And those times weren't as troubled as these.

She concludes sardonically, "The people who burned the cross couldn't have gone past the fourth grade but for the time, they were mighty interested in education" (HB, 195).

The key to understanding O'Connor's views on racial reform is found in appreciating her view on the nature of social change in general, of which the South was the nearest application. She believed that it was easy to succumb to the Enlightenment-inspired fallacy that social change could be produced quickly and easily: "Since the 18th century, the popular spirit of each succeeding age has tended more and more to the view that the ills and mysteries of life will eventually fall before the scientific advances of man" (CW, 815). She argued that it was extraordinarily difficult to achieve social ideals, no matter how appealing they might be, because injustice and abuse may be intertwined with the customs that supply social stability. "[G]ood and evil appear to be joined in any culture at the spine," and if one should try to wrench injustice from the body politic by brute force alone, he might possibly so damage the community as to render impossible successful or permanent reform (MM, 200).

O'Connor often refers to this intangible social skeleton as "manners," and though the manners of the South might be amiss, "traditional manners, however unbalanced, are better than no manners at all." Southerners were, accordingly "traditionally against . . . foreigners from Chicago or New Jersey, all those who come from afar with moral energy that increases in direct proportion to the distance from home" (MM, 200). The manners, or "formality" of the South have been a means of "survival," especially as it has served in some measure to "protect the rights of both races" (MM, 233). She explains, "The uneducated Southern Negro is not the clown he's made out to be. He's a man of very elaborate manners and great formality, which he uses superbly for his own protection and to insure his own privacy." This may not be an "ideal" state of affairs, "but the Southerner has enough sense not to ask immediately for the ideal but only for the possible, the workable" (MM, 234).

In O'Connor's view, the "South has survived in the past because its manners, however lopsided or inadequate they may have been, provided enough social discipline to hold us together and give us an identity." She admits that those manners may now be "obsolete" but "new manners" will have to be acquired to guarantee the civil rights of the black race. O'Connor implicitly accuses reformers in other regions of the country of a superficial understanding of the true nature of reform when she argues that the "rest of the country" thinks that the "race problem is settled" as soon as "the Negro has his rights." But for the Southerner—"whether he's white or colored"—that is "only the beginning" (MM, 234). She rue-fully notes, though, that reports on the progress of manners "seldom make the papers" (MM, 234).

O'Connor's insistence on manners as the axis of reform is pragmatic in-sofar as she believed that to force change upon a population without re-spect for manners would not work, at least in the long run. Such reform might be only paper-thin and as a consequence of its superficiality, later problems might erupt, perhaps more intractable than before. She lamented that the South was "being forced out not only of our many sins, but of our few virtues" (MM, 28-9).

O'Connor often chided Maryat Lee for her impulsive demands for so-cial change. However well intentioned Lee's idealism might have been, O'Connor thought her impatience imprudent. In their long-running habit of making up names for each other, in June of 1961, she addressed Lee "Dear Maryrightaway."[8] Lee acknowledged the friendly rebuke when she wrote back "Dear Patience."[9] Writing to Lee, O'Connor would often coun-sel caution, but always with a dose of good humor. She wrote Lee in 1961 to thank her for a gift and added, "Are you coming here for Easter? If so, you can hold some demonstrations" (HB, 436).

She wrote to provide Lee with an update on the turmoil surrounding public education in Georgia. In October of 1963, she said "Nothing doing so far on the integration front." Then, in reference to Lee's activism, she good-naturedly warned, "Don't come down for any monkey bidnis or we'll put you in jail and hang you for inciting insurrection. I will person-ally volunteer to spring the trap or pull the rope or whatever you do" (HB, 544).

In 1959, Lee offered to help arrange for O'Connor to visit with the rad-ically minded James Baldwin who was touring several of the Southern states. O'Connor's reaction illustrates her concern for respecting her re-gion even while engaged in reform. She is frank and emphatic in declin-ing Lee's offer.

> No I can't see James Baldwin in Georgia. It would cause the greatest trouble and disturbance and disunion. In New York it would be nice to meet him; here it would not. I observe the traditions of the society I feed on—it's only fair. Might as well expect a mule to fly as me to see James Baldwin in Geor-gia." (HB, 329)

She later admitted she preferred Martin Luther King Jr.'s politics to those of James Baldwin. She felt Baldwin's political views were outrageous: "If

Baldwin were white nobody would stand him a minute." She even offered her approval of the young boxing sensation, Cassius Clay as she thought he possessed a generous measure of homespun common sense and did not presume that his fighting genius made him an expert on every other issue. She said, "I prefer Cassius Clay" and then added, "Cassius Clay is too good for the Moslems."[10]

Given O'Connor's esteem for the writing of Jacques Maritain, his thoughtful *Reflections on America* illuminate more fully O'Connor's cautious attitude toward political and social change. Maritain notes that "the most general fact concerning the race question in America is the opposition which exists between the mores and the law." He notes that the legal segregation persisting in the Southern states is not only the "legacy of a social structure which was based on slavery" but also the ingrained customs and traditions to which the daily activities of the white man and the Negro have been adjusted for generations."[11] Maritain suggests the complexity of the problem when he insists, "One must, no doubt, look with understanding and sympathy at the difficulties with which many men of good will, who are aware of their duties toward colored people, but bound by their own local traditions, are confronted in the South." Maritain suggests that the persistence of prejudice is more complex than legal issues because it involves the "demons of the human heart." The darker dimension of human nature that gives rise to invidious prejudice, envy, and contempt is not easily changed and involves the most inscrutable elements of the human psyche.[12]

Given the intricacy of the racial question, Maritain argues that social reform cannot be brought about by legal fiat alone; on the contrary, more is needed than mere political mandate. Here he intersects with O'Connor's view on the importance of intangible mores and customs that are often tied to nongovernmental institutions. He happily observes progress in the informal sectors of society. For example, "as the number of educated Negroes occupying positions of responsibility in the community grows, the very progress toward complete integration gains momentum automatically." "Another sign," notes Maritain, "is the progressive awakening of public opinion, as well as the determination and activity of those self-organized groups of good citizens, especially organized religion, which are, so to speak, the nerve system of the nation" and it is these institutions that will foster the essential "profound inner changes" in the citizenry.[13]

He concludes by admitting that the "Negro question is a thorn in the flesh" of the American nation. He also concedes that the country seeks its solution "more or less gropingly," yet "without respite" as it "struggles doggedly against itself . . . against a certain legacy of evil in its own mores . . . in order to free itself of abuses which are repellent to its own spirit."

In so doing, he asserts, "the country will raise its entire practical behavior to the level of the tenets and principles in which it believes and in the strength of which it was born."[14]

O'Connor's views on the efficacy of human law to bring about meaningful change are, in some measure, an application of St. Thomas's ideas on law found in his "Treatise on Law."[15] The law, Thomas argues, is something "pertaining to reason," meaning that it must be imminently reasonable, especially in its practical application. The motivation, sentiment, or theory behind changes is important, but most important is that, once applied, it must not prove counterproductive to its intention; that is, the change must not make things worse. To further the common good, a law must be practically sound, not merely speculatively persuasive: it cannot merely "sound good in theory."[16]

For law to be sound and effective, it must be enacted and implemented under the shadow of higher laws, both the natural law, which we possess by virtue of our humanity, and the eternal law, from which any meaningful law ultimately finds its source. Accordingly, when human beings enact laws, they should do so with an attitude of humility insofar as the legislator or judge recognizes that his is an attempt—often an awkward one—to express higher principles in imperfectly fashioned laws. If one should try to force social change recklessly, as Asbury did, such arrogance is likely to be harmful, especially because, as Thomas teaches, "Law were made that . . . human audacity might be held in check."[17]

JULIAN ON MEANNESS AND MANNERS

O'Connor's short story "Everything That Rises Must Converge" reinforces her belief, presented in "The Enduring Chill," that personal virtue and social change should not be separated. This is the account of a petulant young man named Julian who escorts his mother on the city bus to the local YWCA but the brevity of the journey in space and time belies the moral distance he travels. His mother has enrolled in an exercise class to lose the weight her doctor warns will trigger a heart attack. Julian loathes the time he spends with his mother and does little to hide his annoyance. On the bus, his mother—afflicted as she is with inherited bigotry—suffers the stress of seeing a black woman wearing the same hat she is sporting, and Julian takes delight in her predicament. He deliberately antagonizes her by sitting close to the Negroes on the bus, thus severely aggravating her consternation. He fails to detect, however, an early warning when her "face seemed to be unnaturally red, as if her blood pressure had risen" (CW, 493). Julian is more liable for his vice than is his mother for hers: his mother's prejudice is inbred and without malice but Julian's is willful. She exercises poor judgment, though, when she gives the woman's child a shiny penny as they disembark. The child's mother interprets her kindness as condescension and angrily knocks her to the pavement.

Rather than offer compassion, Julian seizes the opportunity to condemn his mother's prejudice and imprudence, though his mother, staggering down the sidewalk, is clearly traumatized. But Julian sees no reason to leave her lesson unaccompanied by his mean spirited commentary. In doing so, he states the antithesis of O'Connor's view of social manners, antithetical because of its maliciousness and because of its derisive disrespect for the intricacy and resilience of social manners.

> "What all this means," he said, "is that the old world is gone. The old manners are obsolete and your graciousness is not worth a damn." (CW, 499)

His next admonition to his mother is ironic as he insists, "'You needn't act as if the world had come to an end. . . . Buck up,' he said, 'it won't kill you'" (CW, 500).

But it does kill her. Suddenly, "[h]e was looking into a face he had never seen before" as a "tide of darkness seemed to be sweeping her from him" (CW, 500). Julian's pretensions vanish as he uses terms of endearment to plead with his mother not to die. "'Mother!' he cried. 'Darling, sweetheart, wait!'" But she collapses on the pavement (CW, 500). He tries in vain to run for help but "his feet moved numbly as if they carried him nowhere. The tide of darkness seems to sweep him back to her, postponing from moment to moment his entry into the world of guilt and sorrow."(CW, 500)

In this story, O'Connor warns that social reform undertaken rashly and angrily may be more destructive than helpful. She also reiterates another theme from "The Enduring Chill," but this time more forcefully, that the promotion of public virtue must be accompanied by a commitment to personal character. The reformer cannot deflect responsibility for his own integrity by demanding that the rest of society change instead. He can't behave uncharitably and require charity from others.

ASBURY, AQUINAS, AND ARISTOTLE

The pragmatic reform that O'Connor and Maritain advocate finds its antecedent in Aquinas's teaching on the virtue of prudence. Aquinas explains that prudence is a virtue "most necessary for human life" and is needed because "it matters not only what a man does, but also how he does it." Prudence enables one not only to identify the goal to be achieved, such as social reform, but offers guidance toward the best means to its achievement.[18] O'Connor completed "The Enduring Chill" in the fall of 1958. Just a year earlier, during the period when she would have been writing the story, she said, "I was reading that St. Thomas said Prudence was the highest of the virtues . . . because it articulated all the others. Anyway, the older I get the more respect I have for Old Prudence" (HB, 247).

A more detailed consideration of the virtue of prudence further exposes Asbury's destructive behavior. Aristotle explains that prudence is essential for the man who wishes to act "with regard to the things that are good or bad for man."[19] Even though someone may have theoretically sound ideas, without prudence, he is unable to put those ideas into practice, for prudence bridges between the abstract principle and its implementation. So, to be prudent, one must first understand the principles that govern a given situation and then identify the particulars to which the principles should be applied. [20]

Perhaps Asbury should not be judged too harshly for his imprudent behavior: Aristotle argues that young men in general often lack prudence because of their youth and inexperience. While young men may enjoy success if they undertake professions dealing with abstract duties, they still may lack the practical wisdom essential for other occupations. Aristotle concisely explains, "What has been said is confirmed by the fact that while young men become geometricians and mathematicians and wise in matters like these, it is thought that a young man of practical wisdom cannot be found."[21]

Aristotle's philosophy also suggests that even if Asbury's youth and inexperience had not been an obstacle to his acting prudently, his vicious attitude toward his family and surroundings would have made prudential behavior impossible. Consistently prudential leadership is impossible outside of a life of moral virtue. Prudence is not some isolated tool that may be wielded by a morally weak individual. The best that the man of weak character can exercise is a bastardized form of prudence, a kind of narrow self-interested shrewdness; or, in Asbury's case, mean-spirited self-satisfaction driven by angry disdain for convention. "Practical wisdom," Aristotle explains, "is the quality of mind concerned with things just and noble and good for man, but these are the things which it is the mark of a *good man* to do." (emphasis added). If the aim of practical wisdom is what is good and noble, the bad and ignoble person has no capacity for prudence; indeed, he has no need for it.[22] And so, "the work of man is achieved only in accordance with practical wisdom" coupled with "moral virtue; for virtue makes us aim at the right mark, and practical wisdom helps us take the right means." According to Aristotle, one cannot go without the other. It is simply "not possible to be good in the strict sense without practical wisdom, or practically wise without moral virtue."[23] O'Connor once noted that Shakespeare's *Troilus and Cressida* is "odd" but "inspired." In the play, the Trojan warrior Hector might speak for O'Connor when he warned his colleagues that "modest doubt is called / The beacon of the wise" (HB, 399).[24]

"REVELATION" AND EQUALITY

A discussion of O'Connor's insistence on respect for manners and prudential social change should be coupled with an understanding of her belief in the fundamental equality of all men. This belief is most clearly stated in her moving short story "Revelation," about which she confessed she was "right enthusiastic" (HB, 546).[25] The story was written in the last difficult year of O'Connor's life, which means she was writing, as Sally Fitzgerald explains, "more or less in extremis" (HB, 549). Her friend Caroline Gordon suggested the story was O'Connor's "profoundest" (HB, 562).

In the story, the work of grace forces the protagonist, Mrs. Ruby Turpin, to acknowledge that her social status does not make her superior to those around her in any fundamental way. It is so difficult for Mrs. Turpin to accept this idea of equality that the sudden violent act of a deranged girl is necessary to initiate her harsh lesson. Notwithstanding the disturbing episode, Mrs. Turpin yields to the "revelation" only after a defiant argument with God himself that transpires over a pigsty. At the conclusion of this struggle, Mrs. Turpin understands that human equality is rooted in human mortality.

The first scene of the story takes place in the doctor's waiting room as Mrs. Turpin and her husband Claud await treatment for a leg injury he has sustained from a cow kick. Mrs. Turpin is a large woman and her size reflects her inflated self-importance: "She stood looming at the head of the magazine table set in the center . . . a living demonstration that the room was inadequate and ridiculous" (CW, 633).[26] Upon sitting, Mrs. Turpin looks at the angry girl seated beside her, Mary Grace, with her usual patronizing attitude: "The poor girl's face was blue with acne and Mrs. Turpin thought how pitiful it was to have a face like that at that age. She gave the girl a friendly smile but the girl only scowled the harder" (CW, 635). She reflects that she "herself was fat but she had always had good skin, and, though she was forty-seven years old, there was not a wrinkle in her face except around her eyes from laughing too much" (CW, 635). As they wait on the doctor, Mrs. Turpin harshly ruminates about "niggers" and "white trash," all the while she mentally hums a gospel tune, "And wona these days I know I'll we-eara crown" (CW, 634). O'Connor explains that Mrs. Turpin would sometimes occupy "herself at night naming the classes of people." On the bottom were "colored people," and then "white trash," then "home-owners" and "above them the home-and-land owners, to which she and Claud belonged." Her hierarchy, though, would become confusing after she ranked the rich above her and Claud, but then reflected that "some of the people with a lot of money" could be "common." She would grow more perplexed when she thought that some people with "good blood" might be without money and her puzzlement would deepen even more when she remembered that there "was a colored dentist in town who had two red Lincolns and a swimming pool and a farm with registered white-face cattle on it" (CW, 637).

Mrs. Turpin remarks to another woman in the waiting room, the disturbed girl's mother, that it is "good weather for cotton if you can get the niggers to pick it," but she notes the difficulty in doing so "because they got to be right up there with the white folks" (CW, 638). She also tells the woman that she and Claud had, in addition to their cotton and cows, "a few hogs." When another woman present—a "white trash woman"—retorts that she wouldn't have hogs because they were "nasty stinking things, a-gruntin and a-rootin all over the house," Mrs. Turpin huffs,

> "Our hogs are not dirty and they don't stink. . . . They're cleaner than some children I've seen. Their feet never touch the ground. We have a pig-parlor— that's where you raise them on concrete," she explained to the pleasant lady, "and Claud scoots them down with the hose every afternoon and washes off the floor." (CW, 638)

The troubled girl scowls more intensely at Ruby as she continues to speak invidiously of Negroes. Mrs. Turpin vainly tries to engage the young woman in pleasant conversation but the girl grows more menacing. Mrs. Turpin, though, finds it easy to return to her self-congratulatory reverie and is flooded with gratitude at the thought of her own pleasant character and good fortune.

Suddenly, Mary Grace hurls her book, striking Mrs. Turpin viciously above her left eye, and then bodily attacks both Ruby Turpin and Claud, aggravating his leg injury. A melee ensues until the disturbed girl is restrained and sedated, but not before she raises her head and whispers to

Mrs. Turpin, "Go back to hell where you came from, you old wart hog" (CW, 646).

Mrs. Turpin and Claud are treated for minor injuries and sent home, but, upon returning, Mrs. Turpin cannot dismiss the girl's harsh indictment as if it carried an unwelcome element of truth. "'I am not,' she said tearfully, 'a wart hog. From hell.' But the denial had no force" (CW, 648). After she and Claud rest, Mrs. Turpin marchs to the "pig-parlor," but her intention is to do more than care for the hogs: "She had the look of a woman going single-handed, weaponless, into battle." (CW, 651) She is at war with God. Hosing down the hogs, she addresses the Almighty, "'Why me?' she rumbled. 'It's no trash around here, black or white, that I haven't given to. And break my back to the bone every day working. And do for the church'" (CW, 652). Ruby tries once more to assert the rightness of her doctrine of fundamental social inequality, using the analogy of a wooden fence with its rails ordered hierarchically from top to bottom. She

> braced herself for a final assault and this time her voice rolled out over the pasture. "Go on," she yelled, "call me a hog! Call me a hog again. From hell. Call me a wart hog from hell. Put that bottom rail on top. There'll still be a top and bottom!" A final surge of fury shook her and she roared, "Who do you think you are?" (CW, 653)[27]

At that moment, Ruby Turpin receives a transforming revelation, triggered in a mundane way. She notices her husband's truck in the distance on the highway "heading rapidly out of sight." Something about the image seems to impress upon her the fragility of human existence and the inescapable mortality that all men share, whether black or white.

> Its gears scraped thinly. It looked like a child's toy. At any moment a bigger truck might smash into it and scatter Claud's and the niggers' brains all over the road. (CW, 653)

The possibility of her beloved Claud's carnage mixing with that of her Negro help moves Mrs. Turpin profoundly, suggesting to her that the true basis of the equality of all men is their mortality, the awful brevity of their existence that is a necessary consequence of man's "wart-hog"-like sinfulness. As this knowledge settles upon her, she returns her attention to the pigs and in them she perceives something of the mystery of life itself. She "bent her head slowly and gazed, as if through the very heart of mystery, down into the pig parlor at hogs. . . . They appeared to pant with a secret life" (CW, 653). Mrs. Turpin seems absorbed in "some abysmal life-giving knowledge" and then gazes into the distance as a "visionary light settled in her eyes." She sees "a vast horde of souls" traveling toward heaven and their behavior violates Mrs. Turpin's standards of decorum.

> There were whole companies of white-trash, clean for the first time in their lives, and bands of black niggers in white robes, and battalions of freaks and lunatics shouting and clapping and leaping like frogs. (CW, 654)

Most striking about this group is not the odd assortment of humanity, but those who are bringing up the rear of this procession. It is "a tribe of people whom she recognizes at once as those . . . like herself and Claud." Theirs is a "purgatorial" march as Mrs. Turpin "could see by their shocked and altered faces that even their virtues were being burned away" (CW, 654, HB, 577).[28]

In "Revelation," Mrs. Turpin learns she is not fundamentally superior to "niggers" or "white trash" because she can no more escape her mortality than they can. This is the meaning of the scripture, with which O'Connor was certainly familiar, that asserts, "Here there is no Greek or Jew, circumcised or uncircumcised, barbarian, Scythian, slave or free, but Christ is all, and is in all."[29] Death is the great leveler: Ruby is rendered equal to those she holds in condescension by their common status before God. She also learns that however much she might prize her own virtue, those qualities are but dim reflections of the sturdier and purer character she has yet to attain.

CONCLUSION

In her literature, essays, and correspondence, O'Connor insists that the social reformer should not handle recklessly the intangible infrastructure of public manners. To do so is to endanger the very reform one hopes to attain, because, to lose the social framework of the public edifice is to have no means of housing a better society and thus to risk deep resentment, violence, and even chaos.

As in "The Enduring Chill," so also in "Everything That Rises Must Converge," O'Connor dramatically argues that "manners" are an indispensable element in social change and stability. She suggests that political change must be undertaken with respect to the manners that lend stability to social relations. One will only ignore their critical role with tragic consequences. Julian also serves as a reminder that social change undertaken through flagrant hypocrisy is too severe a contradiction to promise meaningful and lasting improvement. O'Connor contends through her fiction that those who aspire to work for the betterment of society cannot hope to be fruitful in their efforts if they pursue justice in a grossly hypo-critical and unjust manner. Personal hate and contempt cannot be the mo-tivation by which one eradicates public hate and contempt.

Finally, although O'Connor might temper the reformer's zeal with her more cautious approach to social improvement, her insistence on public manners and private virtue must be understood in the context of her be-lief in the basic equality of humanity, a condition derived from their shared mortality, and by implication, their vital dependence upon an im-mortal God. O'Connor's view of human equality was undoubtedly rein-forced each year in the Ash Wednesday service she attended from child-hood, where the priest intones, while making the sign of the cross with ashes on the forehead of each and every parishioner, "Remember man that thou art dust and to dust thou shalt return."

8

Modernity versus Mystery in "A View of the Woods"

"Fiction is the concrete expression of mystery," O'Connor wrote (HB, 144). In arriving at this opinion, O'Connor was inspired by Aquinas who believed that humanity is entangled in this mystery because human beings reside at the boundary of the spiritual and the material. So situated, humans are complex, in contrast to the simplicity of lower embodied creatures and of the higher disembodied angels. At this juncture of the material and the immaterial, human beings are "middle creatures," that is, they "must be understood in relationship not only to what is beneath them but also to what is above them." Humanity, then, involves a kind of mystery, because of its precarious and barely tenable position, situated at the apex of animal life, but also occupying the lowest rung of the theological ladder that ascends to God (HB, 144).[1]

O'Connor's faith, and especially her Catholic upbringing, imbued her with a deep appreciation for mystery. This sense of mystery was reinforced by several of her favorite writers. In *The Grammar of Assent*, which appears in her library collection, John Henry Newman suggests that the overlap of human life and divine life is impossible for the human mind to comprehend fully and so it must be accepted as a mystery; what cannot be understood must be met with faith and devotion. "The pure and indivisible Light is seen only by the blessed inhabitants of heaven," Newman argues, but "here we have . . . such faint reflections of it as its diffraction supplies." Though these reflections may not satisfy the demands of human reason, "they are sufficient for faith and devotion" and though the human mind may try to wrench a more rational explanation from them, "you gain nothing but a mystery."[2]

O'Connor owned a copy of Pascal's *Pensées* and there the French mathematician and philosopher offers a different but complementary perspective on the mystery of human existence and its attendant uncertainty. He observes that human beings "are floating in a medium of vast extent, always drifting uncertainly, blown to and fro." Just when we identify a "fixed point to which we can cling and make fast, it shifts and leaves us behind." Should we pursue it, "it eludes our grasp, slips away, and flees eternally before us."[3]

According to O'Connor, not even Thomas Aquinas can explain away mystery; perhaps it is better said *especially* St. Thomas, because he recognizes the boundary beyond which neither reason nor even revelation can penetrate. O'Connor warned her friend Cecil Dawkins, "I don't want to discourage you from reading St. Thomas, but don't read him with the notion that he is going to clear anything up for you." Her best solution, she offered, was "prayer" (HB, 308). She counseled a young student who wrote her after an appearance at Emory University, "Mystery isn't something that is gradually evaporating. It grows along with knowledge" (HB, 489). The more one knows, the more he realizes what he does not—and cannot—know. Thus, a mature view of the world is one in which the mysterious becomes, in a sense, more mysterious, not less; and, those elements of life shrouded in mystery become darker still. Thinking of O'Connor, Walker Percy observed, "If the scientist's vocation is to clarify and simplify, it would seem that the novelist's aim is to muddy and complicate."[4] In his *Confessions*, St. Augustine admitted that only by faith could he find intellectual satisfaction in the face of inscrutable human suffering. At first the theological explanations for such human conundrums were "sounding strangely" to the point that they "were wont to offend me." But, once he acknowledged "the depth of the mysteries" he was able to submit to their authority and see them as "worthy of religious credence."[5]

For O'Connor, the purpose of fiction is to help the reader cultivate respect for this mystery of human life. She once explained the difference between writers who are merely "regional" writers, and those who use their surroundings as the podium from which to address themes of universal importance. She wrote, "The Southern writer has certainly been provided with a variety of riches, but if his vision goes no farther than these materials, then he would have been as well off without them. . . . Those people become regional writers who don't reveal any element of mystery in the rich material they have at hand."[6]

O'Connor admits, though, just how difficult it is for her to articulate the theological sense of mystery in discourse, and this admission gives the reader more appreciation for why she would resort to fiction as the best means of depicting mystery. She once apologized to Maryat Lee that she had not been able to respond adequately in correspondence to a point of theological debate: "You are of course entirely right that the reply was inadequate and cliché-ridden. It always will be. These are mysteries that I can in no way approach."[7]

The challenge to the fiction writer is especially pressing because, as O'Connor notes, the modern world is "a generation that has been made to feel that the aim of learning is to eliminate mystery." For readers loath to confront mystery, "fiction can be very disturbing" because a writer like O'Connor will be looking for every opportunity to present mystery through the matter of everyday life, "the concrete world of sense experience" (MM, 124-5). In searching for the best material to place upon her literary palette, she found writing about the rural poor "irresistible" because the "mystery of existence is always showing through the texture of their ordinary lives" (MM, 132).

She explains that education may make it more difficult for one to appreciate this existential mystery, apparently because the overeducated mind is impatient with the mundane character of everyday life, finding it commonplace. She writes, "The type of mind that can understand good fiction is not necessarily the educated mind, but it is at all times the kind of mind that is willing to have its sense of mystery deepened by contact with reality, and its sense of reality deepened by contact with mystery" (MM, 79). Elsewhere she speaks of "those depths of mystery which the modern world is divided about—part of it trying to eliminate mystery while another part tries to rediscover it in disciplines less personally demanding than religion" (MM, 145). She argues, "For nearly two centuries the popular spirit of each succeeding generation has tended more and more to the view that the mysteries of life will eventually fall before the mind of man" (MM, 158). O'Connor endeavors to use literature to urge the reader toward the mystery that lies behind the everyday facts and events of life, the mystery that inheres even in custom and prejudice. She admits, "The fiction writer presents mystery through manners, grace through nature, but when he finishes there always has to be left over that sense of Mystery which cannot be accounted for by any human formula" (MM, 153). Even Catholics, she admits, "are very much given to the Instant Answer." But, "[f]iction doesn't have any. It leaves us . . . with a renewed sense of mystery" (MM, 184).

In her short story, "A View of the Woods," O'Connor offers one of her harshest warnings. Through the story, she admonishes the reader that mystery is an inexpugnable part of the human condition, and it is most acutely felt in the face of human suffering. If one should attempt to eradicate human suffering without some thoughtful respect for the mystery with which it is shrouded, the consequences may be more tragic than the suffering itself. In addition to forcing the reader to face the mystery of human suffering, "A View of the Woods" also exposes the reader to the mystery of human nature that makes the prediction and control of human behavior so difficult given the conflicting angelic and bestial elements of man's internal makeup. Most importantly, through an intriguing use of metaphor, O'Connor argues in this story that the proper response to the mystery of human nature and suffering is recourse to another mystery—the mysterious redemptive work of Christ.

In addition, and in keeping with the Thomistic view that evil is the absence of good, this story suggests that when one is faced with life's mystery, if rashness replaces proper consideration, such injudicious conduct can create the vacuum into which evil may rush. Jacques Maritain is especially helpful in explaining this element of the teaching of St. Thomas and, by implication, how it might be illustrated through O'Connor's story. More specifically, Maritain shows how human thoughtlessness first creates the vacuum that is filled later with evil action. Maritain further suggests that the neglect of proper moral consideration is a kind of "nothingness," and as such is a dimension of the moral nihilism so characteristic of the modern age.

O'Connor told a friend that upon the completion of "A View of the Woods," she sent the story to *Harper's Bazaar*, which previously had published other of her stories. Referring to the women who would read the magazine at the beauty parlor, she cautioned, "it may be a little grim for the dryer set." On the other hand, she concluded, those ladies are "a pretty grim set" themselves (HB, 175). She warned Sally and Robert Fitzgerald, "I enclose a little morality play of mine for your Christmas cheer but it is not very cheerful, I'd advise you to leave off reading it until after the season" (HB, 186).

THE STORY

This is a tragic story of an old man, Mr. Fortune, and his granddaughter, Mary Fortune. Mary Fortune's father, Pitts, who is son-in-law to the grandfather, also plays an important role as a foil to his father-in-law. The elements of the story are as mundane as those of any story that O'Connor has written; but, she fashions out of this ordinary material one of her most artistic and philosophically unsettling short stories.

As the story opens, a backhoe is clearing an area of rural pasture. Throughout the story, O'Connor describes the machinery in baleful language. Mary Fortune sits on the hood of her grandfather's car watching "the big disembodied gullet gorge itself on the clay, then with the sound of a deep sustained nausea and a slow mechanical revulsion, turn and spit it out" (CW, 525). In the background are a lake and "a black line of woods which appeared at both ends of the view to walk across the water and continue along the edge of the fields" (CW, 525). This description of the woods appearing to perform the miraculous Christ-like miracle of walking upon water is an early hint that the woods possess divine symbolism, a symbol that will be developed throughout the story, and especially at the end.

Fortune has no respect for anyone in the family except his granddaughter. His daughter, Mary's mother, "had married an idiot named Pitts and had had seven children, all likewise idiots except the youngest, Mary Fortune." The family lives on the grandfather's land and he uses the land to control them, regularly reminding them that it is his, and occasionally vexing them by selling a parcel of it to outsiders. He has reduced his eight-hundred-acre tract by selling "five twenty-acre lots on the back of the place and every time he sold one, Pitt's blood pressure had gone up twenty points" but only because, as the old man explained to his granddaughter, her father "would let a cow pasture interfere with the future" (CW, 528). The grandfather always had thought that Mary Fortune was like him rather than the rest of her family, who "are the kind that would let a cow pasture or a mule lot or a row of beans interfere with progress," but, he adds, "People like you and me with heads on their shoulders know you can't stop the marcher time for a cow" (CW, 528).

What the old man cannot control are the regular beatings that Pitts inflicts on his daughter: "Time and again, Mr. Fortune's heart had pounded to see him rise slowly from his place at the table . . . and abruptly, for no reason, with no explanation, jerk his head at Mary Fortune and say, 'Come with me.'"

> A look that was completely foreign to the child's face would appear on it. The old man could not define the look but it infuriated him. It was a look that was part terror and part respect and part something else, something very like cooperation. (CW, 530)

Mary's father would then take her in his truck out of earshot and beat her. In this lies his revenge upon, and his only control of, his father-in-law, who feels as frustrated as if he himself were doing the beating. Pitts defiantly tells Fortune, "She's mine to whip and I'll whip her every day of the year if it suits me." Mary Fortune, for her part, will never admit to her grandfather that her father beats her and in this she reflects her grandfather's obdurate pride. When he demands to know why she submits to the abuse, she denies the obvious and retorts that "nobody beat me." She also ominously predicts, "Nobody's ever beat me in my life and if anybody did, I'd kill him" (CW, 530).

In this familial duel between grandfather and son-in-law, the elder plans a new move sure to grieve the younger. Whereas previously it was only land to the rear of the tract that has been sold, Fortune is about to close negotiations to sell a parcel to Tilman a local storeowner who will construct a gas station directly in front of the family home. To the family, this two hundred foot stretch of field is "the lawn" and it provides a play area and a grazing field for the few family cows. Most importantly, it allows a view of the woods across the highway. Even though Fortune plans to use the proceeds to build a bank account for his granddaughter, she fiercely objects when he divulges his plans and he finds incomprehensible her insistence on retaining "a view of the woods."

> "We won't be able to see the woods across the road," she said.
> "The old man stared at her. "The woods across the road?" he repeated.
> "We won't be able to see the view," she said.
> "The view?" he repeated.
> "The woods," she said; "we won't be able to see the woods from the porch." (CW, 532)

The old man fumes at her senseless objections and, referring to her father, asks, "Do you think I give a damn hoot where that fool grazes his calves?" Mary Fortune portentously warns, "He who calls his brother a fool is subject to hell fire." Fortune retaliates with a reminder of her meek acquiescence in her frequent whippings. She retorts, "'He nor nobody else has ever touched me' . . . measuring off each word in a deadly flat tone. 'Nobody's ever put a hand on me and if anybody did, I'd kill him'" (CW, 532-3).

Shortly thereafter, at the dinner table, Fortune alarms the family by announcing his plans and Pitts makes it an occasion to abuse his daughter again. He "had stopped eating and was staring in front of him." He looked at Mary Fortune and said, "You done this to us." As the old man watches his son-in-law take his granddaughter away, her submission "made him physically sick." He condemns his daughter for not intervening, in response to which she indicts him for the same passivity. But, he excuses himself with, "I'm an old man with a heart condition" (CW, 533-4).

Fortune's relationship with his granddaughter begins to degenerate in ways that he does not understand and that he cannot control. During a trip to see Tilman, the prospective buyer of the front lot, Fortune instructs his granddaughter to wait in the car, but she leaves him and walks back home. He finds her on the porch, looking out across the yard, and asks why she left. "'I toljer I was going and I went,' she said in a slow emphatic voice, not looking at him, 'and now you can go on and lemme alone.'" Fortune hears something "very final, in the sound of this, a tone that had not come up before in their disputes." As she speaks, Mary is gazing at the skyline, and by describing Mary's gaze in this manner, O'Connor means to focus the reader's attention on the story's unfolding moral drama. Mary sits "staring at the sullen line of black pine woods fringed on top with green. Behind that line was a narrow gray-blue line of more distant woods and beyond that nothing but the sky, entirely blank except for one or two threadbare clouds." O'Connor explains that Mary Fortune "looked into this scene as if it were a person that she preferred to him," and by this the author suggests symbolically her grandfather has threatened something more sacred than their relationship, in spite of her obvious affection for him. But Mr. Fortune cannot comprehend what troubles Mary: "There's not a thing over there but the woods," he protests (CW, 535-7).

That evening at dinner, "nobody addressed a word to him, including Mary Fortune" and he spends the remainder of the evening alone in his room again, justifying to himself his plans. He reasons, "They would not have to go any distance for gas. Anytime they needed a loaf of bread, all they would have to do would be step out their front door into Tilman's back door." Tilman's gas station would bring more traffic, more stores. Selling the lot would "insure the future" (CW, 538-9).

The next morning brings no improvement in Mary Fortune's mood and her disposition is reflected in the weather: The sky "was an unpleasant gray and the sun had not troubled to come out" (CW, 540). Fortune finds Mary on the front porch again, gazing straight ahead, and once again, it was "apparent that this morning she preferred the sight of the woods." He is able to entice her into town to visit the boat store, but once there, she is so despondent and indifferent that Fortune "could not believe that a child of her intelligence could be acting this way over the mere sale of a field." The offer of an ice-cream cone elicits no more interest, nor does a subsidized visit to the ten-cent store. She finally responds to his queries, again insisting, "We won't be able to see the woods any more." The old man is so irked with her attitude that he storms into a nearby office to have a deed drawn up for the real estate transaction. At this point, O'Connor uses the weather yet again, this time to warn the reader of impending disaster: "The sky had darkened also and there was a hot sluggish tide in the air, the kind felt when a tornado is possible" (CW, 541). As the pair are en route to close the deal with Tilman, O'Connor's description of Mary Fortune also transmits a warning of imminent calamity. She has become "withdrawn" and "he might have been chauffeuring *a small dead body* for all the answer he got" (CW, 542, emphasis added).

At the precise moment that Fortune and Tilman shake hands over the sale, Mary Fortune goes berserk. She hurls a bottle at Tilman that he barely avoids and begins to wreck the store. She is "screaming something unintelligible and throwing everything within her reach." Fortune finally subdues her when "he caught her by the tail of her dress and pulled backward out of the store" and then lifts her "wheezing and whimpering" into the car. He drives down the highway for five minutes in silent fury and Mary Fortune is "rolled into a ball in the corner of the seat" and is "snuffling and heaving." He is stunned that a child of his relation would behave so violently and embarrass him so severely. He concludes that he has been overindulgent. "He saw that the time had come, that he could no longer avoid whipping her" and so, when he reaches his own property, he turns off a side path and drives down into the woods to "the exact spot where he had seen Pitts take his belt to her." It is a widened place in the clay road where a car could turn around, "an ugly red bald spot surrounded by long thin pines that appeared to be gathered there to witness anything that would take place in such a clearing" (CW, 544).

Only at this point does the adolescent realize why they have stopped: "Where a few seconds before her face had been red and distorted and unorganized, it drained now of every vague line until nothing was left on it but positiveness, a look that went slowly past determination and reached certainty." She then repeats her warning to her grandfather, "'Nobody has ever beat me,' she said, 'and if anybody tries it, I'll kill him'" (CW, 544). Fortune warns her not to give him "no sass" but his "knees felt very unsteady, as if they might turn either backward or forward." Mary responds by instructing him to remove his glasses. "'Don't give me orders!' he said in a high voice and slapped awkwardly at her ankles with his belt" (CW, 544).

The gesture unleashes a violent fury in Mary Fortune for which the incident in Tilman's store had been only an omen. The young girl is over her grandfather so quickly "that he could not have recalled which blow he felt first, whether the weight of her whole solid body or the jabs of her feet or the pummeling of her fist on his chest. . . . It was as if he were being attacked not by one child but by a pack of small demons all with stout brown school shoes and small rocklike fists" (CW, 544-5).

When she pauses in her assault, Fortune finds the opportunity to grab the advantage. Now on top and looking down at her with her neck in his hands, "he lifted her head and brought it down once hard against a rock. . . . Then he brought it down twice more."

> Then [he was] looking into the face in which the eyes slowly rolling back, appeared to pay him not the slightest attention. (CW, 545)

"'This ought to teach you a good lesson,' he said in a voice that was edged with doubt" (CW, 546). He stands up but feels an "enlargement of his heart" and he falls again as "his heart expanded once more with a convulsive motion." He begins to imagine that he is moving through the woods toward the lake, and even, in his fantasy, "perceived that there would be a little opening there, a little place where he could escape and leave the woods behind him" (CW, 546).

> On both sides of him he saw that the gaunt trees had thickened into mysterious dark files that were marching across the water and away into the distance. He looked around desperately for someone to help him but the place was deserted except for one huge yellow monster which sat to the side, as stationary as he was, gorging itself on clay. (CW, 546)

MYSTERY AND EVIL

There is a similar despair that attends to the conclusion of "A View of the Woods" and the disquieting short story, "The Lame Shall Enter First": neither story offers even the muted hope one finds in other of O'Connor's short stories. On the contrary, the denouement is darker, more tragic. Although in many of her stories, O'Connor often uses evil to set the stage for the introduction of grace, in these two stories the extent of evil leaves less room for the operation of grace. It is as if the evil is more extensive in these stories than others. "The Lame Shall Enter First" is a pungent literary account of the phenomenon of evil; it offers an especially clear illustration of St. Thomas Aquinas's teaching on evil as a deprivation and distortion of good. "A View of the Woods" also suggests the Thomistic teaching on evil and in this case Jacques Maritain's published lecture *Saint Thomas and the Problem of Evil* is especially helpful in understanding O'Connor's reliance upon Thomas. Maritain begins by acknowledging the starting point of the Thomistic doctrine of evil: evil is a defect of good, not a separate entity of its own. In this instance, though, Maritain explains that this defect can be a *voluntary and free* defect, the consequence of an individual's "free choice" and this becomes the "root of evil" that will come to full fruition in one's later activity.[8] One must, St. Thomas explains, "*preconsider a certain defect in the will, a certain deficiency prior to the act of choice which is itself deficient.*" Maritain offers a gloss on Thomas's passage, explaining that the "defect" occurs when one fails, before acting, to consider the principle, or rule, proper to the relevant moral question and so the evil arises from the failure properly to apply moral evaluation to the dilemma at hand.[9]

Accordingly, the freedom of one's will becomes, in a perverse way, the source of evil. The exercise of that will, or more accurately, the *failure* to exercise the will in proper consideration, is a defective use of the will that has as its consequence evil action because one does not make use of "the rule of reason and of divine law" before taking important and far-reaching moral action.

According to Maritain, an individual is not required always to hold moral principles consciously before him any more than a carpenter must carry a ruler with him at all times; rather, what is required is that when it comes time to act, or cut as in the case of the carpenter, then attention must be given to the principle, or ruler, that should guide such action. As he explains, "What is required of the soul is not that it should always look to the rule or have the ruler constantly in hand, but that it should *produce its act* while looking at the rule."[10] St. Thomas elaborates,

> Thus the craftsman does not err in not always having his ruler in hand but in proceeding to cut the wood without his ruler. The faultiness of will does not consist in not paying attention in act to the rule of reason or of divine law, but in this: —that without taking heed of the rule it proceeds to the act of choice.[11]

As a consequence of this defect, the neglect of proper and due consideration, the individual acts without the guidance of either reason or divine law as he "proceeds to the act of choice, which is consequently *deprived* of the rectitude it would have."[12]

Maritain's analysis suggests that the evil act that occurs in the simultaneous deaths of Mr. Fortune and Mary is an act that may have had its roots earlier, in Mr. Fortune's headstrong attempt to manipulate his extended family without proper consideration of the principles that should have guided his weighty actions. It is clear on the afternoon prior to the violent final day that Mr. Fortune does not understand the situation of which he was a part; yet, rather than hesitate until he has the confidence that a clearer grasp of the relevant principles might supply, he pushes ahead with a decision fraught with grim implications for his family.

That afternoon, Fortune retires to his room to rest but he arises several times to look "out the window across the 'lawn' to the line of woods [Mary] said they wouldn't be able to see any more." But he sees nothing but ordinary "woods—not a mountain, not a waterfall, not any kind of planted bush or flower, just woods" (CW, 538). Yet his bewilderment, rather than giving him pause, stiffens his resolve to sell, with the vague plan that he can compensate Mary Fortune "by buying her something" (CW, 538). He is clearly troubled that he does not understand. The third time he gets up to look at the woods, he seems to come the closest to grasping the moral dimensions of his circumstance, as he perceives, however incompletely, something more than a line of trees.

The old man stared for some time, as if for a prolonged instant he were caught up out of the rattle of everything that led to the future and were held there in the midst of an uncomfortable *mystery* that he had not apprehended before. (CW, 538, emphasis added)

This "glimpse" suggests the existence of something vital though un-known, and for this reason he should have hesitated, but he ignores even this partial revelation, making him all the more culpable for his later will-ful behavior and its horrific consequence.

Maritain elaborates upon St. Thomas's principle, thereby offering the O'Connor reader the means by which he might judge Mr. Fortune's be-havior. Once the individual has made the willful choice not to identify and apply the rule, his choice means there now exists an "absence of good," that while not evil in itself, will produce evil if left uncorrected. This "voluntary" choice bears all the characteristics of Thomistic evil—and not coincidentally of nihilism as well, as it

is a certain nothingness, the nothingness of the consideration of the rule, it is a certain nothingness introduced by the creature at the start of his action; it is a mere absence, a mere nothingness, but it is the root proper of evil ac-tion.[13]

Mr. Fortune's behavior, to use Martain's words, bears "in itself the teeth-marks of nothingness." The conclusion to Maritain's explanation of this dimension of Thomistic evil seems an equally apt characterization of For-tune's behavior: "Here we have traced evil to its innermost hiding-place."[14]

By the time Mr. Fortune takes Mary to the woods to beat her, he has lost more than his control over Mary Fortune. His philosophical worldview is crumbling and he has accordingly lost his self-confidence. When he an-nounces to his granddaughter, "Now I'm going to whip you," O'Connor describes his voice as "extra loud" but "hollow" (CW, 544). But by this time it is too late to regain the secure grounding that wisdom can supply and so he blusters his way forward, devoid of divine or reasonable guid-ance and propelled only by the force of his will which he vainly tries to impose upon his doomed granddaughter.

O'CONNOR ON THE MYSTERY OF SUFFERING

His granddaughter's suffering maddens Fortune because he cannot con-trol it and because she submits to it. O'Connor implies that Fortune fails to appreciate the mystery of suffering with its inexplicable and uncontrollable nature. He regards it as a problem to be solved quickly and forcibly, rather than as a complex and difficult mystery requiring forethought before action. After one of her beatings, he wonders to himself,

> What was the matter with her that she couldn't stand up to Pitts? Why was there this one flaw in her character when he had trained her so well in everything else. *It was an ugly mystery.* (CW, 536, emphasis added)

O'Connor offers a correction to Fortune's attitude toward suffering, both by her writing and by her life. She was, of course, well acquainted with "mysterious" suffering because of the enigmatic disease of lupus she inherited from her father that took her own life prematurely at the age of thirty-nine. The late Sally Fitzgerald reported, "When she came home to Georgia for good, it was of course under the hard constraint of disseminated lupus erythematosus, a dangerous [autoimmune deficiency] disease of metabolical origin—incurable but controllable by steroid drugs—which exhausts the energies of its victims and necessitates an extremely careful and restricted life" (HB, xvi). Some of O'Connor's friends were slow to realize the seriousness of her illness because O'Connor either understated it or treated it with humor. From Rome, Italy, she wrote her friends the Cheneys regarding the pilgrimage to which she had reluctantly agreed—"Have endured. Cheers, Flannery."[15] In the last year of her life, Brainard Cheney wrote, "I somehow can't realize the degree of hazard in which you live!"[16] A fellow lupus sufferer with whom O'Connor corresponded, DeVene Harrold, reports that O'Connor was wryly appreciative that if one must suffer a serious disease, the more mysterious the ailment, the better. Harrold reports, "We had lengthy letters and lengthy chats about lupus. They were factual and matter-of-fact. She was of the opinion that it was a fine ailment to have—if you HAD to have one—simply because it was a mystery."[17]

Another of her stories sheds light on O'Connor's view of tragic suffering: "Good Country People," discussed in chapter 5, involves a young woman, Joy, who lives with the suffering of a lost leg. Even worse, she suffers from a weak heart and the doctors had told her mother Mrs. Hopewell "that with the best of care, her daughter Joy might see forty-five." Joy had made it clear were it not for her physical limitations, she would be at a university "lecturing to people who knew what she was talking about . . . far from these red hills and good country people" (CW, 268).

O'Connor suggests that Hulga's suffering becomes the pretext by which she, encouraged by her overeducation, rejects the idea that tragedy can render life richer and more meaningful. Hulga would never have imagined that one might experience joy and suffering simultaneously. Hence, the symbolism inherent in her given name "Joy," a name she rejects in favor of her ugly creation, Hulga. O'Connor, in the penultimate year of her life, wrote to her friend Janet McKane, "Perhaps however joy is the outgrowth of suffering in a special way" (HB, 527). Joy may be the result of embracing one's suffering, but such an experience requires one to choose the transcendent over the material. "We all prefer comfort to joy," O'Connor once observed (HB, 926).

By this time, the writer was intimately acquainted with suffering, though it never seemed to steal her humor.

> I stayed [at Emory Hospital] a month, giving generous samples of my blood to this, that and the other technician, all hours of the day and night, but now I am at home again and not receiving any more awful cards that say to a dear sick friend, in verse what's worse. Now I shoot myself with ACTH once daily and look very well and do nothing that I can get out of doing. (HB, 24)

The ACTH treatments were a blunt instrument to alleviate the suffering of lupus, but she once admitted, "The large doses of ACTH send you off in a rocket and are scarcely less disagreeable than the disease" (HB, 26). She never failed, though, to find redemptive merit in her pain. She wrote to Robert Lowell, "I am making out fine in spite of any conflicting stories. . . . I have enough energy to write with and as that is all I have any business doing anyhow, I can with one eye squinted take it all as a blessing. What you have to measure out, you come to observe more closely, or so I tell myself" (HB, xvi).

One of the most poignant and insightful portraits of O'Connor's suffering was written by Richard Gilman, who came to Milledgeville to interview the author for a *New York Review of Books* piece on O'Connor's collection of essays, *Mystery and Manners*. Gilman was apprehensive about meeting the writer because he knew that by that time (four years before her death) "she was crippled and that the disease had distorted her face." He admitted, "I found myself glancing past her face, averting my eyes when she moved laboriously about, not wanting yet to see her." But then, Gilman explained, "something broke and I was looking at her, at her face, twisted to one side, at her stiff and somewhat puffy hands and arms, and at her thinning and lusterless hair." In a remarkable observation that articulates O'Connor's own vision for suffering, he admits that even as he resisted "an occasional spasm of pity . . . her appearance was absorbed for me into her presence and—I don't use the word lightly—transfigured by it." He wrote, "Tough-minded, laconic, with a marvelous wit and an absolute absence of self-pity, she made me understand, as never before or since, what spiritual heroism and beauty can be."[18]

Walker Percy only met O'Connor once, but he thought she was "amazing," and he seemed to perceive the connection between her suffering and the richness it lent to her work. He notes that during the entirety of her short publishing career, she was dying an untimely death. As early as the age of twenty-five, she had been hospitalized in Atlanta with a major attack of the same intractable disease that had taken her father. The occasion of their meeting was a lecture she delivered at Loyola in New Orleans. Percy recalls, "I could recognize the symptoms of advanced lupus. . . . She had lost most of the tissue of her chin" and "her face was very strange."

> I remember we were going into this lecture hall, and she came in from a side entrance. Somebody was with her from the university and helped her. She had crutches and they helped her up to the podium, where she sort of hung on and delivered a stunning lecture. . . . Then she answered questions and was just extraordinary.[19]

O'Connor once commented on the subject of suicide in a letter to Betty Hester. She writes, "My Mother said to [the wife of a suicide] that she didn't see how anybody with any faith in God could do such a thing." O'Connor concluded insightfully, "His tragedy was I suppose that he didn't know what to do with his suffering (HB, 287).[20] Indeed, O'Connor was quick to express gratitude for her illness because it made her life more meaningful. She explains, "In a sense sickness is a place, more instructive than a long trip to Europe, and it's always a place where there's no company, where nobody can follow." She adds, in a startling observation, that illness is an opportunity to experience the mercy of God. She elaborates, "Sickness before death is a very appropriate thing and I think those who don't have it miss one of God's mercies" (HB, 163). Such an attitude is remarkable given the extent of O'Connor's suffering; she once added a poignant postscript in a letter to her friend Louise Abbot: "Prayers requested. I am sick of being sick" (CW, 1210).

For many, though, the temptation to nihilistic or existentialist skepticism is strongest when one looks in the mysterious face of suffering. This was the rock on which the brilliant rhetorician Augustine of Hippo foundered for years. He first embraced the Manichean remedy that God and the Devil are coequal opponents; human suffering occurs when the fight tilts toward the latter. After St. Augustine concluded that the Manichean solution was simplistic, he converted to Christianity, accepting the Judeo–Christian doctrine that human suffering can never be fully understood but should lead to an increasingly greater dependence upon

God, not a rejection of his existence nor a resignation that life is tragic and absurd.

C. S. Lewis's *The Problem With Pain*, which appears in O'Connor's personal library with many annotations, is an apologetic for a God whose benevolence is not contradicted by intense human suffering. When O'Connor read it, one might reasonably surmise that she read not with detached philosophical curiosity, but with immediate personal interest. Lewis argues that suffering is not incompatible with a loving God because it is tied inextricably to the very dignity and complexity of human life. He explains, "Try to exclude the possibility of suffering which the order of nature and the existence of free wills involve, and you find that you have excluded life itself." In this regard, Lewis reinforces one of O'Connor's favorite themes: divine love is not primarily a sentimental phenomenon; instead, it may be a no-nonsense reminder of the reality of the human condition. Lewis says, "If God is Love, He is, by definition, something more than mere kindness." Lewis adds, "He has paid us the intolerable compliment of loving us, in the deepest, most tragic, most inexorable sense."[21]

MODERNITY AND REDEMPTION

In his advice on dealing with uncertainty, the political philosopher Niccolò Machiavelli anticipates O'Connor's concerns in "A View of the Woods" and, more generally, introduces the modern response to mystery. Machiavelli might have been speaking for Mr. Fortune when he advises, "I judge . . . that it is better to be impetuous than cautious, because fortune is a woman; and it is necessary, if one wants to hold her down, to beat her and strike her down." Machiavelli continues, "And one sees that she lets herself be won more by the impetuous than by those who proceed coldly."[22]

Those still confident with the exaggerated rationalism that began with Descartes hope to eliminate all mystery from life. The modern world has been riding an ever-cresting wave of technology that has emboldened man to try and conquer all human suffering and want. O'Connor warns that there will always be limits to progress, and, even more to the point, that there is a "view of the woods" that cannot and should not be eradicated by science and technology. If this view is lost along with the humility that should attend it, one risks a disaster worse than the pain and suffering he is trying to erase. The final event of this story is darkly ironic precisely because the grandfather, in trying to force "progress" without regard for the mystery of human nature and suffering, confirms that mystery by perpetrating a suffering far more ghastly than that which he tried to eliminate.

O'Connor's warning against overweening confidence in so-called progress is symbolized by her disturbing descriptions of the bulldozer, placed like bookmarks at the beginning and end of the story. As the story opens, Mary Fortune watches "the big disembodied gullet gorge itself on the clay, then with the sound of a deep sustained nausea and a slow mechanical revulsion, turn and spit it out." At the conclusion of the tale, the grandfather's last view is of "a huge yellow monster which sat to the side, as stationary as he was, gorging itself on clay" (CW, 525, 546).[23]

"A View of the Woods" suggests that the mystery of suffering often is intertwined with another element of life's mystery, namely, the inscrutability of human nature. O'Connor once noted, "Good fiction deals with human nature" (MM, 126). And so, at one point in their death struggle, when Mary still has the upper hand, she pauses long enough to ask if her grandfather "has had enough." The old man sees something of his own nature in her face but it is an element he could not understand. "The old man looked up into his own image. It was triumphant and hostile" (CW, 545). All through the story her grandfather had willed himself to believe that she carried only the Fortune inheritance, not the legacy of the Pitts family as well. But he is never entirely confident in this opinion, at times only hopeful. His confident belief that she shared his own character is "like the gentle little tide on the new lake" but he is also troubled that perhaps he could not completely predict or control her nature. He is reluctantly aware that she is perhaps a "Pitts," also, and this troubled the surface serenity of his belief as it "pulled back like an undertow" (CW, 533). An unfamiliar voice emanates from Mary threatening his confident worldview with its announcement of the intractability of human nature embodied in his granddaughter's defiance:

> "You been whipped," it said, "by me," and then it added, bearing down on each word, "and I'm PURE Pitts." (CW, 545)

The name "Pitts" corresponds with the "Pit," the place of judgment resigned for those who follow their irrational instincts. Associating one's name with the Pit evokes the lower, darker side of human nature that we would all change—if we could. But it is the folly of presumption that these wayward leanings that make human existence so mysterious can be erased or easily controlled. Mr. Fortune not only misunderstands the girl's nature, he is also blind to the vicious dimension of his own character. Hence the severe irony when he asserts, "There's not an ounce of Pitts in me," as he murders his own granddaughter by slamming her head down cruelly on a rock (CW, 545). O'Connor offers another clue to the problem of human nature in this story by assigning the old man a "heart condition." His physical ailment is symbolic of the sickness with which his humanity is afflicted. The author would most likely have been familiar with the oft-quoted verse from the Book of Jeremiah, "The heart is deceitful above all things and beyond cure / Who can understand it?"[24]

O'Connor develops her concern over the mystery of human nature in other places. Her short story, "The Life You Save May Be Your Own" revolves around on the machinations of Tom T. Shiftlet, a one-armed vagabond who takes advantage of a mother and her handicapped daughter by marrying the daughter only to abandon her after he has stolen the family's car. Shiftlet, as his name suggests, is a cunning swindler who distresses even himself by his wayward conduct. When he first meets the mother and daughter he proposes to do handyman tasks in exchange for food and shelter. At that time, he offers an inadvertent warning to the older woman, and in doing so, provides a general comment on the darker side of human nature. He explains the work of thoracic surgeons in Georgia's capital,

> "There's one of these doctors in Atlanta that's taken a knife and cut the human heart—the human heart," he repeated, leaning forward, "out of a man's chest and held it in his hand," and he held his hand out, palm up, as if it were slightly weighted with the human heart, "and studied it like it was a day-old chicken, and lady," he said, allowing a long significant pause in which his head slid forward and his clay-colored eyes brightened, "he don't know no more about it than you or me." (CW, 174)

Shiftlet later applies the illustration to himself when he says, "If they was to take my heart and cut it out . . . they wouldn't know a thing about me" (CW, 180).

O'Connor embeds yet a third—and the most important—component of mystery in "A View of the Woods." She provides a fascinating gloss on this story when she answered a correspondent's misguided question regarding whether Pitts, Mary Fortune's father, was a "Christ symbol." "I had that role cut out for the woods," she explains. She continues by noting that Pitts cannot represent Christ because he "is a pathetic figure by virtue of the fact that he beats his child to ease his feelings about Mr. Fortune. He is a Christian and a sinner, pathetic by virtue of his sins." Accordingly, a "Christ figure" can't be "pathetic by virtue of his sins." It is the woods themselves that "walk across the water," she explains. Furthermore, O'Connor explains that the old man only runs to the edge of the water in his imagination, and the writer changed the verb to the "conditional" to make this clear.[25] Hence "the old man felt *as if he were being pulled*, felt *as if he were running* as fast as he could . . . [but Fortune] dies by

Mary Fortune's side" all the while that the woods are, in his imagination, imitating Christ's miraculous feat of walking upon water (CW, 546; HB, 189-190, emphasis added). The woods, then, simultaneously represent "Christ" and "mystery," two mutually compatible designations, since the Church identifies both the person and the redemptive work of Christ as theological mysteries.

The grandfather's failure to grasp the redemptive symbolism of the tree line might help the reader understand why O'Connor's judgment on the grandfather is so harsh: by destroying the woods he is rejecting Christ's redemption. O'Connor apparently struggled over the inclusion of Mary Fortune's quotation of the scripture to her grandfather, "He who calls his brother a fool is subject to hell's fire."[26] She was reluctant to remove it, though, since the grandfather's arrogant and violent rejection of redemptive mystery warranted punishment. She concludes, "Some prediction of hell for the old man is essential to my story" (HB, 187). Whereas "Pitts and Mary Fortune realize the value of the woods," the grandfather does not. When the grandfather looks those three times out of his bedroom window at the woods on that restless afternoon, the limited insight he gains upon his third gaze suggests that the woods hold a theological mystery, especially given the obvious theological significance of the number three.

By the third instance, the tree line emerges more clearly as a metaphor for Christ and his passion; he died, as the Scriptures report, upon a "tree."[27] O'Connor writes that the tree line appears to the grandfather "as if someone were wounded behind the woods and the trees were bathed in blood." It is an "unpleasant vision" for the old man because it undermines his fragile self-assurance by calling attention to his need for redemption. As O'Connor herself explains, only "the woods and the woods alone are pure enough to be a Christ symbol if anything is" (CW, 538, HB, 190).

The grandfather might have profited from G. K. Chesterton's admonition, "Mysticism keeps men sane. As long as you have mystery you have health; when you destroy mystery you create morbidity."[28] O'Connor argued many times that the human condition generates a longing, however vague, for redemption. The proper response to mystery, according to this short story, is the recognition and acceptance of man's need for another mystery, the mystery of redemption.

9

Redemption and the Ennoblement of Suffering in "The Artificial Nigger"

"You will observe that I admire my own work as much if not more than anybody else does," O'Connor wrote. "I have read 'The Artificial Nigger' several times since it was printed, enjoying it each time as if I had had nothing to do with it" (HB, 78). She called this story her "favorite" and "probably the best thing I'll ever write"(HB, 101, 208).

The "Artificial Nigger" is a beautiful story of the weakness of human nature and its remedy in the mystery of suffering made possible by the Incarnation. One reason O'Connor enjoyed her story as much as she did may be because she found success in a difficult endeavor:

> One of the awful things about writing when you are a Christian is that for you the ultimate reality is the Incarnation, the present reality is the Incarnation, and nobody believes in the Incarnation; that is nobody in your audience. (HB, 92)

This story is perhaps the best illustration of O'Connor's willingness to place a "skandalon," or a stumbling block, in the path of the reader: those who are put off by the title, and who may even err badly in calling O'Connor a "racist" on the basis of this story, are guilty of the worst kind of knee-jerk reaction. Far from being a racist tale, in "The Artificial Nigger," O'Connor pays the African-American race the highest possible compliment: out of their tragedy, O'Connor finds the opportunity for redemption. She identifies their misery with the sufferings of Christ, and their severe suffering provides "an action of grace" (HB, 160).

"What I had in mind to suggest with the artificial nigger," O'Connor explains, "was the redemptive quality of the Negro's suffering for us all" (HB, 78). But this was a task she approached with caution. As one of the better students of O'Connor has noted, "she understood many of the injustices done to [black Americans] by her society," but did not presume to understand their suffering and psyche well enough "to try to write from their perspective."[1] Nonetheless, O'Connor chose to write about the suffering of the black man from her own theological worldview, on a topic she considered of the utmost importance. She admitted unabashedly, "I see from the standpoint of Christian orthodoxy." Such a perspective meant that life must be "centered in our Redemption by Christ and that what I see in the world I see in its relation to that." Accordingly, the author felt there was little room for compromise: "I don't think that this is a position that can be taken halfway or one that is particularly easy in these times to make transparent in fiction" (CW, 805). Since, as she noted "we have all been expelled from the Garden of Eden" then the central Christian mystery must be that those so expelled "are found by God to be worth dying for" (MM, 146).[2]

THE STORY

The story involves only two individuals who are identified by name. The first is Mr. Head and the other is his grandson, Nelson. Mr. Head appears first as he awakens very early in the morning to leave their rural home for a day trip by train to Atlanta. O'Connor characterizes the old man as lacking the modesty that should temper his self-possession and protect him from the humiliation soon to come. She ingeniously does so in her description of his clothing. Mr. Head's trousers are pictured on the back of a chair "like the garment some great man had just flung to his servant." The moon, in contrast to his trousers, is less pretentious as "the face on the moon was a grave one. It gazed across the room and out the window where it floated over the horse stall and appeared to contemplate itself with the look of a young man who sees his old age before him." But the moon, confronted with Mr. Head's unsightly pride, "paused as if it were waiting for his permission to enter" (CW, 210). The description of Mr. Head's habit of awakening reinforces his pretension as he arose without the aid of an alarm clock because "[s]ixty years had not dulled his responses; his physical reactions, like his moral ones, were guided by his will and strong character." His eyes

had a look of composure and of ancient wisdom as if they belonged to one of the great guides of men. He might have been Vergil summoned in the middle of the night to go to Dante, or better, Raphael, awakened by a blast of God's light to fly to the side of Tobias. (CW, 210)

This comparison is ironic, for Mr. Head is neither a Vergil, Dante's illustrious escort in the *Divine Comedy*; nor a Raphael, Tobit and Sarah's heavenly guide from the Old Testament *Book of Tobit*. If he had had the literary vocabulary, though, he might have fancied himself as such, especially since he presumes to serve as a self-fashioned moral guide for Nelson in Atlanta. If anything, he is a parody of Vergil and Raphael, not an imitation.

After getting ready for the trip, "Mr. Head lay back down, feeling entirely confident that he could carry out the moral mission of the coming day." This mission consists of demonstrating to Nelson that, even though the boy had been born in the city, the city's attraction was no more than an illusion; and, for that reason he ought to "be content to stay at home for the rest of his life." Then Nelson will find out "you ain't as smart as you think you are" and so the trip should be "a lesson that the boy would never forget" (CW, 211).

Nelson, for his part, is a child "who was never satisfied until he had given an impudent answer" (CW, 211). Although the two of them are grandfather and grandson, "they looked enough alike to be brothers and brothers not too far apart in age" (CW, 212). In describing them in this way, O'Connor suggests that there is less moral dissimilarity between them than Mr. Head would suppose. Nelson demonstrates a kind of comic childish pride, as he races to dress before his grandfather and begins cooking corn pone and frying meat in "his new suit and his new gray hat pulled low over his eyes" and "drinking cold coffee out of a can." But Mr. Head is possessed of a kind of juvenile conceit himself: although he warns Nelson before the trip not to get lost in the big city, it is the elder who will be humiliated because of his disorientation and self-righteousness cowardice. There is also a universal dimension to Mr. Head's foibles, and the way in which he will be rescued from his predicament is a universal remedy. O'Connor means for the reader to identify himself, both with Mr. Head's weakness and its remedy. This is the reason for his name, "Mr. Head," an appellation generic enough to symbolize anyone and everyone.

Although Mr. Head is able to maintain his confidence and superiority on the train, as soon as he disembarks his plan begins slowly to unravel. It does so in apparently trivial ways, but the insignificance of the events belies the significance of O'Connor's morality tale. He first forgets the bag lunch he had packed for the two and leaves it on the train. Next, he directs Nelson to a penny-weighing machine they find at one of the storefronts.

Mr. Head's ticket puzzles him. It said, "'You weigh 120 pounds. You are upright and brave and all your friends admire you.'"

> He put the ticket in his pocket, surprised that the machine should have got his character correct but his weight wrong, for he had weighed on a grain scale not long before and knew he weighed 110. (CW, 219-220)

The machine, of course, is wrong on both counts and its flattering message anticipates Mr. Head's approaching moral collapse.

MR. HEAD'S HUMILIATION

The grandfather is dismayed that Nelson seems infatuated with the city rather than repulsed by it. He attempts a weak bluff when he shows him a sewer entrance and then warns that all city dwellers are in danger of being "sucked into the sewer and never heard from again." Nelson is momentarily shaken but recovers as he concludes that "you can stay away from the holes" and so quickly regains his exasperating stubbornness (CW, 220). The pair soon lose their way and circle through a neighborhood of prostitutes and juvenile delinquents. Nelson suspects their predicament: "'We done been here!' he shouted." He adds accusingly, "I don't believe you know where you're at!" (CW, 221).

In their rural home, Mr. Head and Nelson were unaccustomed to seeing Negroes, so that beginning with the train ride the black man acquires a kind of mystical quality for the two. There, Nelson sees a black man for the first time and he stares, not just in fascination, but with something akin to awe. Once lost in the city, the neighborhood grows increasingly black. "Colored children played in the gutters and stopped what they were doing to look at them" and "[b]lack eyes in black faces were watching them from every direction" (CW, 221). Their discomfort increases when they realize they have forgotten their lunch. Nelson angrily accuses his grandfather, "First you lost the sack and then you lost the way" (CW, 222). His grandfather refuses to ask one of the "niggers" for directions, so Nelson asks a local woman. At first, the woman teases him, albeit in a kindly way, but as Nelson looks at her in wonder, he finds a strange comfort, a comfort that anticipates the resolution of the story in which redemption will be channeled through a black man, albeit an artificial one.

> He suddenly wanted her to reach down and pick him up and draw him against her and then he wanted to feel her breath on his face. He wanted to

look down and down into her eyes while she held him tighter and tighter. He had never had such a feeling before. (CW, 223)

O'Connor wrote to her friend Ben Griffith, "You may be right that Nelson's reaction to the colored woman is too pronounced, but I meant for her in an almost physical way to suggest the mystery of existence to him" (CW, 931). She also explained that the black woman is necessary to add a dramatic tension to the story as she added, "I felt that such a black mountain of maternity would give him the required shock to start those black forms moving up from his unconscious" (HB, 78).

Although the woman gives the two a general orientation toward the train station, they walk a considerable distance with no confidence that they are any closer, and they become distraught once more. Nelson is tired, hungry, and thirsty, and he demands that they stop and rest; whereupon, he immediately falls into an exhausted sleep. Mr. Head, now shaken and insecure, devises a quick but ill-conceived plan to regain his authority over the boy. He hides behind a trashcan and awakens his grandson with a loud noise, thinking that if he awakes alone, he will appreciate the old man: "He justified what he was going to do on the grounds that it is sometimes necessary to teach a child a lesson he won't forget, particularly when the child is always reasserting his position with some new impudence" (CW, 225).

But Nelson awakens so fitfully at the noise that he "shot up onto his feet with a shout . . . whirled several times and then, picking up his feet and throwing his head back, he dashed down the street like a wild maddened pony" (CW, 225). In his panic, he becomes "a streak of gray" and his grandfather cannot catch him. Mr. Head then sees a tumult ahead where the boy has collided with an elderly woman. Nelson is on the ground in a daze and the woman, sitting amidst her scattered groceries, screams that her ankle is broken, and that the boy's daddy must pay for the episode. She and the other bystanders call loudly for a policeman: "A crowd of women had already gathered to see justice done" to the "juvenile delinquent" and his family (CW, 226).

Mr. Head cautiously creeps forward and "his head had lowered itself into his collar like a turtle's; his eyes were glazed with fear and caution." Nelson digs his fingers into his legs but his grandfather shocked them all, especially his grandson, by denying the obvious relationship. "'This is not my boy,' he said. 'I never seen him before'" (CW, 226).

The women dropped back, staring at him with horror, as if they were so repulsed by a man who would deny his own image and likeness that they could not bear to lay hands on him. Mr. Head walked on, through a space they silently cleared, and left Nelson behind. Ahead of him he saw nothing but a hollow tunnel that had once been the street. (CW, 226)

After Mr. Head has disgraced himself by his betrayal, Nelson follows him but by about twenty feet, and, "Mr. Head's shoulders were sagging and his neck hung forward at such an angle that it was not visible from behind." Nelson's eyes beat into his back "like pitchfork prongs" and, despite his thirst, he refuses to drink from the same spigot as his grandfather who feels "the depth of his denial." Still lost, he anticipates that if they miss the train they will be beaten and robbed. A now broken Mr. Head thinks such a fate would be just for him but not for Nelson as the "speed of God's justice was only what he expected for himself, but he could not stand to think that his sins would be visited upon Nelson" (CW, 227). For his part, Nelson's mind "had frozen around his grandfather's treachery as if he were trying to preserve it intact to present at the final judgment" (CW, 228).

The urban ghetto gradually gives way to white suburbs and Mr. Head, now reduced to a pale reflection of his former prideful self, sees "a bald-headed" man with "golf knickers" and confesses, "I'm lost and can't find my way and me and this boy have got to catch this train and I can't find the station." The grandfather learns that he and Nelson are only three blocks away from a suburban train stop and he "stared as if he were slowly returning from the dead." But Nelson's eyes "were triumphantly cold. There was no light in them, no feeling, no interest. . . . Home was nothing to him" (CW, 229).

Nelson's attitude suggests that Mr. Head's humiliation is not complete. It would be a kind of moral and spiritual shortcut for him to regain his frail confidence simply because he had found the train station again; and so, the brief light in Mr. Head's mood is instantly redarkened by the reminder of what Nelson has suffered because of his grandfather's Judas-like betrayal. His grandfather is in misery, but a misery that is preparing him for grace. He "felt he knew now what time would be like without seasons and what heat would be like without light and what man would be like without salvation" (CW, 229).

AN ENCOUNTER WITH REDEMPTION

O'Connor explained in correspondence that "Mr. Head's redemption is all laid out inside the story," and the redemptive high point of the narrative occurs when he experiences his greatest despair (CW, 1108). In his unhappiness, his attention is suddenly arrested by an image, "like a cry out of the gathering dusk" for which the previous encounters with Negroes had been a harbinger (CW, 229). The image is a small statue, the type that in O'Connor's day was a ubiquitous yard decoration in the South, a plaster image of a Negro boy about Nelson's size. It has a tragic appearance as it is "pitched forward at an unsteady angle since the putty that held him to the wall had cracked. One of his eyes was entirely white and he held a piece of brown watermelon" (CW, 229).

> Mr. Head stood looking at him silently until Nelson stopped at a little distance. Then as the two of them stood there, Mr. Head breathed, "An artificial nigger!" (CW, 229)

The statue appears timeless and universal, and is conspicuous for the suffering that it evinces: "It was impossible to distinguish whether the statue were meant "to be someone young or old; he looked too miserable to be either." Though when it was first made the designer had attempted to give it a cheery look, time had transformed the statue so that it wore a miserable cast: "He was meant to look happy because his mouth was stretched up at the corners but the chipped eye and the angle he was cocked at gave him a wild look of misery instead" (CW, 229). Both Nelson and his grandfather are awe-struck, having never seen this type of Southern icon.

Wondrously, they are drawn together, as if the pain represented by the statue were efficacious in overcoming the congenital insecurity and enmity that keeps them separated. Enthralled by the statue, Nelson echoes, "An artificial nigger!" (CW, 229). The statue emits a charisma, flowing from an unknown source, which brings success out of their failure.

> They stood gazing at the artificial Negro as if they were faced with some great mystery, some monument to another's victory that brought them together in their common defeat. They could both feel it dissolving their differences like an action of mercy. (CW, 230)

Stumbling across the statue, Mr. Head and Nelson experience a mysterious encounter with the redemptive work of Christ, made real to them in two distinct, but unified, ways. First, the statue represents Christ himself, the "Suffering Servant" of the Book of Isaiah whose task it is to "spread over the whole earth . . . the news of the Redemption."[3] The Old Testament passage is a foreshadowing of the coming and work of Christ, as is much of the book of Isaiah. It begins in a tone of incredulity and wonder—not unlike that of Nelson and Mr. Head—because of what the prophet anticipates. The writer asks, "Who has believed our message / and to whom has the arm of the LORD been revealed?" Although God's

Servant "grew up . . . like a tender shoot," and despite his divine origin, "[h]e was despised and rejected by men, a man of sorrows, and familiar with suffering." He suffered on behalf of "our transgressions," and "he was crushed for our iniquities." It is his suffering "that brought peace" and "by his wounds we are healed."[4]

The Apostle Paul explains, by his own experience, the second manner in which the statue represents the redemptive power of suffering to the pair. He claims that his own suffering that he has incurred in his apostolic activity constitutes a share in, and a continuation of, the suffering of Christ. As such, it facilitates the continuing availability of redemptive grace to the young churches under his care. St. Paul tells the Philippian church that he aspires to "the fellowship of sharing in [Christ's] sufferings." He further tells the Colossian church that he rejoices in that he has suffered because "I fill up in my flesh what is still lacking in regard to Christ's afflictions, for the sake of his body, which is the church."[5] O'Connor follows St. Paul and the Catholic tradition in believing that the suffering of ordinary men and women extends the redemptive grace of Christ's own suffering, not because such suffering is efficacious in itself, but because it helps release the work of the original redemptive suffering of Jesus. As she once explained, "I believe that everybody, through suffering, takes part in the Redemption" (CW, 921). Accordingly, O'Connor is offering the hope in this story that the decades of suffering of the African-American race in America might hold a kind of redemptive grace of its own, hence the power of the "artificial nigger."

By virtue of his encounter with the statue, Mr. Head realizes that his own goodness has largely been an illusion, but until the illusion is dispelled, he is unable to receive the mercy he so badly needs. He "had never known before what mercy felt like because he had been too good to deserve any, but he felt he knew now" (CW, 230). The statue underscores the common need for mercy he and Nelson both share since each has been burdened, in his own way, by his spiritual poverty. Thus, "Mr. Head looked like an ancient child and Nelson like a miniature old man." But this action of mercy for Nelson also means that some measure of the innocence appropriate to a child his age is restored; and so, he experiences "a hungry need" for "assurance," and his eyes "seemed to implore" Mr. Head "to explain once and for all the mystery of existence" (CW, 230). He even loses his contempt for his rural life as Mr. Head had hoped he would, although the shift in attitude is accomplished, ironically, at Mr. Head's expense, not because of his wise guidance. Nelson exclaims, "I'm glad I've went once, but I'll never go back again!" (CW, 231).

Just that morning, Mr. Head's persona had crowded out of the predawn sky the moon that cowered before his arrogance; but after a pensive return trip that ends well after nightfall, the two disembark the train to find the moon in its former glory. As they set foot at their own train station, the moon, at that moment, "restored to its full splendor, sprang from a cloud and flooded the clearing with light." The rest of the celestial bodies, as if unopposed by human conceit, are resplendent as the sky is "hung with gigantic white clouds illuminated like lanterns" (CW, 230).

O'Connor once mused, "I guess Mr. Head is a kind of Peter," suggesting that Mr. Head, like the overconfident apostle who denied Christ three times, was brought to a state of abject humiliation in which his prideful bluster was replaced by an utter spiritual helplessness to help him recognize that only mercy could redeem him.[6] As he steps off the train, the action of grace in Mr. Head's life is in full motion, having brought about a degree of self-knowledge that might have crushed him had he not been able to respond with humility. The grace is a work of redemption flowing from the suffering represented by the black man's tortured past, accordingly, Mr. Head recognizes that the mercy he has received "grew out of agony" (CW, 230).

> He had never thought himself a great sinner before but he saw now that his true depravity had been hidden from him lest it cause him despair. He realized that he was forgiven for sins from the beginning of time, when he had conceived in his own heart the sin of Adam, until the present, when he had denied poor Nelson. He saw that no sin was too monstrous for him to claim as his own, and since God loved in proportion as He forgave, he felt ready at that instant to enter Paradise. (CW, 231)

O'Connor's description of the grace Mr. Head receives calls to mind Romano Guardini's description of the work of grace, or "graciousness" as he calls it. According to Guardini, "this graciousness is discovered in what may be called the moment of perfect peace." Such an experience is "a state, in which life is made aware of itself in its richness and perfection and as serene and free." As a result of such grace, "A man feels that all is well; he has no unfulfilled desires; existence is complete." As with Mr. Head, there "has been no notable change in things or in the man himself but a balance has been achieved" that carries a "promise of an ultimate fulfillment" and is in some way connected to "some ultimate and unique reality" because it involves a "mysterious presence."[7]

FICTION AND REDEMPTION

In a light mood in 1957, O'Connor referred to the upcoming trip to Europe she had reluctantly agreed to take, saying, "My mother and me facing

Europe will be just like Mr. Head and Nelson facing Atlanta."[8] O'Connor elsewhere, and more seriously, explained the ordinary manner by which she arrived at the statue as the icon of Christ's redemption:

> My mother went cow-buying a couple of years ago and asked an old man for directions how to get to a certain man's house. He told her to go thus and so and that she couldn't miss it because it was the only house in town with an artificial nigger. (HB, 140)

After this episode, O'Connor "was so intrigued" with the statuette "that I made up my mind to use it." She explained that "it's a terrible symbol of what the South has done to itself. I think it's one of the best stories I've written, and this because there is a good deal more in it than I understand myself" (HB, 140). She added elsewhere that "there is nothing that screams out the tragedy of the South like what my uncle calls 'nigger statuary'" (HB, 101).

In tying a cheap regional relic to the noble theme of Christ's redemption, O'Connor is trying to overcome the almost insurmountable challenge of the Christian author who feels compelled to present convincingly this theological wonder to a skeptical audience. She writes, "Redemption is meaningless unless there is cause for it in the actual life we live, and for the last few centuries, there has been operating in our culture, the secular belief that there is no such cause."

> When you can assume that your audience believes the same thing you do, you can relax a little and use more normal ways of talking to it; when you have to assume that it does not, then you may have to make your vision apparent by shock."[9]

Commenting on this story, the author tried to explain the nature of what transpired with Mr. Head. She said, "Mr. Head is changed by his experience even though he remains Mr. Head. He is stable but not the same man at the end of the story." But she added, "Part of the difficulty of all this is that you write for an audience who doesn't know what grace is and don't recognize it when they see it" (HB, 275).

Not only was O'Connor concerned with an apathetic response to man's need for redemption, she also knew that the attitude might be more hostile, and she often illustrates this hostility in her fiction. In *The Violent Bear It Away*, Rayber, the skeptic schoolteacher says, "I'm no fool. I don't believe in senseless sacrifice. A dead man is not going to do you any good." In his furious resistance to the prophetic calling, Tarwater tries to escape "the bleeding stinking mad shadow of Jesus" (CW, 395, 465). Hazel Motes's attitude toward redemption suggests that the idea is antithetical to the nihilistic gospel. Haze asserts that his new church is the one "that the blood of Jesus don't foul with redemption" (CW, 59). O'Connor explained that *Wise Blood* is "entirely Redemption-centered in thought." She admitted, though, that among the book's critics and readers, "Not too many people are willing to see this," and she wonders out loud if perhaps it is hard to see because H. Motes is such an admirable nihilist." Even his "nihilism," though, "leads him back to the fact of his Redemption" (HB, 69-70).

If Hazel Motes' desperate nihilism prompts a frontal attack on the concept of redemption, it is because such an idea is a threat to the success of the nihilist project. To be sure, Nietzsche had complained of "a justice that accepts the innocent as a vicarious sacrifice; someone who orders his disciples to drink his blood; prayers for miraculous interventions; sins perpetrated against a god, atoned for by a god; fear of a beyond to which death is the portal; the form of the cross as a symbol in a time that no longer knows the function and the ignominy of the cross—how ghoulishly all this touches us, as if from the tomb of a primeval past!" He concludes, as if with mock incredulity, "Can one believe that such things are still believed?"[10]

O'Connor artfully depicts the aversion to redemption in her somber and captivating short story "The Displaced Person." The tale is about a mid-century Polish refugee family who come to work as laborers on Mrs. McIntyre's farm. The father of the family, Mr. Guizac, is an exceptionally hard worker, motivated by a mixture of gratitude and an old world work ethic. Soon, however, his cultural differences stir up envy and hostility in both the mean-spirited Mrs. McIntyre and her self-serving white help, the Shortleys. Mrs. McIntyre learns that Mr. Guizac had arranged for one of the Negro help to take his niece's hand in marriage in order to rescue her from the German concentration camps. The landowner is infuriated, giving no thought to the dire plight of the girl. Mrs. McIntyre decides to fire him, but before she does, Mr. Guizac is violently killed by an unsecured tractor carelessly parked by Mr. Shortley. The accident looks suspiciously like negligent homicide because the farm owner and work personnel do nothing either to prevent the accident or to warn the victim.

Mr. Guizac suffers a kind of martyr's fate at the hand of narrow-minded and prejudiced people; even more, O'Connor uses his death as a symbol of the redemption of Christ. Indeed, O'Connor cleverly identifies Mr. Guizac's untimely death with Christ's passion. Mrs. McIntyre tries to inform Father Flynn, the Catholic priest who arranges Mr. Guizac's job on the farm, that despite Mr. Guizac's excellent work, the refugee would not be able to stay. During their conversation, the two "talk past each other," so to speak, with the priest ruminating about Christ and Mrs. McIntyre complaining about Mr. Guizac. Father Flynn is so taken with the display of one of the farm peacocks that he interrupts his conversation:

> "Christ will come like that!" he said in a loud gay voice and wiped his hand over his mouth and stood there, gaping. (CW, 317)

His conversant is startled and annoyed.

> Mrs. McIntyre's face assumed a set puritanical expression and she reddened. Christ in the conversation embarrassed her the way sex had her mother. (CW, 317)

After a few more befuddled exchanges, the identification of Mr. Guizac with Christ is complete.

> "Mr. Guizpac didn't have to come here in the first place," she said, giving him a hard look.
> The cock lowered his tail and began to pick grass.
> "He didn't have to come in the first place," she repeated, emphasizing each word.
> The old man smiled absently. "He came to redeem us," he said and blandly reached for her hand and shook it and said he must go. (CW, 317)

Later, Mrs. McIntyre tells Father Flynn that the refugee's dismissal is imminent. The same conversational conflation occurs, although this time, perhaps more purposefully. Father Flynn uses the occasion of their meeting to speak of Christ's redemption.

> "For," he was saying as if he spoke of something that had happened yesterday in town, "when God sent his Only Begotten Son, Jesus Christ Our Lord"—he slightly bowed his head—"as a Redeemer to mankind, H . . ."
> "Father Flynn!" she said in a voice that made him jump. "I want to talk to you about something serious!"
> . . .
> "As far as I'm concerned," she said and glared at him fiercely, "'Christ was just another D.P." (CW, 320)

After the grisly death of Mr. Guizac, Mrs. McIntyre's farm goes to ruin. As if torn apart by an unspoken but shared guilt, all of her help abandon her, the farm falls into bankruptcy, and her health rapidly declines. Her only consolations are the regular visits from Fr. Flynn who would sit at her bedside and "explain the doctrines of the Church" (CW, 327).

O'Connor explains in correspondence, "The displaced person did accomplish a kind of redemption in that he destroyed the place, which was evil, and set Mrs. McIntyre on the road to a new kind of suffering." But she admits that the act of redemption was understated and she wonders aloud if she had accordingly failed in her purpose. She balanced the possibility of artistic failure, however, with the recognition that "there is certainly no reason why the effects of redemption must be plain to us and I think they usually are not" (HB, 118).

AQUINAS ON REDEMPTION

If O'Connor's world was not only apathetic toward the promise of redemption but also hostile to the idea, perhaps it is because in order to accept redemption one must admit sin and recognize evil. O'Connor writes, "Part of the mystery of existence is sin. When we think about the Crucifixion, we miss the point of it if we don't think about sin" (HB, 143). Modern science has tried to explain away sin and O'Connor notes, "When Jung says that the Church reduces evil to talk about original sin and Adam's relatively insignificant 'slip-up' with Eve, he is showing that he knows nothing about what the Church teaches" (HB, 382). Mr. Head and Nelson provide a universal portrait of the divisive nature of sin. They are separated one from the other and Mr. Head is devoid from real insight about his own character deformation. Consequently, he has no meaningful relationship with God.

But sin is an alien notion to many. O'Connor claims that her region of the country, the South, has been better able to recognize sin as such rather than re-define it in terms of social inadequacies. She explains, "The notion of the perfectibility of man came about at the time of the Enlightenment in the eighteenth century. This is what the South has traditionally opposed." Thus, for O'Connor and her regional countrymen, the "fall" means a fall from innocence into sin. "How far we have fallen" means the fall of Adam, the fall from innocence, from sanctifying grace. The South "still believes that man has fallen and that he is only perfectible by God's grace, not by his own unaided efforts." By contrast,

> [t]he Liberal approach is that man has never fallen, never incurred guilt, and is ultimately perfectible by his own efforts. Therefore, evil in this light is a problem of better housing, sanitation, health, etc. and all mysteries will eventually be cleared up. (CW, 302–3)

So she speaks for herself and other fiction writers when she claims, "There is something in us, as story-tellers and as listeners to stories, that demands the redemptive act, that demands that what falls, at least be offered the chance to be restored." Not only are many writers prompted by a sense of the need for redemption, but readers are similarly troubled even if they fail to see how desperate is their need and how real is the problem of evil. She explains, "The reader of today looks for this notion, and rightly so, but what he has forgotten is the cost of it. His sense of evil is diluted or lacking altogether and so he has forgotten the price of restoration" (CW, 303). Whereas O'Connor believes "that you destroy your freedom by sin, . . . the modern reader believes . . . that you gain it in that way" (MM, 116).

"The Artificial Nigger" may be O'Connor's most explicitly religious tale for in it she retells the plight of man's separation from God and his fellow man because of prideful sin, and the mysterious means by which he is restored, which is the suffering that leads to Christ's redemption made available through grace. Her special pleasure in crafting this narrative helps the reader to understand her deep grief over the apostasy of her generation. She confesses, "I suppose what bothers us so much about writing about the return of modern people to a sense of the Holy Spirit is that the religious sense seems to be bred out of them in the kind of society we've lived in since the eighteenth century" (CW, 299). Religion is "bred out of them double quick now by the religious substitutes for religion." Consequently, the Christian writer's task is daunting because "[t]here's nowhere to latch on to, in the characters or the audience."

> If there were in the public just a slight sense of ordinary theology; . . . if they only believed at least that God has the power to do certain things. There is no sense of the power of God that could produce the Incarnation and the Resurrection. (CW, 300)

As St. Thomas explains, the redeeming work of Christ had to wait its time, until it became clear to an unbelieving world that it was in need of redemption, due to its own sin. St. Thomas quotes St. Augustine when the latter says, "*There was no cause of Christ's coming into the world, except to save sinners. Take away diseases, take away wounds, and there is no need of medicine.*"[11] Thomas continues, "Therefore God became incarnate at the most fitting time; and it was not fitting that God should become incarnate at the beginning of the human race. . . . For medicine is given only to the sick. Hence Our Lord Himself says (Matth. Ix. 12, 13): They that are in health need not a physician, but they that are ill. . . . For I am not come to call the just, but sinners."[12] Aquinas's explanation of this important matter of timing is true both for the human race in general, and for the individual sinner.

In "The Artificial Nigger," Mr. Head represents both the individual case, and symbolically, the corporate state of mankind as well. Aquinas explains that it was important that redemption be offered at the appropriate time; if it were offered prematurely, man's pride will interfere, given that his pride is a constituent part of his sinful condition. And so, "on account of the manner of man's sin, which had come of pride, . . . man was to be liberated in such a manner that he might be humbled, and see how he stood in need of a deliverer." Man is humbled, "so that having recognized his infirmity he might cry out for a physician, and beseech the aid of grace."[13] Therefore when Mr. Head asks directions saying, "'I'm lost and can't find my way," his confession is as much in reference to his spiritual state as to his physical disorientation. His next exclamation underscores the desperation of his soul, made ripe by his Atlanta fiasco. He cries, "Oh Gawd I'm lost! Oh hep me Gawd I'm lost!" Surely, O'Connor means for this to be Mr. Head's spiritual confession as he is finally faced with the frailty of his soul. His circumstances have violently stripped away his pretense and he has arrived at the state St. Thomas prescribes: "For if the physician were to give the medicine at the very outset of the ailment, it would do less good, and would hurt rather than benefit. And hence the Lord did not bestow upon the human race the remedy of the Incarnation in the beginning, lest they should despise it through pride, if they did not already recognize their disease."[14] T. S. Eliot reinforces the importance of a man understanding the severity of his disease before he seeks a cure: "Our only health is the disease / If we obey the dying nurse / Whose constant care is not to please / But to remind of our, and Adam's curse / And that, to be restored, our sickness must grow worse."[15]

"COMPASSION" VERSUS REDEMPTION

O'Connor asserted her "vocation" was to deliver the message of the "The Artificial Nigger" in the manner in which she wrote it (HB, 227). She found it much more typical in her day for writers to insist on sentiment in their novels, rather than the comparatively hard message of redemption. She notes, "It's considered an absolute necessity these days for writers to have compassion."

> Compassion is a word that sounds good in anybody's mouth and which no book jacket can do without. It is a quality which no one can put his finger on in any exact critical sense, so it is always safe for anybody to use. (CW, 817)

In O'Connor's view, the contemporary insistence upon compassion is a secular panacea for the demand for redemption. Instead of demanding moral change, the modern "writer excuses all human weakness because human weakness is human." But this is at best a kind of "hazy compassion," and "in this popular spirit, we mark our gain in sensibility and our loss in vision." Although "other ages" may have *felt less,* they *saw more,* which is to say they saw with the "unsentimental eye . . . of faith." But now that faith is absent, "we govern by tenderness." Since that tenderness is "cut off from the person of Christ," it is supported only by faithless, abstract theories. This is a dangerous condition because "[w]hen tenderness is detached from the source of tenderness," it is prone to become paternalistic and abusive. Hence, "its logical outcome is terror. It ends in forced labor camps and in the fumes of the gas chamber" (CW, 831-2, emphasis added).

Walker Percy picks up this concern in his novel *The Thanatos Syndrome,* a mystery novel of sorts about a scheme run by a cadre of psychiatrists in which the doctors tamper with the water supply of a rural region of Louisiana. The water is altered, producing a chemical reaction in the brain so that crime decreases and academic and athletic performance improves. But as a side effect, the men and women who are so affected become more sheep-like and their daily experience less thoughtful and more trivial; daily conversation is full of platitudes. Worse, the scientific elite's "compassion" begins to deteriorate to the sexual abuse of the women and children under their care. One of the doctors involved in perpetrating the experiment explains "that for the first time we have actually achieved the full meaning of the Greek word *eu* in euthanasia. . . . I think good is better than bad, serenity better than suffering."[16]

A prophetic warning in the novel comes from Father Smith, an eccentric and slightly imbalanced Catholic priest who lives in a fire tower in a manner reminiscent of Simeon Stylites, the fifth-century Syrian ascetic who sat upon a nine-foot pillar for thirty-six years so that he could fast and pray in relative solitude. Dr. Thomas More, the novel's protagonist, eventually uncovers the social experiment and, on one occasion, visits Father Smith in his cramped elevated accommodations. Father Smith warns that "people of the loftiest sentiments, the highest scientific achievements, and the purest humanitarian ideals" in modern society may have become the most dangerous. He suggests that in some instances, it is precisely those who have taken "the oath of Hippocrates" who are guilty of the benevolent abuse of those under their care without "a single letter of protest in the august *New England Journal of Medicine.*" He repeats O'Connor's assertion asking,

"Do you know where tenderness always leads?"
"No, where?" I ask, watching the stranger with curiosity.
"To the gas chamber."
"I see."
"Tenderness is the first disguise of the murder."[17]

In Walker Percy's novel *The Moviegoer*, the protagonist, a New Orleans stockbroker, disappoints his aunt by his personal irresponsibility. In chastising him, she generalizes her discontent by observing that although "our moral fiber is rotten" and the "national character stinks to high heaven," we are nonetheless "kinder than ever."[18] O'Connor, though, would agree with Percy in that the so-called compassion that has trumped redemption as the remedy for mankind's ills is a weak species of sentiment, not a vigorous expression of passion. In another of Percy's stories, as one of the characters, Ewell McBee berates the young millionaire Will Barrett, Barrett is struck by a "strange thought": "Perhaps Ewell was the last hater. Has a time come when not only has love left the world but hatred also and nothing is left but niceness?"[19] Indeed, for O'Connor, one of the worst manifestations of vapid sentimentalism is pornography, an activity that has everything to do with feeling but little to do with genuine human passion—and nothing to do with virtue. Accordingly, O'Connor worries about writing for an audience prone to "confuse virtue with satisfaction," For that reason, the writer will be of little service if he writes "soggy, formless, and sentimental literature" (CW, 804).

When her friend Betty Hester left the Catholic Church after only a short period, O'Connor noted with some disgust that since Hester's "release," she now "loves everything and is a bundle of empathy for everything" (HB, 459). O'Connor also attacked this problem metaphorically: in her celebrated short story "A Good Man is Hard to Find," the self-centered grandmother's cat's name is "Pitty Sing," a name evocative of cloying sentimentality, and it is the cat whose behavior is the proximate cause of the entire family's being at the mercy of the villain who ruthlessly executes them (CW, 144).

One reason O'Connor despises the modern identification of virtue with sentiment is because sentiment becomes a substitute for action, a surrogate for charity. If in the face of need, one can emote sufficiently, a concrete charitable response is unnecessary. T. S. Eliot notes that the modern individual remains in a "shadow" between the initial "feeling" that his circumstances evoke, and a meaningful response to the same. Eliot writes, "Between the conception / And the creation / Between the emotion / And the response / Falls the Shadow."[20] O'Connor admits that the confusion between charity and sentimentality "is one reason I am chary of

using the word, love, loosely. I prefer to use it in its practical forms, such
as prayer, almsgiving, visiting the sick and burying the dead and so
forth." In a book O'Connor admired, Guardini notes that "human love
has been stifled, resting content with sympathy."[21] O'Connor admitted, "I
must say that the thought of everyone lolling about in an emotionally satisfying faith is repugnant to me. I believe that we are ultimately directed
Godward but that this journey is often impeded by emotion" (HB, 102,
CW, 952).

EVIL AND SUFFERING

Before Mr. Head and Nelson leave the presence of the statuette, Mr. Head
"looked at Nelson and understood that he must say something to the
child to show that he was still wise and in the look the boy returned he
saw a hungry need for that assurance. Nelson's eyes seemed to implore
him to explain once and for all the mystery of existence" (CW, 230). Mr.
Head's response might be taken by the reader as demeaning:

> Mr. Head opened his lips to make a lofty statement and heard himself say,
> "They ain't got enough real ones here. They got to have an artificial one."
> (CW, 230)

Mr. Head's pronouncement is anything but narrow and mean-spirited.
On the contrary, he is commenting upon the tragedy of the black American experience. If he could have articulated it differently, Mr. Head
would have said, "Not only has the Negro been oppressed in his daily
experience, but, as if the white race were still unsatisfied, they must also
re-create that black oppression and humiliation in this cheap art form."
O'Connor's use of the word "nigger" in this story, far from being gratu-
itously "racist," is meant to underscore the awful evil of enslavement,
oppression and prejudice. She was not in the habit of using the designation "nigger," even though it was everyday Southern nomenclature for
Negro help; rather, when the term appears in her literature, disagreeable
if not repulsive characters employ it. Her characters often use the word
to reveal their souls—perverse and desperately in need of redemption.
Here, the appellation is meant to evoke the evil nature of the American
black experience.

Finally, "The Artificial Nigger" demonstrates C. S. Lewis's argument in
The Problem of Pain that the act of suffering *per se* is not evil, though it may
be caused by evil. O'Connor believes that one's response to suffering is often the very means of overcoming evil, because pain prompts human be-

ings to reach beyond themselves into the transcendent. In Dostoyevsky's *Notes From Underground*, the narrator challenges the superficiality of the modern age when he rhetorically asks, "Which is better; cheap happiness or sublime suffering?"[22] Given the chance, O'Connor would identify the latter as the more meaningful life. Human misery is the very phenomenon that releases the grace needed to overcome the emptiness of the human soul. Thus what Eric Voegelin calls "the mystery of representative suffering," far from being equivalent to evil, may be its redemptive remedy.[23]

10

Grace, the Devil,
and the Prophet

"All my stories are about the action of grace on a character who is not willing to support it, but most people think of these stories as hard, hopeless, brutal, etc" (HB, 275). In describing her work in this way, O'Connor is placing herself squarely in the Christian tradition, given that the scriptures teach that grace is the "new law" of the New Testament, replacing the more inflexible Old Testament law. Because of the flawed human condition, he is in desperate and constant need of grace. Indeed, for the most part, O'Connor equates the concept of "good" with the phenomenon of grace; in her view, it is only by grace that one is able to do what is good or to be good. St. Augustine reinforces her position when he asserts that without grace we "can do absolutely no good thing, whether in thought, or will and affection, or in action."[1]

Goodness, O'Connor believes, is the proper condition of the human soul, but this belief runs counter to the philosophical anthropology of the modern age, ever since Descartes dealt a mortal blow to the concept of the soul. The French philosopher divided the human being into an innovative but flawed dualism of mind and body that ignored the soul, so that its importance as the philosophical living principle of a human being faded by neglect. Walker Percy notes "the dread chasm that has rent the soul of Western man ever since the famous philosopher Descartes ripped body loose from mind and turned the very soul into a ghost that haunts its own house."[2]

O'Connor, therefore, vigorously employs all of her artistry to demonstrate that grace comes in order that one's soul might be healed. In her works, grace is "a tricky fictional agent" that, however subtly, intrudes upon the men and women of her literary world.[3] In her personal copy of his work, O'Connor has annotated Voegelin's observation that Christianity offers the possibility of the "formation of the human soul through grace."[4] Since the modern world, though, denies the existence of the human soul, it is not surprising that it sees no need for grace.[5] For that reason, O'Connor uses exaggerated language and imagery to wrench the attention of a world spiritually dull.

Scripture explains that grace is *poikileis,* meaning that it is "many-colored" or "diversified."[6] Indeed, grace comes in so many shapes, sizes, and expressions, that its operation is a true mystery. The Catholic Church, following St. Augustine and St. Thomas, tries various ways to explain the operation of grace. These explanations help one to appreciate just how rich is the phenomenon of grace, but they all fall short of truly explaining its nature. St. Thomas offers that grace is either "prevenient" grace, meaning it comes before, or "subsequent grace," meaning that it follows. Prevenient grace is that grace that initiates a work of self-knowledge, healing, or conversion in one's life; subsequent grace follows the initial event and takes the work to greater completeness.[7] The Catholic catechism divides grace into "habitual" grace and "intervening" grace. Habitual grace is the grace that is available continually; intervening grace is that which is given on especially needful occasions. St. Augustine, never as systematic as St. Thomas would be, is content to say that through the operation of merciful grace, God "anticipates us . . . that we may be healed; but then He will also follow us, that being healed we may grow healthy and strong. He anticipates us that we may be called; he will follow us that we may be glorified. He anticipates us that we may lead godly lives; He will follow us that we may always live with Him."[8]

O'Connor both illustrates these traditional ideas of the many-colored operation of grace in her fiction, and she also adds to the corpus of teaching on grace by illustrating imaginatively how it might operate. She felt that an arresting approach was essential given "the nature of the modern audience which is for the most part ignorant that there is such a thing as grace."[9] Grace is integral to Hazel Motes reversal from his willful self-destructive pursuit of nothingness. Even though Hazel has an inner instinct to do what is good and avoid evil—his "wise blood"— he needs grace to carry his quest to completion. The journey to this destination, however, is strewn with impediments, like Sabbath Hawks, who exposes the feebleness of Hazel's will and reason. Parker, in the short story "Parker's Back," also pursues a certain longing for God but he tries to satisfy that urge with tattoos. Aquinas might be commenting on both Haze and Parker when he explains, "Man therefore needs the divine assistance, lest with such impediments in his way, he fail altogether in the gaining of his last end."[10]

In "Revelation" the violent act of the deranged Mary Grace prompts Mrs. Turpin's lesson in humiliation, but subsequent grace occurs when Mrs. Turpin is resting in her bedroom. It appears again during her argument with God over the pigpen. In "Parker's Back," it is a kind of prevenient grace at work when Parker's tractor explodes against the tree and subsequent grace is active when his friends throw him from the pool hall as if he were Jonah cast from the ship in the storm. In "The Artificial Nigger" prevenient grace initially flows from the redemptive suffering symbolized by the pathetic statue. This grace humbles Mr. Head and then reconciles him with his grandson; subsequent grace is at work during the train ride home.

Through her literature, O'Connor also responds to the important question, "Is grace available to the non-believer?" O'Connor's answer is an emphatic "yes" and her belief is informed by her understanding of the phenomenon of "natural grace." She makes a distinction between "supernatural" and "natural" grace, explaining that natural grace must be depicted "the way it comes—through nature" (HB, 144). The availability of natural grace is a corollary of the existence of the natural law. It refers to a residue of grace, owing its existence to the Creator, which though divine in origin, is natural in its occurrence. Natural grace resides in every human soul. Like the natural law that provides man with the rudimentary instincts of right and wrong, natural grace provides a kind of assistance that facilitates the pursuit of the precepts of the natural law. It also affords man with occasional flashes of self-knowledge that he might otherwise never acquire. In O'Connor's stories, it is uncertain just where the dividing line occurs between natural grace and the more supernatural sanctifying grace since both are wrapped in mystery; thus, her uncertainty is a reflection of the theological imprecision inherent in any conception of grace. Where it begins and ends, and at what point natural grace is superseded by more direct divine action, seem impossible to pinpoint.[11]

Grace, for St. Augustine, "liberates and controls nature."[12] For Romano Guardini, there is an element of grace in creation, in "being." Indeed, he asks, "In what kind of world could this phenomenon not exist?" Such grace, suggested by scripture, points to

the "invisible being" of God which "from the creation of the world is clearly seen in His works and through the Spirit, namely, His eternal power and His divinity." (Rom. I 19-20)[13]

Pascal adds, "Grace will always be in the world, and nature also, so that the former is in some sort natural."[14] I referred in the introduction of this book to the horrible events of September 11, 2001. As terrible as those tragedies were, given the chance, O'Connor might also point to the extraordinary heroism and benevolence of that time as examples of natural grace, the occurrence of a level of goodness that transcended the ordinary character and inclinations of the men and women involved.

St. Augustine explains that the assistance of such grace by no means compromises man's freedom. Divine assistance is just that—*assistance*—provided to help a man toward his end, but such "aid . . . does not exclude the act of our will," rather, it facilitates its operation. Through the exercise of the free will, one still retains the right and the ability to cooperate with grace or to resist it.[15] Even more, Guardini explains that certain "atmospheres" can discourage the operation of grace, especially an atmosphere characterized by the unwarranted exercise of power. Such a state stultifies the free operation of natural grace.[16] Several of O'Connor's stories reflect Guardini's warning: for example, Mr. Fortune's preoccupation with Machiavellian-like control over his family delimits the possibility of grace, hence the story's tragic conclusion. Sheppard's attempt to willfully reform Johnson and force his own child to lay his grief aside and assume another identity constitutes a destructive obsession with the exercise of power. Mrs. McIntyre unlawfully controls Mr. Guizac's destiny and acquiesces in his death. She may also be complicit in the ruin of his niece by preventing her desperate marriage arrangement. As far as the reader knows, Mrs. McIntyre dies in misery, although Father Flynn's visits hold the possibility of eleventh-hour redemption. Guardini and O'Connor both echo, in their own way, the admonition from scripture, important enough to appear in the Bible in three separate instances: "God opposes the proud / but gives grace to the humble."[17] Shakespeare's Angelo suggests the lamentable state when grace is suppressed, and in doing so, he might as well have been predicting Mrs. McIntyre's fate. He observes, "Alack, when once our grace we have forgot, / Nothing goes right: we would, and we would not."[18]

The reader who understands O'Connor's message might be tempted to despair, seeing the difficult plight of modern man, but St. Thomas provides the assurance that the same grace that assists a man upon his return will lend him hope that the return is possible and thus overcome the hopelessness that might otherwise discourage him.[19] Even with this hope, though, ordinary virtue may not always be sufficient to keep one from evil; for that reason, grace is also an aid in the tenacious virtue of perseverance that fortifies one against discouragement.[20]

SELF-KNOWLEDGE

O'Connor's grace appears in her stories as interventions in everyday life, often through everyday means, that assist in the acquisition of the self-knowledge without which growth in virtue is impossible (CW, 817). As the learned essayist Michel de Montaigne confessed, "I would rather be an authority on myself than on Cicero."[21] In the same play cited above, Shakespeare admonishes, "Go to your bosom / Knock there, and ask your heart what it doth know."[22]

Although many of O'Connor's stories have a tragic or quasi-tragic ending, they are usually not without a glimmer of hope and this hope usually comes in the form of self-knowledge. The self-centered grandmother in the short story "A Good Man is Hard to Find" experiences a flash of compassionate self-understanding even though it was only a second or two before her death (CW, 152). Even after Calhoun and Hulga are ensnared by the spirit of nihilism with which they have dangerously trifled, both see a glimpse of redemptive grace. In "The Partridge Festival," Calhoun has a final fleeting vision that is suggestive of a divine presence, something that has been waiting patiently for him, "a face whose gift of life had pushed straight forward to the future to raise festival after festival. Like a master salesman, it seemed to have been waiting there from all time to claim him" (CW, 796). After her misfortune, Hulga looks out the hayloft window and sees Pointer "struggling successfully over the green speckled lake," as if he were walking on water, an event suggesting that she, having lost her supercilious pretension, has now been touched by the grace prompted by Pointer's abuse (CW, 283). Asbury, sick and supine on his bed because of his arrogance but now devoid of his self-deceptive sense of superiority, watches as "the Holy Ghost . . . continued, implacable, to descend" (CW, 572).

In placing such emphasis in her stories on the attainment of self-knowledge, O'Connor puts her finger on a most basic human impulse. For human beings, the need to know oneself—one's strengths, weaknesses, assets, and inadequacies—is an irrepressible and universal longing. This need is an impulse of the human soul, and even more, a sine qua non of maturity and an essential step in regaining intimacy with God himself. This is a lesson O'Connor seems to have been willing to apply to herself. Shortly before her death, she signed one of her cards from Piedmont Hospital "Mrs. Turpin," the O'Connor character who undergoes such a striking acquisition of self-knowledge, an experience whereby her arrogance is demolished by the grace that wrenches her from her self-righteousness. In identifying herself with Mrs. Turpin, O'Connor may have been admitting her own felt need for self-knowledge, a yearning perhaps made more intense by her physical distress and the experience of living so close to death.[23] She seems to have had her role as an artist in mind when she asserts, "Self-knowledge is a great curb to irresponsible self-expression, for to know oneself is, above all, to know what one lacks."[24] "Greenleaf" is one of

O'Connor's most violent accounts of the acquisition of self-knowledge and O'Connor speculated that she also might identify herself with the protagonist Mrs. May, whose self-knowledge is delivered with the goring of a bull (CW, 506).[25] Pascal observes that self-knowledge is the starting point from which we understand our place in the universe.

> Let man, returning to himself, consider what he is in comparison with what exists; let him regard himself as lost, and from this little dungeon, in which he finds himself lodged, I mean the universe, let him learn to take the earth, its realms, its cities, its houses and himself at their proper value.[26]

It may be that this aspiration for self-knowledge explains the presence each day of many thousands visiting the confessional, or frequenting its secular analog, the therapist's office.

Many critics have noted O'Connor's interest in depicting man's fallen state and need for grace. Less attention, though, has been given to her portrayal of the heroic. O'Connor's pantheon of heroes includes all of those who have responded positively to their opportunity for grace and there are many such heroes in her fiction. They include Haze Motes, Tarwater, Mr. Head, Mrs. Turpin, the Grandmother, Asbury, Parker, and Harry Ashfield, the spiritually hungry little boy in the short story "The River" who drowns himself in an attempt at self-baptism, looking for "the Kingdom of Christ" (CW, 170). Accordingly, O'Connor would agree with Walker Percy's warning that it is a grave sin indeed to disdain grace. The warning comes in *Love in the Ruins* when the protagonist's daughter, Samantha, before she dies, warns her father,

> "Just promise me one thing, Papa."
> "What's that?"
> "Don't commit the one sin for which there is no forgiveness."
> "Which one is that?"
> "The sin against grace."

Scripture offers a similar admonition when it warns the reader to "receive not the grace of God in vain."[27] These O'Connor heroes, however, may not resemble romantic or idealized models of the heroic. They more fit the pattern, described by W.B. Yeats in a poem O'Connor learned in school and was fond of quoting: her heroes are "wild beasts" who are "slouching toward Bethlehem to be born" (HB, 90).[28]

EVIL AND GRACE

While self-knowledge is the first step in human and spiritual development, O'Connor believes, as we have seen, that a man must also regain

knowledge of good and evil, and the apprehension of one concept de-
pends upon an understanding of the other. Aquinas teaches that God
himself does not separate the knowledge of good from the knowledge of
evil. He discusses this idea in the chapter of the *Summa Contra Gentiles* entitled "That God Knows Evil Things." The chapter begins, "When good is
known, the opposite evil is known;" and, since "God knows all particular
good things, to which evil things are opposed," then "God knows evil
things." Even God's knowledge of what is good would be incomplete
without a full appreciation of what is evil. Though the two concepts may
be contraries, they are mutually dependent, as man's desire for a more
perfect knowledge of good is linked to a more complete knowledge of
evil.[29] Now that we have eaten from the tree of good *and evil*, the apple
can't be put back on the branch, as much as we might wish to do so.

Since evil is the absence of good, good may be recognized best when it
is not there. Goodness may be appreciated fully only by its negation. If the
extent of the disease is not known or understood, it is unlikely that the
cure will be applied properly and so O'Connor shows in a variety of ways
that good is evil's remedy. O'Connor introduces her characters to goodness by means of grace, and that grace is most often prompted by evil. By
her own explanation, she is "interested in characters who are forced out
to meet evil and grace;" this requires them to act on "a trust beyond themselves—whether they know very clearly what it is they act upon or not"
(CW, 816). O'Connor elaborates, "I am interested in the indication of
Grace, the moment when you know that Grace has been offered and accepted. . . . These moments are prepared . . . by the intensity of the evil circumstances" (HB, 367-8). O'Connor would agree with St. Augustine when
he asserts, "There are . . . evils which are of use by the wondrous mercy of
God."[30] The deranged murderer Singleton in "The Partridge Festival" is
"a lecherous old nut" but by his obscene behavior he explodes "the young
people's absurd notions of him." He is, according to O'Connor, "one of
those devils who go about piercing pretensions" (HB, 443). In "The Artificial Nigger," the train that carries the pair to Atlanta is a necessary evil.
Hence, when Mr. Head and Nelson have returned from their trial in Atlanta, the train is rebuked back into submission. O'Connor writes that it
"disappeared like a frightened *serpent* into the woods" (CW, 231; emphasis added). O'Connor acknowledged the unpleasant means by which
grace intervenes in human life: "The reader wants his grace warm and
binding, not dark and disruptive" (CW, 862).

This explains even more fully why the acquisition of personal self-
knowledge may be so violent: it is often the presence of evil in its count-
less manifestations that is directly responsible for the unexpected and
unwelcome circumstances acting as the catalyst for seeing oneself in a
better light. Manley Pointer is one of the most malevolent characters in

O'Connor's literature, but it took his vulgar and violent act to expose Hulga's spiritual handicap. She has neglected her own spiritual well being to the extent that she instead cared for her artificial leg "as someone else would his soul" (CW, 281). Exactly how she responds to the intervention of grace wrapped in such a disturbing character is unknown; but the reader does know that she has lost her surrogate spirituality along with her leg.

In light of O'Connor's reliance on Thomas's teaching that evil is the privation of good, it is not difficult to see why the nihilistic flight from good and evil might degenerate into no more than a crude celebration of evil, as Jacques Maritain suggests in his essay highlighted in chapter 8. A syllogism explains the process: if evil is the absence of good, and if nihilism seeks to rid the world of traditional concepts of good, then *nihilism can only be defined as evil.* This is Dostoevsky's apparent conclusion, since it is the Devil himself who explains to Ivan Karamazov the sinister nature of the doctrine the young nihilist pursues.[31] O'Connor implies the slide from nihilism to evil in her short vignette "Why Do the Heathen Rage?" The story is about a stroke victim brought home by his family from the hospital. Despite the family's loss of its patriarch, the grown son refuses to take familial responsibility. O'Connor writes that Walter, the feckless young man, "courted good and evil impartially and saw so many sides of every question that he could not move." His mother concludes, "Any evil could enter that vacuum" (CW, 799). Guardini explains that a human being cannot sustain the "vacancy" hollowed out by the attempt to move beyond good and evil. Into this "no man's land . . . stalks another initiative, the demonic."[32]

THE DEVIL

Just as an understanding of good leads one ultimately to the knowledge of God, in a similar way, an appreciation of evil leads one to the reality of the Devil. O'Connor insists that a recovery of good and evil is impossible without belief in the Devil—not as an abstract metaphor, but as a person sophisticated enough to alter his strategy and appearance to fit the circumstance. She argues, "[W]e need a sense of evil which sees the devil as a real spirit who must be made to name himself, and not simply to name himself as vague evil, but to name himself with his specific personality for every occasion" (MM, 117). St. Thomas teaches that God is the "extrinsic principle" of "good," just as the Devil is the "extrinsic principle of evil." The definition of good and evil will be complete only with reference to those entities, God and the Devil, who are their agents.[33] O'Connor explains, "In my stories a reader will find that the devil accomplishes a good deal of groundwork that seems to be necessary before grace is effective" (MM, 117). She stated elsewhere that "the Devil teaches most of the lessons that lead to self knowledge" (HB, 439).

One of the most violent episodes in O'Connor's second novel *The Violent Bear It Away* occurs when the young Tarwater hitches a ride with a stranger. The driver drugs Tarwater and then rapes him, but the boy awakens determined to answer God's call on his life. O'Connor tried to explain to a reader why she had to include such a distasteful episode in the book. She conceded that she could sympathize with the "feeling of repulsion at the episode of Tarwater and the man in the lavender and cream-colored car." She continues, "It was a very necessary action to the meaning of the book, however, and one which I would not have used if I hadn't been obliged to." "The man who gives him the lift," she adds, "is the devil, and it takes this action of the devil's to make Tarwater see for the first time what evil is."

> He accepts the devil's liquor and he reaps what the devil has to give. Without this experience of evil, his acceptance of his vocation in the end would be merely a dishonest manipulation by me. Those who see and feel what the devil is turn to God. Tarwater learned the hard way but he has a hard head.[34]

In "The Lame Shall Enter First" among the many strategic advantages that Rufus holds over Sheppard is the latter's disbelief in the devil. In this tale, O'Connor progressively reveals the presence of the devil himself. In keeping with his pinched rationalism, Sheppard proposes to Rufus, "Maybe I can explain your devil to you" (CW, 601). But it is clear that Sheppard understands nothing about the devil. On several occasions, O'Connor describes Johnson in serpentine language; for example, his speech sounds like a "hiss" (CW, 624). The delinquent later warns a skeptical Sheppard, "The devil has you in his power." By the end of the story, Sheppard has become a believer. In the final lines of the story, the word "devil" is capitalized, turning the word from a generic designation to a proper name: "He saw the clear-eyed *Devil*, the sounder of hearts, leering at him from the eyes of Johnson" (CW, 632; emphasis added).

O'Connor, though, was well aware that in holding a literal belief in the devil, she was swimming against a tide of cynicism. Her character Mrs. McIntyre in "The Displaced Person" speaks for a world that not only disbelieves in the devil, but also ignores the question of his existence: "She had never given much thought to the devil for she felt that religion was essentially for those people who didn't have the brains to avoid evil without it" (CW, 294). O'Connor writes in an approving book review of *Evidence of*

Satan in the Modern World, by Léon Christiani, "It is ironical that in these evil times we should need fresh evidence of the existence of Satan, but such is the case because of his success in persuading us he does not exist." O'Connor adds that Christiani's book is useful reading because "the reader leaves this book with his belief in Satan considerably fortified."[35] She complains that "the modern reader is so far de-Christianized that he doesn't recognize the Devil when he sees him" (HB, 361). One reviewer of O'Connor's works notes that she believed that "to a world which does not yet accept the idea of the devil, she had better emphasize his allegorical appearance."[36] O'Connor thought it important to treat the devil allegorically as a strategy for proving his existence because, "The devil's greatest wile . . . is to convince us that he does not exist" (MM, 112). In *The Violent Bear It Away*, the devil approaches the young would-be prophet Tarwater in the guise of the unseen "stranger's" voice, tempting him to ignore his prophetic calling. He attempts to cloak himself in anonymity by quietly suggesting his nonexistence: "No no no, the stranger said, there ain't no such thing as a devil. I can tell you that from my own self-experience. I know that for a fact" (CW, 354).[37]

O'Connor believed both in the Devil as well as in the dominions over whom he exercises authority to carry out his subversion of virtue and piety. She wrote to a former classmate, "As to the devil, I not only believe he is but believe he has a family, which in the extent and scope of its activity, is a power to be reckoned with."[38] O'Connor once wrote to Betty Hester, "I am sure that an angelic world is no part of your belief but of course it is very much a part of mine" (HB, 128). In correspondence to John Hawkes on November 28, 1961, O'Connor, in sorting out a point of philosophical disagreement notes that between her and her correspondent, there is a "difference in our two devils." She continues,

> My Devil has a name, a history and a definite plan. His name is Lucifer, he's a fallen angel, his sin is pride, and his aim is the destruction of the Divine plan. Now I judge that your Devil is co-equal to God, not his creature; that pride is his virtue, not his sin; and that his aim is not to destroy the Divine plan because there isn't any Divine plan to destroy. My Devil is objective and yours is subjective. You say one becomes "evil" when one leaves the herd. I say that depends entirely on what the herd is doing.

O'Connor explains to Hawkes that his is a democratized conception of evil of the worst sort. For Hawkes, evil is a matter of public opinion, anchored in nothing more predictable or secure than the whims of the majority.

> The herd has been known to be right, in which case the one who leaves it is doing evil. When the herd is wrong, the one who leaves it is not doing evil but the right thing.

Never one to mince words, O'Connor suggests to Hawkes that he himself was guilty of such "herd mentality." She writes, "If I remember rightly, you put that word, evil, in quotation marks, which means the standards you judge it by there are relative; in fact you would be looking at it there with the eyes of the herd" (HB, 455).

O'Connor once wrote, "My subject in fiction is the action of grace in territory held largely by the devil" (MM, 118). Her motivation for so doing came from her opinion that "[m]ost of us have learned to become dispassionate about evil" (CW, 830). In O'Connor's view, not only has the wave of nihilism washed away the image of God, but it has also obliterated a genuine belief in the reality of Satan. Belief in both, however, is vital for navigation through the difficult waters of the modern age. Even though O'Connor followed the Thomistic teaching that evil has no substance of its own, she believed that the Devil, by contrast, is a concrete entity with will and purpose.

For O'Connor, then, the devil is neither a philosophical concept nor a metaphor for human misconduct. He is a being. Walker Percy's character Lancelot adds a startling corollary to O'Connor's belief in the devil and her worry over nihilism. He implies that although the modern world has busied itself putting God to death, nobody gave a thought to killing Satan, which means that if he does indeed exist, he may have freer hand than at any time in history.[39] Guardini notes that the nineteenth century, "self-confident in its unshaken faith in progress, ridiculed the figure of 'the demon' whom we shall name by his correct name, Satan." Yet, as he explains, individuals "capable of insight do not laugh" because they "know that he exists, and actively so." Guardini notes the irony of an age that prides itself on "realism" yet "fails to face up to the truth" about the devil.[40]

THE PROPHET

Flannery O'Connor was a young woman on a mission as well as an accomplished artist; she was equally interested in the moral and the aesthetic, writing not only to entertain, but also to persuade. She argued, "I don't think you should write something as long as a novel around anything that is not of the gravest concern to you and everybody else and for me this is always the conflict between an attraction for the Holy and the disbelief in it that we breathe in with the air of the times" (HB, 349).

O'Connor may have inadvertently referred to her own modest contributions in literature when she wrote, "What St. Thomas did for the new learning of the thirteenth century we are in bad need of some one to do for the twentieth" (HB, 306). Whereas Thomas's first audience had been the Church, O'Connor aims her message primarily at the un-churched, or at least the "under-churched." Her family acquaintances complained that she should write "something nice;" likewise, the visiting nuns who provided Sunday religious instruction at Sacred Heart Church in Milledgeville asked why she did not write on more pleasant or inspirational subjects, like the lives of the saints. O'Connor consistently responded that she wrote, most of all, for a pagan world divorced from a meaningful spiritual life, not for those who already enjoyed it. In her well-worn edition of St. Augustine's *Confessions*, she underlined a prayer in Book I, which reads, "deliver those too who call not on Thee yet, that they may call on Thee and Thou mayest deliver them."[41]

In an essay entitled "Novelist and Believer," O'Connor offers a spiritual taxonomy of the modern world in which unbelieving men and women fall into one of three categories. She first identifies the individual who sees "a spiritual dimension within himself but fails to recognize a being outside himself whom he can adore as Creator and Lord; consequently he has become his own ultimate concern." This man, O'Connor explains, says with the nineteenth-century British poet, Swinburne, "Glory to man in the highest, for he is the master of things" (MM, 159). The second man admits that God exists but he persists in a kind of lazy agnosticism because he chooses not to believe that a divine being can be known through scripture, Church doctrine, the experience of the Church sacraments, or even in meaningful literature. Such a man "wanders about in a maze of guilt he can't identify, trying to reach a God he can't approach, a God powerless to approach him" (MM, 159). These are the passive, aimless denizens of the modern world of whom T. S. Eliot prophesied: "We are the hollow men / We are the stuffed men / Leaning together / Headpiece filled with straw."[42]

O'Connor identifies yet a third category of modern men and women. These individuals, though unbelievers, cannot remain content in disbelief. They desperately search "in all experience for the lost God" (MM, 158). Walker Percy had such people in mind with his creation, Will Barrett, who though a millionaire, is profoundly unhappy with a life whose attractions consist of a lower golf handicap or opportunities for easy romance. Consequently, Barrett abandons his Mercedes, isolates himself in a woodland cave, and decides he will either wait for an answer to the question of God's existence or die in the attempt.[43] O'Connor seems especially interested in using her fiction to lead these "searchers and discoverers" to the place where she took Tarwater in *The Violent Bear It Away* when his hunger became so great "that he could have eaten all the loaves and fishes after they were multiplied" (CW, 478).

Mrs. Flood of *Wise Blood* speaks for O'Connor in describing the nihilistic forlornness of the modern world. She tells Haze Motes, "The world is a empty place" (CW, 128). Though her diagnosis of the state of modernity is indeed bleak and disturbing, O'Connor does not write as someone without hope. If she seems at times pessimistic, hers is what Guardini calls a "valid pessimism without which nothing great is ever achieved." It is a "bitter urging" that "enables the courageous heart and the creative spirit to persevere in all worthy ventures."[44] She would agree with Aquinas, that, "The diminution . . . of good by evil cannot go on indefinitely," even though it may appear that in "moral matters this diminution of good by evil may proceed to infinity." She would, however, further agree with Aquinas that the longer man persists in moral deviancy, the more difficult will be his return to his "proper and due end."[45]

Eric Voegelin's explanation of the role of the prophets of Israel and their relevance to today's threat of modern nihilism might apply just as well to Flannery O'Connor's role in Western society at the turn of the millennium. He explains that the prophets suffered with God "under the defection of Israel." They were spared "the intellectual confusion about the meaning of history," in the same way that the prophet today carries the knowledge that Nietzsche's claim to have murdered God is a "rebellious fantasy." Voegelin continues, "There are times when the divinely willed order is humanly realized nowhere but in the faith of solitary sufferers." Such "faith in the time of crisis" forces a prophet "to oppose the order of society," consoled by the knowledge that "[s]uffering in solitude [means] suffering, in communion with God, under the disorder of a community" in which the prophet retains his membership.[46] Surely O'Connor understood this kind of prophetic suffering when she described her character Tarwater as destined "to the torture of prophecy" (CW, 465). With O'Connor in mind, Walker Percy adds to Voegelin's observations an earthier but no less incisive observation of the prophet's role. The novelist as prophet "is like the canary that coal miners used to take down into the shaft to test the air. When the canary gets unhappy, utters plaintive cries, and collapses, it may be time for the miners to surface and think things over."[47] O'Connor owned several books by French novelist Georges Bernanos. The opening line of one could apply to her. It reads, "A prophet isn't really a prophet until after his death; until then he is not very frequently consulted." Bernanos notes that the modern world has "businessmen and policemen in abundance," what it needs to hear is the "liberating voice" of a prophet.[48]

At the age of seventeen, two years after the untimely death of her father to whom she was endeared, O'Connor wrote in her personal journal, employing the tough style that would characterize her later writing. She said, "The reality of death has come upon us and a consciousness of the power of God has broken our complacency like a bullet in the side." Yet, the trauma of her personal loss filled her not only with sorrow but also with awe for a God who cannot be managed or anticipated: "A sense of the dramatic, of the tragic, of the infinite, has descended upon us, filling us with grief, but even above grief, wonder." This episode in her life seems to have deepened her faith and intensified her reliance upon God as she concluded, "Our plans were so beautifully laid out, ready to be carried to action, but with magnificent certainty God laid them aside and said, "You have forgotten—mine?"[49]

Flannery O'Connor, then, does not challenge her readers with anything more than what she herself experienced, so that by fiction, prose, correspondence, and personal example she calls her readership to confront the nihilistic despair of the modern world by rededicating themselves to God's purpose for the human race—even in the most difficult of circumstances, personal tragedy. As Sally Fitzgerald notes, with whose family O'Connor lived from 1948 to 1949, the role of the prophet is to bear witness to vital, living truth by both words and example. She writes, "Flannery O'Connor defined the prophet as one whose function is not to foresee the future but to see into the depths of finite reality, of men and manners, to the spirit that enlivens then, and to bear witness to that insight, whether in utterance or in the life he leads."[50]

CONCLUSION

In O'Connor's view, modern's man active pursuit of nihilism, allegorically depicted in *Wise Blood*, has not occurred all at once. Rather, the seductive slide toward nihilism involves first the ancient and universal problem of human pride that can only be effectively countered with the self-knowledge borne of humility. O'Connor also indicts the impatience that overeducated pseudointellectuals have for flawed social conventions. This impatience with the human condition breeds a contempt for human weakness and an intolerance for the slow pace of meaningful social change. Such is the attitude of Asbury whose demand for the instant eradication of all social inequality leaves him physically disabled. O'Connor demolishes, moreover, the Enlightenment-inspired rationalism that falsely promises facile solutions to intractable human nature, solutions that may be doomed to do more harm than good because they are constructed out of the thin gossamer-like fabric of unproven, abstract theory woven in a crassly materialistic world. This is a world in which a self-styled therapist like Sheppard denies the essence of human life, the human soul, and thus brings disaster on himself and those he loves. As O'Connor argues in "Good Country People," such misleading rationalism finds its genesis in Descartes's violent separation of faith and reason.

The descent into nihilism is hastened when man at his most hubristic tries to conquer the unconquerable: the mystery of human existence, rendered most "mysterious" when human suffering is involved. This is the great sin of the grandfather in "A View of the Woods" who destroys the one he most loves by trying to solve the mystery of her suffering through nothing more than the reckless and ill-considered assertion of his own will over her life and circumstances. His is the attempt to exercise a kind of backwoods "will to power," that admits no limitations, recognizes no principles, and most crucially, sees no need for the caution that would curb his destructive overconfidence.

The complete response to nihilism must point to the human need for redemption, as O'Connor so beautifully illustrates in "The Artificial Nigger." Man's state is such that neither compassion nor intellectual self-confidence is sufficient to provide him stable grounding in a precarious world. Accepting such a diagnosis, however, requires an attitude of humility, and O'Connor believes that those unwilling or unable to adopt such a posture may require the humiliating intervention of violent grace, as did Mr. Head and so many of the odd citizens who populate her fictional world.

Although in her stories O'Connor regularly satirizes condescending and presumptuous characters, her sharpest response to Nietzsche's elitist aspirations of the overman is her character Enoch. With the creation of this odd moronic character, who does not fail to leave the reader bemused, O'Connor argues that nihilism will produce, not superior human beings, but men who regress to the more bestial part of their nature.

Indeed, O'Connor calls Nietzsche's bluff. Nietzsche argues that if we are willing to destroy, we will then be free to create. His nihilism, as Stanley Rosen argues, "is fundamentally an attempt to overcome or to repudiate the past on behalf of an unknown and unknowable yet hoped-for future."[51] O'Connor believes that if we destroy, we will be left with nothing more than the consequence of our destruction since no one but God is capable of *creatio ex nihilo*.[52] This is especially clear in *Wise Blood* where the nihilist "evangelist" discovers that there is *nothing* beyond good and evil once he has preached his sacrilegious doctrine of "The Church of Jesus Christ Without Christ." Nothing exists beyond the destruction, nothing beyond the "nothingness." In T. S. Eliot's play "The Rock," the Chorus explains, "In all of my years, one thing does not change. However you disguise it, this thing does not change: / The perpetual struggle of Good and Evil."[53]

Francois Mauriac observed, in a volume found in O'Connor's library, "Modern man has cut off communication with God by a basic negation."[54] Nihilism's path has been prepared by groundless rationalism, vaunting hubris, neglect of grace, ignorance of evil, and disbelief in the Devil. Instead of creating a better man who lives beyond good and evil, nihilism has caused a spiritual, moral, and intellectual regression that has produced, not an "overman," but a generation of Enochs who have traded their rich spiritual and cultural heritage for a pathetic "new jesus." To undo this reverse evolution, O'Connor argues that novelist and believer alike must regain "a distrust of the abstract, a respect for boundaries, [and] a desire to penetrate the surface of reality and to find in each thing the spirit which makes it itself and holds the world together" (MM, 168). This means arresting the flight from God, recognizing the limitations inherent in the human condition, and reacquiring reverence for the unfathomable mystery of the Infinite. In doing so, O'Connor hopes with Aquinas that man may yet reacquire the understanding that his "last end is the uncreated good, namely, God, Who alone by His infinite goodness can perfectly satisfy man's will."[55]

Endnotes

NOTES TO CHAPTER 1

1. The President's speech to Congress and the nation was delivered on September 13, 2001. The excerpt of the speech in which the phrase occurs is copied below:

> These terrorists kill not merely to end lives but to disrupt and end a way of life. With every atrocity they hope that America grows fearful, retreating from the world and forsaking our friends. They stand against us because we stand in their way. We're not deceived by their pretenses to piety. We have seen their kind before. They are the heirs of all the murderous ideologies of the 20th century. By sacrificing human life to serve their radical visions, by abandoning every value except the will to power, they follow in the path of fascism, Nazism and totalitarianism. And they will follow that path all the way to where it ends: in history's unmarked grave of discarded lies.

2. Friedrich Nietzsche, *Beyond Good and Evil*, Walter Kaufmann, trans. (New York: Vintage Books, 1966).

3. "Aquinas and Nietzsche," a Paper read to the Aquinas Society of London on April 15, 1944 (London: Blackfriars, 1955), pp. 10, 11.

4. "Break on Through (To the Other Side)," written and composed by Jim Morrison, John Densmore, Ray Manzarek, and Robbie Kieger. Copyright © 1970 by Doors Music Company, ASCAP.

5. Marion Montgomery, *Why Flannery O'Connor Stayed Home* (La Sale, Ill.: Sherwood Sugden, 1981), p. 216.

6. Walker Percy, *Lancelot* (New York: Farrar, Straus and Giroux, 1977), p. 138.

7. 1 Cor. 13:12 (King James Version).

8. St. John of the Cross, *The Collected Works of St. John of the Cross*. Kieran Kavanaugh, O.C.D., and Otilio Rodriguez, O.C.D., trans. (Washington, D.C.: Institute of Carmelite Studies, 1991), p. 137.

9. Reported by Robert Giroux in his introduction to O'Connor's *The Complete Stories* (New York: Farrar, Strauss and Giroux, 1971), p. xv.

10. Flannery O'Connor, "The Catholic Novelist in the South," in *Collected Works* (New York: Literary Classics of the United States, 1988), p. 853.

11. Joseph Conrad, "Preface," *The Nigger of the Narcissus*, Robert Kimbrough, ed. (New York: W. W. Norton, 1979), 145–8.

12. Review of *Sister Clare*, by Loreta Burrough, in *The Bulletin*, April 16, 1960, in *Flannery O'Connor: Her Life, Library and Book Reviews*, Lorine M. Getz, ed. (New York: Edwin Mellen Press, 1980), p. 149.

13. Aristotle, *The Poetics*, James Hutton, trans. (New York: W. W. Norton, 1982).

14. Public address to Georgia State College for Women. No date supplied. In correspondence, given to Rebeka Poller February 1957, pp. 8–9.

15. In her copy of the *Summa*, O'Connor has annotated the section that associates prophecy with the imagination. It is Question 12, Article 11, "Reply Obj," *Introduction to St. Thomas Aquinas*, Anton C. Pegis, ed. (New York: Modern Library, 1948), p. 92. She also owned a three volume edition of *De veritate* and she seems to have had in mind Article IV, "Is Some Natural Disposition Needed For Prophecy," "Answers to Difficulties," Art. 2, St. Thomas Aquinas, *Truth* (Chicago: Henry Regnery, 1953), p. 127.

16. Sarah Gordon, "Maryat and Julian and the 'not so bloodless revolution,'" *Flannery O'Connor Review* (volume 21, 1992), pp. 25–36.

17. Maryat Lee, "Flannery, 1957," *The Flannery O'Connor Bulletin*, 5 (autumn, 1976), p. 49.

18. "Review of *The Phenomenon of Man*," by P. Teilhard de Chardin, in *The American Scholar*, fall, 1961, in *Flannery O'Connor: Her Life, Library and Book Reviews*, Lorine M. Getz (New York: Edwin Mellen Press, 1980), p. 149.

19. With this sentiment in mind, Henry King Stanford wrote to thank O'Connor for her appearance at his university, Birmingham-Southern, on November 25, 1958. He quipped, "All of us here are grateful to you for taking time out to speak to our students and budding (?) writers. You may have done literature a great service if you nipped some of them in the bud" (December 5, 1958).

20. (New York: Meridian Books, 1955), p. 126.

21. Flannery O'Connor, "Some Aspects of the Grotesque in Southern Fiction," in *Flannery O'Connor: Collected Works* (New York: Library of America, 1988), p. 814.

22. O'Connor, "Some Aspects of the Grotesque," p. 819.

23. Flannery O'Connor, Review of *Sister Clare*, by Loreta Burrough, in *The Bulletin*, April 16, 1960, in *Flannery O'Connor: Her Life, Library and Book Reviews*, Lorine M. Getz, ed. (New York: Edwin Mellen Press, 1980), p. 149.

24. G. K. Chesterton, *Orthodoxy* (Westport, Conn.: Greenwood Press, 1974), p. 293.

25. Blaise Pascal, *Pensées and the Provincial Letters*, W. F. Trotter and Thomas M'Crie, trans. (New York: Modern Library, 1941), No. 397, No. 139.

26. To Mr. Billy Koon, December, 15, 1962, from Milledgeville.

27. *The Correspondence of Flannery O'Connor and the Brainard Cheneys*, C. Ralph Stephens, ed. (Jackson: University Press of Mississippi, 1986), p. 6.

28. Maryat Lee, "Flannery, 1957," *The Flannery O'Connor Bulletin* 5 (autumn, 1976), p. 54.

29. Walker Percy, *Conversations with Walker Percy*, Lewis A. Lawson and Victor A. Kramer, eds. (Jackson: University Press of Mississippi, 1985), p. 214.

30. Walker Percy, *The Message in the Bottle* (New York: Farrar, Straus & Giroux, 1954), p. 118.

31. "Visit to Flannery O'Connor Proves a Novel Experience," Margaret Turner/May 1960, From the *Atlanta Journal and Constitution*, 29 May 1960, sec. G, 2, in *Conversations with Flannery O'Connor*, Rosemary M. Magee, ed. (Jackson: University Press of Mississippi, 1987), pp. 41–43.

32. To Shirley Abbott Tomkieviez, May 3, 1956, from Milledgeville.

33. *Flannery O'Connor: Her Life, Library and Book Reviews*, Lorine M. Getz, ed. (New York: Edwin Mellen Press, 1980), pp. 8–9.

34. Address to Georgia State College for Women. No date supplied. In Correspondence, given to Rebeka Poller, February 1957, pp. 5, 8–9.

35. To Maryat Lee, Wednesday, 1958 (no month supplied), from Milledgeville.

36. "Such Nice People," *Time* 6 (June 1955): 114. Review not signed.

37. Matt. 6:22–23 (New International Version).

38. "Six Unpublished Letters of Flannery O'Connor," in *The Flannery O'Connor Bulletin*, with commentary by James F. Farnham, 12 (autumn 1983), p. 62.

NOTES TO CHAPTER 2

1. Nietzsche's notorious statement may be found, e.g., at Friedrich Nietzsche, *The Gay Science* (New York: Vintage Books, 1974), pp. 167, 181; *Thus Spake Zarathustra*, in *The Portable Nietzsche*, Walter Kaufmann, trans. (Middlesex, G.B.: Penguin Books, 1954), p. 124.

2. To Shirley Abbott Tomkieviez, March 17, 1956, from Milledgeville.

3. Eric Voegelin, *Plato and Aristotle: Volume Three, Order and History* (Baton Rouge: Louisiana State University Press, 1957), p. 188.

4. John Herman Randall Jr., *The Making of the Modern Mind: A Survey of the Intellectual Background of the Present Age* (Boston: Houghton Mifflin, 1926), pp. 563–4. My thanks to Lamonica Jenkins Sanford at GC & SU for her assistance in obtaining this information from Flannery O'Connor's school records.

5. Randall, *The Making of the Modern Mind*, pp. 563–4.

6. Flannery O'Connor, *The Presence of Grace and Other Book Reviews*, compiled by Leo J. Zuber, Carter W. Martin, ed. (Athens: University of Georgia Press, 1983), p. 168.

7. Gerhart Niemeyer, *Between Nothingness and Paradise* (South Bend, Ind.: St. Augustine's Press, 1998), pp. viii, 221.

8. Randall, *The Making of the Modern Mind*, p. xx.

9. Friedrich Nietzsche, *Human, All-Too-Human*, in *The Portable Nietzsche*, Walter Kaufmann, trans. (Middlesex, G.B.: Penguin Books, 1954), p. 52.

10. Friedrich Nietzsche, *Beyond Good and Evil: Prelude to a Philosophy of the Future*, Walter Kaufmann, trans. (New York: Vintage Books, 1966), p. 60.

11. Friedrich Nietzsche, *The Gay Science*, Walter Kaufman, trans. (New York: Vintage Books, 1974), pp. 184, 187.

12. Friedrich Nietzsche, *The Antichrist*, in *The Portable Nietzsche*, Walter Kaufmann, trans. (Middlesex, G.B.: Penguin Books, 1954), p. 585.

13. Randall, *The Making of the Modern Mind*, pp. 586, 584.

14. Nietzsche, *Zarathustra*, p. 143.

15. Nietzsche, *Zarathustra*, p. 144.

16. Nietzsche, *Zarathustra*, p. 14.

17. Nietzsche, *Zarathustra*, p. 146.

18. Nietzsche, *Zarathustra*, p. 188.

19. Nietzsche, *Zarathustra*, pp. 435, 436. Also see, Nietzsche, *Beyond Good and Evil*, p. 68.

20. Frederick Copleston, S.J., *A History of Philosophy, Volume VII, Modern Philosophy: From the Post-Kantian Idealists to Marx Kierkegaard, and Nietzsche* (New York: Doubleday, 1994, first published in 1965), p. 393.

21. Copleston, *History*, p. 395.

22. Nietzsche, *Zarathustra*, pp. 309, 304.

23. Nietzsche, *Zarathustra*, pp. 124, 158.

24. Nietzsche, *Zarathustra*, pp. 135–6.

25. Nietzsche, *Zarathustra*, p. 135.

26. Nietzsche, *Zarathustra*, p. 141; also see Nietzsche, *Beyond Good and Evil*, pp. 115, 118.

27. Nietzsche, *Zarathustra*, pp. 398, 164, 302.

28. Nietzsche, *Zarathustra*, p. 171; *Twilight of the Idols*, p. 563; *Zarathustra*, p. 313; all in *The Portable Nietzsche*.

29. Nietzsche, *Beyond Good and Evil*, pp. 9–31.

30. Friedrich Nietzsche, *The Birth of Tragedy and the Case of Wagner* (New York: Vintage Books, 1967).

31. Aristotle, *The Poetics*, James Hutton, trans. (New York: W. W. Norton, 1982).

32. Nietzsche, *Birth of Tragedy*, pp. 67–71, 24. Passages such as these make it easy to understand why Nietzsche was later embarrassed by the style of this book; however, his regret does not extend to the doctrine he promotes, only the "saccharine to the point of effeminacy" character of certain sections of his prose. See "Attempt at Self-Criticism," p. 19.

33. *Euripides V*, David Grene and Richmond Lattimore, eds., *The Bacchae*, William Arrowsmith, trans. (Chicago: University of Chicago Press, 1959), Line 653, 776; "Introduction to *The Bacchae*," p. 145. I should acknowledge that in *The Birth of Tragedy*, Nietzsche disapproves of several of the elements of Euripides' portrayal of Dionysus, e.g., the god's effeminate appearance, as well as the Euripides atypical use of the Chorus, who serve, not as a kind of dramatic conscience, but as Dionysus's sycophants.

34. Nietzsche, Friedrich, *The Birth of Tragedy*, p. 124.

35. Nietzsche, *Birth of Tragedy*, pp. 70–71.

36. Nietzsche, *Twilight of the Idols*, pp. 561–2.

37. Nietzsche, *Zarathustra*, p. 300, pp. 156–7, 167.

38. Copleston, *History*, p. 397.

39. Nietzsche, *The Gay Science*, p. 244.

40. Nietzsche, *Zarathustra*, p. 199.

41. Nietzsche, *Gay Science*, p. 219.

42. Nietzsche, *Twilight of the Idols*, p. 530.

43. Aristotle also influences anyone influenced by Aquinas, given that much of Aquinas' work is his attempt to integrate the Greek philosopher's thought with Christian theology. When her health began to decline, O'Connor was advised by her physician to use crutches in an attempt to stop the degeneration of her hip. She wryly noted, "I am learning to walk on crutches and I feel like a large stiff anthropoid ape who has no cause to be thinking of St Thomas or Aristotle" (HB, 104).

44. *The Correspondence of Flannery O'Connor and the Brainard Cheneys*, C. Ralph Stephens, ed. (Jackson: University Press of Mississippi, 1986), p. 52.

45. O'Connor apparently did most of her reading in St. Thomas from the *Introduction to St. Thomas Aquinas*, Anton C. Pegis, ed. (New York: Modern Library, 1948). The dust jacket reads, "The essence of the *Summa Theologica* and the *Summa Contra Gentiles* in a volume of more than 700 pages." The book is a thorough compilation of St. Thomas' work, including his treatises on "God," "Creation," "Man," "The End of Man," "Human Acts," "Habits and Virtues," "Law," and "Grace."

46. Stanley Rosen, *Nihilism: A Philosophical Essay* (New Haven, Conn.: Yale University Press, 1969), p. xiv.

47. Eric Voegelin, *The World of the Polis: Volume Two, Order and History* (Baton Rouge: Louisiana State University, 1957), p. 281.

48. G. K. Chesterton, *Orthodoxy* (Westport, Conn.: Greenwood Press, 1974), p. 32.

49. "A Paper read to the Aquinas Society of London on April 15th, 1944," (London: Blackfriars, 1955). I was gratified to find this article in O'Connor's collection, especially as the discovery was made late in this project after the general thesis was set and the bulk of the book written. It is difficult to imagine that O'Connor would have stumbled across an article such as this one. It is much more likely that it was deliberately given to her by a colleague, or even more probable, that she ordered this reprint herself. I later learned that before my own special interest in the Copleston lecture, Marion Montgomery had earlier found Copleston's article noteworthy, as he explains in *Why Flannery O'Connor Stayed at Home* (La Salle, Ill.: Sherwood Sugden, 1981).

50. Copleston, "Aquinas and Nietzsche," p. 5.

51. Copleston, "Aquinas and Nietzsche," pp. 6–7.

52. Copleston, "Aquinas and Nietzsche," p. 8.

53. Address to Georgia State College for Women. No date supplied. In Correspondence, given to Rebeka Poller, February 1957, pp. 8–9.

54. Aquinas, *Contra Gentiles*, 3:11, "That Evil is Founded in Some Good."

55. Nietzsche, *Zarathustra*, p. 170.

56. Nietzsche, *Zarathustra*, p. 171.

57. Nietzsche, *Zarathustra*, p. 171.

58. Nietzsche, *Zarathustra*, p. 400.

59. Nietzsche, *Zarathustra*, p. 304.

60. Gerhart Niemeyer, *Between Nothingness and Paradise* (South Bend, Ind.: St. Augustine's Press, 1998), pp. 16, 19.

NOTES TO CHAPTER 3

1. To be sure, O'Connor explicitly likens two of her other characters to Jonah as well, Tarwater (CW, 462) and Parker (CW, 672). Although I am not aware of such an explicit reference linking Hazel Motes to Jonah, he is cast in a similar role. It is worth noting Romano Guardini's proposal that at the end of the modern age the Old Testament will take on a new significance (Romano Guardini, *The End of the Modern World* [Wilmington, Del.: ISI Books, 1998], pp. 107–8).

2. Eric Voegelin, *The Ecumenic Age: Volume Four, Order and History* (Baton Rouge: Louisiana State University Press, 1974), p. 6.

3. Brainard Cheney's Review of Flannery O'Connor's *Wise Blood*, in *Shenandoah*, 3 (autumn, 1952), Appendix A, *The Correspondence of Flannery O'Connor and the Brainard Cheneys*, C. Ralph Stephens, ed. (Jackson: University Press of Mississippi, 1986), pp. 195–7.

4. Fyodor Dostoyevsky, *The Brothers Karamazov* (London: Penguin Books, 1993, first published in 1880), p. 616.

5. St. Thomas Aquinas, *Summa Theologica* (Westminster, Md.: Christian Classics, 1981), I-II, qu. 94, a. 2.

6. Aquinas, *Summa Theologica*, I-II, qu. 4, a. 2; qu. 8, a. 1.

7. Variously ascribed to Chesterton, St. Francis, and St. Augustine, the only documented source of this quotation is the book *The World, The Flesh, and Father Smith* by Bruce Marshall (Boston: Houghton Mifflin, 1945), p. 108 (www.chesterton.org/qmeister2/questions.htm).

8. My thanks to Gregory R. Johnson for offering this insight at a Liberty Fund colloquium entitled "Liberty, Responsibility, and the Human Condition," Mulberry Inn, Savannah, Ga., 9–12, 2000. Also see MM, 72.

9. To Robie McCauley, January 2, 1961, from Milledgeville.

10. Although O'Connor disapproved of the cover of the first British paperback edition of *Wise Blood*, the image on the cover did seem to capture the seductive role that Sabbath plays. As O'Connor described it, "Sabbath is thereon turned into Marilyn Monroe in underclothes" (HB, 408).

11. Frederick Copleston, S.J., *A History of Philosophy, Volume VII, Modern Philosophy: From the Post-Kantian Idealists to Marx Kierkegaard, and Nietzsche* (New York: Doubleday, 1994, First published in 1965), pp. 15–16.

12. Copleston, *History*, pp. 15–16.

13. *Thus Spake Zarathustra*, in *The Portable Nietzsche*, Walter Kaufmann, trans. (Middlesex, G.B.: Penguin Books, 1954), pp. 124, 126.

14. We should note here that, immediately before she consummated Haze's seduction, Sabbath Hawks slid into bed with him and said, "Take off your hat, *king of the beasts*" (CW, 96; emphasis added).

15. John Herman Randall Jr., *The Making of the Modern Mind: A Survey of the Intellectual Background of the Present Age* (Boston: Houghton Mifflin, 1926), pp. 584, 585–6.

16. John 20:7 (New Revised Standard Version).

17. Genesis 5:22–24. There is another Enoch in Genesis 4:17, 18, who built a city after his own name. Because of his parentage, this Enoch is not only an obscure figure, but also has a more dubious legacy. I think that in *Wise Blood*, O'Connor must have the other Enoch in mind, whose memory is celebrated in Hebrews, chapter 11, v. 5.

18. The association between Enoch and Nietzsche's overman has also been noted by Marion Montgomery: see *Why Flannery O'Connor Stayed at Home* (La Salle, Ill.: Sherwood Sugden, 1981), pp. 394–5.

19. O'Connor is quoting Robert Fitzgerald.

20. St. Thomas Aquinas, *Summa Contra Gentiles*, 1:60, "That God is Truth" (John 14:6). Also see 1:61, "That God is pure Truth," and 1:62, "The Truth of God is the First and Sovereign Truth." www.nd.edu/Departments/Maritain/etext/gc.htm.

21. Eric Voegelin, *Israel and Revelation: Volume One, Order and History* (Baton Rouge: Louisiana State University Press, 1956), xiv.

22. "On Truth and Lie in an Extra-Moral Sense," in *The Portable Nietzsche*, Walter Kaufmann, trans. (New York: Penguin Books, 1954), pp. 46–6.

23. Copleston, *History*, p. 18.

24. Blaise Pascal, *Pensées and the Provincial Letters*, W. F. Trotter and Thomas M'Crie, trans. (New York: Modern Library, 1941), No. 200.

25. Aquinas, *Summa Theologica*, I, qu. 79; qu. 19, a. 5, 6.

26. Hannah Arendt, *Eichmann in Jerusalem: A Report on the Banality of Evil* (New York: Penguin Books, 1994, first published in 1963), pp. 105, 163.

27. Arendt, *Eichmann*, p. 150.

NOTES TO CHAPTER 4

1. First reported in Robert Giroux's letter to Flannery O'Connor of April 28, 1952, no location provided.

2. Robert Giroux to Flannery O'Connor, May 10, 1951, no location provided.

3. Reported in Marion Montgomery, *The Flannery O'Connor Bulletin* 9 (autumn, 1980), p. 25.

4. Matt. 7:4 (King James Version).

5. Randall, *Modern Mind*, p. 586.

6. *The Correspondence of Flannery O'Connor and the Brainard Cheneys*, C. Ralph Stephens, ed. (Jackson: University Press of Mississippi, 1986), p. 3.

7. Nietzsche, *Zarathustra*, in *The Portable Nietzsche*, p. 188.

8. Aristotle, *The Politics*, Carnes Lord, trans. (Chicago: University of Chicago Press, 1984), Book 8.

9. Eric Voegelin, *Plato and Aristotle: Volume Three, Order and History* (Baton Rouge: Louisiana State University Press, 1957), p. 355.

10. Josef Pieper, *Leisure, The Basis of Culture*, Alexander Dru, trans. (New York: A Mentor Book, 1952); Neil Postman, *Amusing Ourselves to Death* (New York: Viking Press, 1986).

11. Blaise Pascal, *Pensées and the Provincial Letters*, W. F. Trotter and Thomas M'Crie, trans. (New York: Modern Library, 1941), Nos. 139, 142.

12. Pieper, *Leisure*, p. 41.

13. Jacques Maritain, *Reflections on America* (Garden City, N.Y.: Image Books, 1964), pp. 89–91.

14. Nietzsche once noted the Christian admonition, "'If thy eye offend thee, pluck it out,'" and then argued, "Fortunately, no Christian acts in accordance with this precept." O'Connor's Hazel Motes is her literary response to Nietzsche's challenge. *Zarathustra*, p. 486.

15. St. Thomas Aquinas, *Summa Contra Gentiles*, 3:37, "That the Final Happiness of Man consists in the Contemplation of God." www.nd.edu/Departments/Maritain/etext/gc.htm.

16. St. Thomas Aquinas, *Summa Theologica* (Westminster, Md.: Christian Classics, 1981), III, qu. 3, a. 5.

17. To Dr. George Beiswanger, August 22, 1952, no location provided.

18. St. John of the Cross, *The Collected Works of St. John of the Cross*, Kieran Kavanaugh, O.C.D., and Otilio Rodriguez, O.C.D. (Washington, D.C.: Institute of Carmelite Studies, 1991), p. 27.

19. Flannery O'Connor, *The Presence of Grace and Other Book Reviews*, compiled by Leo J. Zuber, Carter W. Martin, ed. (Athens: University of Georgia Press, 1983), p. 28.

20. The other woman was Simone Weil. Stein's study on St. John's *The Science of the Cross* is in O'Connor's personal library.

21. Flannery O'Connor, *The Presence of Grace and Other Book Reviews*, compiled by Leo J. Zuber, Carter W. Martin, ed. (Athens: University of Georgia Press, 1983), p. 97.

22. St. John of the Cross, *The Collected Works*, Kieran Kavanaugh, O.C.D., trans. (Washington, D.C.: ICS Publications, 1991), stanza 1, p. 113.

23. St. John of the Cross, *Collected Works*, p. 119.

24. St. John of the Cross, *Collected Works*, p. 113.

25. St. John of the Cross, *Collected Works*, p. 119.

26. St. John of the Cross, *Collected Works*, pp. 136, 134.

27. St. John of the Cross, *Collected Works*, p. 137.

28. St. John of the Cross, *Collected Works*, p. 158.

29. St. John of the Cross, *Collected Works*, p. 159.

30. St. John of the Cross, *Collected Works*, p. 70.

31. St. John of the Cross, *Collected Works*, p. 131.

32. T. S. Eliot, *The Complete Poems and Plays, 1909–1950* (New York: Harcourt, Brace & World, 1971), p. 4.

33. Flannery O'Connor, *The Presence of Grace and Other Book Reviews*, compiled by Leo J. Zuber, Carter W. Martin, ed. (Athens: University of Georgia Press, 1983), pp. 52, 85.

34. Romano Guardini, *The Lord* (Washington, D.C.: Regnery Publishers, 1996, originally published in 1952), p. 609.

NOTES TO CHAPTER 5

1. From Robert Giroux, March 3, 1955, no location provided.
2. See Edith Hamilton, *Mythology* (Boston: Little, Brown, 1998, first published in 1942), pp. 34, 36–37.
3. From Allen Tate, February 22, 1955, no location provided.
4. Prov. 6:27, 28 (New International Version).
5. Walker Percy, *More Conversations with Walker Percy*, Lewis A. Lawson and Victor A. Kramer, eds. (Jackson: University Press of Mississippi, 1993), p. 224.
6. Fyodor Dostoyevsky, *The Brothers Karamazov* (London: Penguin Books, 1993, first published in 1880), p. 741.
7. Dostoyevsky, *The Brothers Karamazov*, p. 749.
8. Dostoyevsky, *The Brothers Karamazov*, pp. 749–50.
9. George Bernard Shaw, *Man and Superman* (New York: Bretano's, 1928), p. 13.
10. Shaw, *Man and Superman*, p. 107.
11. Shaw, *Man and Superman*, pp. 219, 177–244. Tanner later exclaims, "If there's no harm in it there's no point in doing it" (p. 60).
12. Nietzsche, *Zarathustra*, p. 200.
13. St. Thomas Aquinas, *Summa Theologica* (Westminster, Md.: Christian Classics, 1981), II- II, qu. 144, a. 1–2.
14. Aquinas, *Summa Theologica*, II-II, qu. 160.
15. Aquinas, *Summa Theologica*, II-II, qu. 160, a. 1, 2; qu. 161, a. 4; qu. 162.
16. C. S. Lewis, *The Problem of Pain* (New York: The Macmillan Company, 1962), p. 57.
17. Eric Voegelin, *The World of the Polis: Volume Two, Order and History* (Baton Rouge: Louisiana State University Press, 1957), pp. 157–8.
18. Percy, *More Conversations*, p. 160. Also see Stanley Rosen, *Nihilism: A Philosophical Essay* (New Haven, Conn.: Yale University Press, 1969), in which the progression from Descartes to Nietzsche is argued thoroughly. William Sessions told me that he once lent O'Connor his copy of *The Dream of Descartes* by Jacques Maritain, the thesis of which is consistent with the argument made here (Mabelle L. Andison, trans. [New York: Philosophical Library, 1944]).
19. John Herman Randall Jr., *The Making of the Modern Mind: A Survey of the Intellectual Background of the Present Age* (Boston: Houghton Mifflin Company, 1926), p. 240ff.
20. René Descartes, *Discourse on the Method for Rightly Conducting One's Reason and for Seeking Truth in the Sciences*, Donald A. Cress, trans. (Indianalopolis: Hackett Publishing, 1980, originally published in 1637), pp. 4, 7, 5.
21. Randall, *Modern Mind*, pp. 224, 220.
22. Randall, *Modern Mind*, pp. 241–242.
23. Randall, *Modern Mind*, p. 244.
24. Descartes, *Discourse*, p. 17.
25. Randall, *Modern Mind*, p. 286.

26. Descartes, *Discourse*, p. 12.

27. Flannery O'Connor, *The Presence of Grace and Other Book Reviews*, Leo J. Zuber, ed. Review of *The Range of Reason*, in *The Bulletin*, November 25, 1961 (Athens: University of Georgia Press, 1983), p. 124.

28. T. S. Eliot, "The Hollow Men," in *The Complete Poems and Plays, 1909–1950* (New York: Harcourt, Brace & World, 1971), p. 58. In respect to O'Connor's interest in Eliot, she wrote her former classmate Betty Boyd Love from the hospital, "I have been reading Murder in the Cathedral and the nurses thus conclude I am a mystery fan. It's a marvelous play if you don't know it, better if you do" (HB, 23).

29. George Bernard Shaw, *Man and Superman: A Comedy and A Philosophy* (London: Penguin Books, 2000) p. 245.

30. Martin Heidegger, *Existence and Being* (Chicago: Henry Regnery, 1949), p. 359; "What is Metaphysics?" R. F. C. Hull and Alan Crick, trans., pp. 355–92.

31. Heidegger, "What is Metaphysics," p. 380.

32. Heidegger, "What is Metaphysics," pp. 361, 366.

33. Heidegger, "What is Metaphysics," p. 361.

34. Aquinas, *Summa Theologica*, I-II, qus. 1–5.

35. The individual designated as "A" in O'Connor's collected correspondence was later identified as Betty Hester who lived in Atlanta, Georgia.

36. I am appreciative of the opportunity to have spoken with the late "Uncle George" Haslam about O'Connor. Haslam was an instructor in Journalism during O'Connor's career at Georgia State College for Women (as it was then called), advisor to the student newspaper *The Corinthian*, in which she wrote, and occasional dinner guest with the O'Connor family.

NOTES TO CHAPTER 6

1. Flannery O'Connor, "The Catholic Novelist in the South," in *Collected Works* (New York: Literary Classics of the United States, 1988), p. 855. All subsequent parenthetical references refer to this edition.

2. Denis de Rougement, *Devil's Share: An Essay on the Diabolic in Modern Society* (New York: Meridian Books, 1956), pp. 25–26, 28.

3. St. Thomas Aquinas, *Summa Theologica* (Westminster, Md.: Christian Classics, 1981), I, qu. 19, a. 9; qu. 49, a. 1.

4. St. Augustine, *The City of God* (Garden City, N.Y.: Image Books, 1958), pp. 217, 248, 508.

5. St. Augustine, *Confessions*, F. J. Sheed, trans. (Hackett Publishing, 1993), XII, XIII.

6. Aquinas, *Summa Theologica*, I, qu. 49 a. 1.

7. Ibid.

8. Ibid.

9. Aquinas, *Summa Theologica*, I, qu. 19, a. 9.

10. Aquinas, *Summa, Theologica*, I, qu. 19, a. 2.

11. Aquinas, *Summa Theologica*, I, qu. 49, a. 3.

12. Arisotle, *De Anima*, Hugh Lawson-Tancred, trans. (London: Penguin Books, 1986), 402a, p. 126.

13. St. Augustine, *The Greatness of the Soul*, Joseph M. Colleran, trans. (New York: Newman Press, 1950), Chaps. 4, 5–6, pp. 18–20.

14. Aristotle, *De Anima*, Hugh Lawson-Tancred, trans. (London: Penguin Books, 1986), 402a, p. 126.

15. Aquinas, *Summa Theologica*, I, qus. 75–76.

16. Michel de Montaigne, "On Glory," in *The Complete Essays*, M. A. Screech, trans. (London: Penguin Books, 1987), p. 705.

17. Aristotle, *De Anima*. Hugh Lawson-Tancred, trans. (London: Penguin Books, 1986). Also, see *Thomas Aquinas: On Human Nature*, Thomas S. Hibbs, ed. (Indianapolis: Hackett Publishing, 1999). See especially editor's introduction, pp. vii–xxi.

NOTES TO CHAPTER 7

1. Walker Percy, *Conversations with Walker Percy*, Lewis A. Lawson and Victor A. Kramer, eds. (Jackson: University Press of Mississippi), p. 232.

2. Titles by all three authors appear in her personal library. The most, fifteen titles, are by Mauriac.

3. T. S. Eliot, "East Coker," in "Four Quartets," in *The Complete Poems and Plays, 1909–1950* (New York: Harcourt, Brace & World, 1971), p. 128.

4. Joseph Conrad, *Nostromo* (New York: Penguin Books, 1990), p. 269.

5. Walker Percy, *Conversations with Walker Percy*, Lewis A. Lawson and Victor A. Kramer, eds. (Jackson: University Press of Mississippi), p. 232.

6. The candidate with the "good looks" won the election, Ernest Vandiver.

7. I am appreciative of Ralph C. Wood's apologetic written to explain that O'Connor's racial views, far from being "racist," were just the opposite—a Christian response to the evil of racism. I am less troubled than Wood, however, by O'Connor's correspondence, nor am I convinced that she needed to "repent" of supposedly untoward views as a result of her adult Christian experience. See "Where Is the Voice Coming From? Flannery O'Connor on Race," *The Flannery O'Connor Bulletin*, 22 (1993–94), pp. 90–118. Anyone seeking a balanced view of O'Connor's views on equality should read thoroughly, among other things, her short story, "Revelation," and take note of how harshly O'Connor "punishes" her character Ruby Turpin for her racial prejudice.

8. To Maryat Lee, June 10, 1961, from Milledgeville.

9. To Flannery O'Connor June 17 [n.d. supplied, 1961(?)], Maryat Lee, from Chester.

10. To Maryat Lee, 21 May [n.d. (1968?)], from Milledgeville. To another correspondent, O'Connor was more frank. She said, "I can't stomach Baldwin." "Six Unpublished Letters of Flannery O'Connor," in *The Flannery O'Connor Bulletin*, with commentary by James F. Farnham, 12 (Autumn 1983, pp. 60–66), p. 64.

11. Jacques Maritain, *Reflections on America* (Garden City, N.Y.: Image Books, 1964), p. 29.

12. Ibid, p. 30.

13. Ibid, pp. 32–34.

14. Ibid, p. 34.

15. Aquinas, *Summa Theologica*, I-II, qus. 90–108. Cf. Aristotle's *Politics*, 1268b125–1269a125, Carnes Lord, trans. (Chicago: University of Chicago Press, 1984).

16. Aquinas *Summa Theologica*, II-I, qu. 91, a. 1.

17. Aquinas *Summa Theologica*, II-I, qu. 95, a. 1.

18. Aquinas, *Summa Theologica*, II-II, qu. 57, a. 3–5.

19. Aristotle, *The Nichomachean Ethics*, David Ross, trans. (Oxford, G.B.: Oxford University Press, 1984), 1140a20ff; p. 142, 114ob6ff, p. 143.

20. Aristotle, *Nichomachean Ethics*, 1141b33ff, p. 146.

21. Aristotle, *Nichomachean Ethics*, 1142a7ff, p. 148.

22. Aristotle, *Nichomachean Ethics*, 1143b18ff, p. 154.

23. Aristotle, *Nichomachean Ethics*, 1143b35, p. 155; 1144b29, p. 158.

24. David Bevington, ed. (Walton on Thames, Surrey, G.B.: Arden Shakespeare, 1998), 2:2:15. For some reason, O'Connor's works of Shakespeare do not currently appear in her personal library, but she was a serious reader of his works. For example, she writes her friend Janet McKane, "I've been reading Shakespeare myself lately. . . . I've got *King Lear, Richard II, Anthony & Cleopatra* and *The Tempest*." She also expressed her intention to add more volumes to her collection (CW, 1191).

25. O'Connor reported to Maryat Lee, "I have writ a story ["Revelation"] with which I am, for the time anyway, pleased pleased pleased" (HB, 551).

26. "Uncle George" Haslam once told me that O'Connor got the characters for this story from a visit to the local doctor's office at which he himself was also present. His account is strengthened by O'Connor's writing Betty Hester, "The last time I went to the doctor here, Ruby and Claud were in there" (HB, 552).

27. Though Ruby is subjected to a uncomfortable re-adjustment of her philosophy, O'Connor respects her and sympathizes with her character's struggle, which she likens to Jacob's struggle with the Angel of the Lord (Gen. 32:22–31): She writes, "You got to be a very big woman to shout at the Lord across a hogpen" (HB, 577).

28. O'Connor wrote Betty Hester "I started to let ["Revelation"] end where the hogs pant with a secret life, but I thought something else was needed" (HB, 549).

29. Colossians, 3:11, New International Version.

NOTES TO CHAPTER 8

1. St. Thomas Aquinas, *Summa Theologica*, "Treatise on Man," I, qus. 75–89 (Westminster, Md.: Christian Classics), 1981. Also see Aristotle, *De Anima*, Hugh Lawson-Tancred, trans. (London: Penguin Books, 1986). I am grateful to Professor John Desmond for helping me to understand this short story at a Liberty Fund Colloquium entitled, "Liberty, Responsibility, and the Human Condition," November 9–12, 2000, Mulberry Inn, Savannah, Ga.; although he may not agree with the conclusions I have drawn.

2. John Henry Newman, *The Grammar of Assent* (New York: Image Books, 1955), pp. 116–7.

3. Blaise Pascal, *Pensées, and the Provincial Letters*, W. F. Trotter and Thomas M'Crie, trans. (New York: Modern Library, 1941), No. 72, p. 25.

4. Walker Percy, "A Novel About the End of the World," in *The Message in the Bottle: How Queer Man Is, How Queer Language Is, and What One Has to Do with the Other* (New York: Farrar, Straus and Giroux, 1954), p. 108.

5. St. Augustine, *Confessions*, Edward B. Pusey, trans. (New York: Picket Books, 1952), p. 90.

6. Address to Georgia State College for Women, no date supplied. In correspondence, given to Rebeka Poller, February 1957, p. 3.

7. To Maryat Lee, June 28, 1957, from Milledgeville, in "Flannery 1957," *The Flannery O'Connor Bulletin*, 5 (autumn, 1976), p. 57.

8. Jacques Maritain, *Saint Thomas and the Problem of Evil* (Milwaukee, Minn.: Marquette University Press, 1942), p. 23. Maritain's reported sources for this essay, though not clearly denoted, are *Summa Theologica*, I, qu. 48, a. 1, a. 2, a. 6; qu. 49, a. 1; I–II, qu. 112, a. 3; *Contra Gentiles*, III, cap. 7, 8, and 9; *Quaestiones Disputatae, de Malo*, 1, 1; 1, 3.

9. Maritain, *Problem of Evil*, pp. 24, 25.

10. Maritain, *Problem of Evil*, p. 27.

11. Maritain, *Problem of Evil*, pp. 27–8. The maxim that good carpenters follow today would take the analogy one step further: "Measure twice, cut once."

12. Maritain, *Problem of Evil*, p. 29.

13. Maritain, *Problem of Evil*, pp. 29–31.

14. Maritain, *Problem of Evil*, pp. 33–35.

15. To Mr. And Mrs. B. Cheney, no day or month supplied, 1958, from Rome.

16. *The Correspondence of Flannery O'Connor and the Brainard Cheneys*, C. Ralph Stephens, ed. (Jackson: University Press of Mississippi, 1986), p. 188.

17. From De Vene Harrold (De Vene Harrold, P.O. 1622, St. Augustine, Fla. 32084), no date supplied, no recipient supplied.

18. "On Flannery O'Connor," by Richard Gilman/September, 1960, From *The New York Times Review of Books*, 21 August 1969, 24–26, in *Conversations with Flannery O'Connor*, Rosemary M. Magee, ed. (Jackson: Jackson Press of Mississippi, 1987), pp. 53–54.

19. Walker Percy, *More Conversations with Walker Percy*, Lewis A. Lawson and Victor A. Kramer, eds. (Jackson: University of Mississippi Press, 1993), pp. 205–6.

20. This is a tragically ironic excerpt given that Hester herself committed suicide long after O'Connor's death, in 1998.

21. C. S. Lewis, *The Problem of Pain* (New York: MacMillan, 1962), pp. 34, 41.

22. Niccolò Machiavelli, *The Prince*, Harvey C. Mansfield Jr., trans. (Chicago: University of Chicago Press, 1985), p. 101.

23. A long-time resident of Milledgeville, who as a teenage girl knew O'-Connor and her family, has suggested that O'Connor's graphic descriptions of the excavation came from her observation of the construction of the Sinclair Dam outside of town that took place in the period during which O'Connor was writing.

24. Jer. 17:9 (New International Version).
25. What O'Connor calls here the "conditional" is, to be precise, the subjunctive.
26. The reference is found in Matt. 5:22.
27. For example, Acts 5:30 (New International Version).
28. G. K. Chesterton, *Orthodoxy* (Westport, Conn.: Greenwood Press, 1974), p. 48.

NOTES TO CHAPTER 9

1. *Flannery O'Connor: Her Life, Library and Book Reviews*, Lorine M. Getz (New York: Edwin Mellen Press, 1980), pp. 30, 45.
2. Address to GSCW, no date supplied. In correspondence, given to Rebeka Poller, February 1957, pp. 8.
3. See Ralph C. Wood, *The Comedy of Redemption: Christian Faith and Comic Vision in Four American Novelists* (Notre Dame, Ind.: Notre Dame Press, 1988), p. 118; also, Eric Voegelin, *Israel and Revelation: Volume One, Order and History* (Baton Rouge: Louisiana State University, 1956), p. 506.
4. Isaiah 53:1–5 (New International Version).
5. Philippians 3:10, Colossians, 1:24 (New International Version). Also see Pope John Paul II's Apostolic Letter "Salvici Doloris," February 11, 1984 ("On the Meaning of Human Suffering").
6. *The Correspondence of Flannery O'Connor and the Brainard Cheneys*, C. Ralph Stephens, ed. (Jackson: University Press of Mississippi, 1986).
7. Romano Guardini, *Freedom, Grace, Destiny*, John Murray, S.J., trans. (New York: Pantheon Books, 1961), pp. 109–110.
8. *The Correspondence of Flannery O'Connor and the Brainard Cheneys*, C. Ralph Stephens, ed. (Jackson: University Press of Mississippi, 1986).
9. Address to Georgia State College for Women, no date supplied. In Correspondence, given to Rebeka Poller, February 1957, pp. 7–9.
10. Nietzsche, *Human, All-Too-Human*, in *The Portable Nietzsche*, Walter Kaufmann, trans. (Middlesex, G.B.: Penguin Books, 1954), pp. 52–53.
11. St. Thomas Aquinas, *Summa Theologica* (Westminster, Md.: Christian Classics, 1981), II-II, qu. 1, a. 3.
12. Aquinas, *Summa Theologica*, II-I, qu. 1, a. 5.
13. Aquinas, *Summa Theologica*, II-I, qu. 1, a. 5.
14. Aquinas, *Summa Theologica*, II-I, qu. 1, a. 5.
15. T. S. Eliot, "East Coker," in *The Complete Poems and Plays, 1909–1950* (New York: Harcourt, Brace & World, 1971), p. 127.
16. (New York: Farrar Strauss Giroux, 1987), p. 351.
17. Ibid., pp. 127–9.
18. New York: Vintage Books, 1998, p. 223. O'Connor wrote to Betty Hester, "If you ever can get at the Atlanta Public Liberry [sic] Walker Percy's book, *The Moviegoer*, I wish you would check it out and send it to me. This is probably one we should both read" (HB, 442).
19. Walker Percy, *The Second Coming* (New York: Farrar, Straus and Giroux, 1980), p. 179.

20. T. S. Eliot, "The Hollow Men," in *The Complete Poems and Plays* (New York: Harcourt, Brace, & World, 1952), p. 59.

21. Romano Guardini, *The End of the Modern World* (Wilmington, Del.: ISI Books, 1998), p. 99.

22. Fyodor Dostoevsky, *Notes From Underground* (New York: W. W. Norton, 1989), p. 88.

23. Eric Voegelin, *Israel and Revelation: Volume One, Order and History* (Baton Rouge: Louisiana State University Press, 1956), p. 514.

NOTES TO CHAPTER 10

1. St. Augustine, *On Rebuke and Grace*, Chapter 3, in *A Select Library of the Nicene and Post-Nicene Fathers of The Christian Church*, Philip Schaff, ed., volume v "Saint Augustine: Anti-Pelagian Writings (Grand Rapids, Mich.: Wm. B. Eerdmans, 1971), p. 473.

2. Walker Percy, *Love in the Ruins: The Adventures of a Bad Catholic at a Time Near the End of the World* (New York: Farrar, Straus & Giroux, 1971) p. 191.

3. See Marion Montgomery, "Grace: A Tricky Fictional Agent," in *The Flannery O'Connor Bulletin* (volume ix, autumn 1980), pp. 19–29.

4. Eric Voegelin, *Plato and Aristotle: Volume Three, Order and History* (Baton Rouge: Louisiana State University Press, 1957), p. 364.

5. St. Thomas Aquinas, *Summa Theologica* (Westminster, Md.: Christian Classics, 1981), I-II, qus. 109–110.

6. 1 Pet. 4:10, NIV; G. Abbott-Smith, *A Manual Lexicon of the New Testament* (Edinburgh, G.B.: T. & T. Clark, 1956).

7. Aquinas, *Summa Theologica*, I-II, qu, 111, a. 3.

8. St. Augustine, *On Nature and Grace*, Chapter 35, in *A Select Library of the Nicene and Post-Nicene Fathers of The Christian Church*, Philip Schaff, ed., volume v "Saint Augustine: Anti-Pelagian Writings (Grand Rapids, Mich.: Wm. B. Eerdmans, 1971), p. 133.

9. "Six Unpublished Letters of Flannery O'Connor," in *The Flannery O'Connor Bulletin*, with commentary by James F. Farnham, 12 (autumn 1983), pp. 60–66.

10. Aquinas, *Summa Contra Gentiles*, 3: 158, "That Man cannot be delivered from Sin except by Grace," 3:148, "That Man Stands in Need of Divine Grace for the Gaining of Happiness." www.nd.edu/Departments/Maritain/etext/gc.htm.

11. O'Connor's conception of grace is supported by St. Thomas Aquinas's rather subtle discussion of natural grace. See *Summa Theologica*, I-II, q 109, a. 1, 2. My thanks to John Roos at the University of Notre Dame, for helping me understand Thomas' teaching on natural grace, even though he may not agree with the way in which I apply the concept to O'Connor's thought.

12. St. Augustine, *On Nature and Grace*, in "Extract From Augustine's Retractions," Book II, Chap. 42, p. 116. To be sure, St. Augustine's anti-Pelagian writings, considered as a whole, support the notion that grace was a part of creation, that it

was implanted in Adam's soul, and that original sin has not evacuated grace from creation at large or from the human soul, though the depth of sin has made supernatural grace essential.

13. Romano Guardini, *Freedom, Grace, and Destiny*, John Murray, S.J., trans. (New York: Pantheon Books, 1961), pp. 113, 133.

14. Pascal, *Pensées and the Provincial Letters*, W. F. Trotter and Thomas M'Crie, trans. (New York: Modern Library, 1941), No. 520.

15. Aquinas, *Summa Contra Gentiles*, 3:149, "That the Divine Will does not compel a Man to Virtue"; 3:160, "That it is reasonably reckoned a Man's own Fault if he be not converted to God, although he cannot be converted without Grace."

16. Romano Guardini, *Freedom, Grace, and Destiny*, John Murray, S.J., trans. (New York: Pantheon Books, 1961), pp. 113–114, 132. O'Connor appears to have highlighted the discussion on page 113 of her copy of this book.

17. Prov. 3:34, 1 Pet. 4:6, 1 Pet 5:5, NIV.

18. *Measure for Measure* (New York: Penguin Books, 1970), 4:4:33–4.

19. Aquinas, *Summa Contra Gentiles*, 3:154, "That Divine Grace Causes in Us a Hope of Future Blessedness."

20. Aquinas, *Summa Contra Gentiles*, 3:146, "That Sins are Punished Also by the Experience of Something Painful."

21. Michel de Montaigne, "Of Experience," *The Complete Essays* (London: Penguin Books, 1991), pp. 1207–1269.

22. *Measure for Measure* (New York: Penguin Books, 1970), 2:2:136–7.

23. To Maryat Lee, May 21, 1964, From Piedmont Hospital. This is a postcard on which O'Connor signed her name as "Mrs. Turpin."

24. Address to Georgia State College for Women, given to Rebeka Poller. No date supplied, p. 5. See O'Connor to Rebeka Poller, Milledgeville, February 1957.

25. The authoress received the O. Henry prize for its publication in the *Kenyon Review* in 1956; the prize was accompanied by a $300 check (HB, 129).

26. Pascal, *Pensées, and the Provincial Letters*, No. 199.

27. Walker Percy, *Love in the Ruins* (New York: Farrar, Straus & Giroux, 1971), p. 373–4; 1 Corinthians 6:1, KJV.

28. "The Second Coming," in *The Collected Poems of W. B. Yeats*, Richard Finneran, ed. (New York: Simon & Schuster, 1996), p. 187.

29. Aquinas *Summa Contra Gentiles*, 1:71, "That God Knows Evil Things."

30. St. Augustine, *On Nature and Grace*, Chapter 27, in *A Select Library of the Nicene and Post-Nicene Fathers of The Christian Church*, Philip Schaff, ed., volume v "Saint Augustine: Anti-Pelagian Writings (Grand Rapids, Mich.: Wm. B. Eerdmans, 1971), p. 130.

31. Fyodor Dostoyevsky, *The Brothers Karamazov* (London: Penguin Books, 1993, first published in 1880), p. 741.

32. Romano Guardini, *The End of the Modern World* (Wilmington, Del.: ISI Books, 1998), p. 126.

33. Aquinas, *Summa Theologica*, I, qu. 90; also see I, qu. 114.

34. To Mrs. William R. Grace Terry, August 27, 1962, From Milledgeville.

35. Review of *Evidence of Satan in the Modern World*, by Léon Christiani, Macmillan, New York City, in *The Bulletin*, March 2, 1962, in *Flannery O'Connor: Her Life,*

Library and Book Reviews, Lorine M. Getz (New York: Edwin Mellen Press, 1980), p. 182.

36. Brainard Cheney's review of Flannery O'Connor's *Wise Blood*, in *Shenandoah*, 3 (autumn, 1952), Appendix A, *The Correspondence of Flannery O'Connor and the Brainard Cheneys*, C. Ralph Stephens, ed. (Jackson: University Press of Mississippi, 1986), pp. 198–9.

37. Jeffrey Russell, a leading scholar on literary and philosophical views of the devil, writes, "Flannery O'Connor urged the Devil's existence in the midst of a society increasingly dominated by materialism and relativism. . . . In this society, resolutely determined to deny the reality of radical evil, evil has seldom been more manifest." Jeffrey Burton Russell, *The Prince of Darkness: Radical Evil and the Power of Good in History* (Ithaca, N.Y.: Cornell University Press, 1988), p. 272.

38. To Betty Boyd Love, June 8, 1949, From NYC. William Sessions once loaned O'Connor his book *Satan*, a compilation of orthodox Church teaching on the Devil, the tone of which is consistent with her literal view of Satan (no author provided [New York: Sheed and Ward, 1952]).

39. Walker Percy, *Lancelot* (New York: Farrar, Straus, and Giroux, 1977), p. 139.

40. Guardini, *The End*, p. 126.

41. Edward B. Pusey, trans. (New York: Picket Books, 1952), p. 10.

42. T. S. Eliot, "The Hollow Men," in *The Complete Poems and Plays, 1909–1950* (New York: Harcourt, Brace & World, 1971), p. 56.

43. Walker Percy, *The Second Coming* (New York: Farrar, Straus and Giroux, 1980).

44. Guardini, *The End*, p. 94.

45. Aquinas, *Summa Contra Gentiles*, 3:12, "That Evil Does not Entirely Swallow Up Good."

46. Eric Voegelin, *Israel and Revelation: Volume One, Israel and Revelation* (Baton Rouge, Louisiana State University Press), 1956.

47. Walker Percy, "Notes for a Novel About the End of the World," in *The Message in the Bottle: How Queer Man Is, How Queer Language Is, and What One Has to Do with the Other* (New York: Farrar, Straus and Giroux, 1954), p. 101.

48. Georges Bernanos, "France Before the World of Tomorrow," in *The Last Essays of Georges Bernanos*, Joan and Barry Ulanov, trans. (Chicago: Henry Regnery, 1955), p. 1.

49. Sally Fitzgerald, "Room with a View," in *The Flannery O'Connor Bulletin* 10 (autumn, 1981), p. 17.

50. Ibid., p. 22.

51. Stanley Rosen, *Nihilism: A Philosophical Essay* (New Haven, Conn.: Yale University Press, 1969), p. 140.

52. See, for example, Aquinas *Contra Gentiles*, 2:16, "That God Has Brought Things Into Being Out of Nothing"; and 2:21 "That It Belongs to God Alone to Create."

53. T. S. Eliot, *The Complete Poems and Plays: 1909–1950* (New York: Harcourt, Brace & World, 1971), p. 98.

54. Francois Mauriac, *What I Believe*, Wallace Fowlie, trans. (New York: Farrar, Straus, 1963), p. 95.

55. Aquinas, *Summa Theologica*, I-II, qu. 3, a. 1.

Index

About the Author

Henry T. Edmondson III teaches political philosophy at Georgia College and State University, Milledgeville, Georgia, which is Flannery O'Connor's alma mater. His previous writing in literature and philosophy includes the edited volume *The Moral of the Story: Literature and Public Ethics* (Lexington Books, 2000). He is founder and director of the summer study abroad program European Government and Culture, and he is a native of Augusta, Georgia, where he lives with his wife, Dorothy Marie, and their four children, Nathan, Erin, Jason, and Kerrie.

DATE DUE
